Frommer's®

Spanish PhraseFinder & Dictionary

1st Edition

WILEY

Wiley Publishing, Inc.

Published by:

Wiley Publishing, Inc.

111 River St.
Hoboken, NJ 07030-5774

ISBN-13: 978-0-471-77330-6
ISBN-10: 0-471-77330-1

Series Editor: Maureen Clarke
Photo Editor: Richard H. Fox
Cover design by Fritz Metsch

Interior Design, Content Development, Translation, Copyediting, Proofreading,
Production, and Layout by:
Publication Services, Inc., 1802 South Duncan Road, Champaign, IL 61822
Linguists: Nanette Monet & Justin Serrano

For information on our other products and services or to obtain technical support,
please contact our Customer Care Department within the U.S. at 800/762-2974, outside the U.S. at 317/572-3993 or fax 317/572-4002.
Wiley also publishes its books in a variety of electronic formats. Some content that
appears in print may not be available in electronic formats.

Manufactured in the United States of America

5   4

Contents

An Invitation to the Reader

In researching this book, we discovered many wonderful sayings and terms useful to travelers in Spain or Latin America. We're sure you'll find others. Please tell us about them, so we can share the information with your fellow travelers in upcoming editions. If you were disappointed with an aspect of this book, we'd like to know that, too. Please write to:

Frommer's Spanish PhraseFinder & Dictionary, 1st Edition
Wiley Publishing, Inc.
111 River St. • Hoboken, NJ 07030-5774

An Additional Note

The packager, editors, and publisher cannot be held responsible for the experiences of readers while traveling. Your safety is important to us, however, so we encourage you to stay alert and be aware of your surroundings. Keep a close eye on cameras, purses, and wallets, all favorite targets of thieves and pickpockets.

Frommers.com

Now that you have the language for a great trip, visit our website at **www.frommers.com** for travel information on more than 3,000 destinations. With features updated regularly, we give you instant access to the most current trip-planning information available. At Frommers.com, you'll also find the best prices on airfares, accommodations, and car rentals—and you can even book travel online through our travel booking partners. At Frommers.com, you'll also find:

- Online updates to our most popular guidebooks
- Vacation sweepstakes and contest giveaways
- Newsletter highlighting the hottest travel trends
- Online travel message boards with featured travel discussions

INTRODUCTION: HOW TO USE THIS BOOK

As a Romance language, Spanish is closely related to Latin, French, Italian, Portuguese, and Romanian. But not one of these European tongues is used with half the frequency of Spanish—with more than 332 million speakers, including more than 23 million in the United States. Variations spoken by Mexicans, Spaniards, Ecuadorians, Puerto Ricans, and other Latino ethnic groups are considerable. For simplicity's sake, we have used a universal form of Latin American Spanish throughout this book. But a native Spaniard has reviewed our translations, noting where they're radically different from what is spoken in Spain.

Our intention is not to teach you Spanish; we figure you'll find an audio program for that. Our aim is to provide a portable travel tool that's easy to use. With most phrasebooks, you practically have to memorize the contents before you know where to look for a term on the spot. This phrasebook is designed for fingertip referencing, to help you find the language you need fast.

Part of this book organizes terms by chapters, as in a Frommer's guide—getting a room, getting a good meal, etc. Within those sections, we tried to organize phrases according to how frequently readers are likely to use them. But let's say you're in a cab and received the wrong change, and don't know where to look in the money chapter. With Frommer's PhraseFinder, you can quickly look up "change" in the dictionary, and learn how to say "Sorry, but this isn't the right change." Then you can follow the cross reference for numbers, and specify how much you're missing.

What will make this book most practical? What will make it easiest to use? These are the questions we asked ourselves as we assembled these travel terms.

Our immediate goal was to create a phrasebook as indispensable as your passport. Our far-ranging goal, of course, is to enrich your experience of travel. And with that we offer the following wish: *¡Que tenga un buen viaje!*

CHAPTER ONE

SURVIVAL SPANISH

If you tire of toting around this phrasebook, tear out this chapter. You should be able to navigate your destination with only the terms found in the next 35 pages.

BASIC GREETINGS

For a full list of greetings, see p111.

Hello.	**Hola.**
	OH-lah
How are you?	**¿Cómo está?**
	KOH-moh ehs-TAH
I'm fine, thanks.	**Estoy bien, gracias.**
	ehs-TOY BYEHN, GRAH-syahs
And you?	**¿Y usted?**
	ee oos-TEHD
My name is ____.	**Me llamo ____.**
	meh YAH-mo
And yours?	**¿Y usted?**
	ee oos-TEHD
It's a pleasure to meet you.	**Es un placer conocerle.**
	EHS oon plah-SEHR koh-noh-SEHR-leh
Please.	**Por favor.**
	pohr fah-VOHR
Thank you.	**Gracias.**
	GRAH-syahs
Yes.	**Sí.**
	see
No.	**No.**
	noh

Okay.	**OK.**
	OH-keh
	De acuerdo.
	deh ah-KWEHR-doh
	Okay.
	OH-keh
No problem.	**No hay problema.**
	noh aye proh-BLEH-mah
I'm sorry, I don't understand.	**Lo siento, no entiendo.**
	loh SYEHN-toh no ehn-TYEHN-doh
Would you speak slower please?	**¿Puede hablar un poco más lento?**
	PWEH-deh ah-BLAHR oon POH-koh mahs LEHN-to
Would you speak louder please?	**¿Puede hablar un poco más alto?**
	PWEH-deh ah-BLAHR oon POH-koh mahs AHL-toh
Do you speak English?	**¿Usted habla inglés?**
	oos-TEHD AH-blah eeng-GLEHS
Do you speak any other languages?	**¿Usted habla otro idioma?**
	oos-TEHD AH-blah OH-troh ee-DYOH-ma
I speak ____ better than Spanish.	**Yo hablo ____ mejor que español.**
	yoh AH-bloh ____ meh-HOHR keh ehs-pah-NYOL
Would you spell that?	**¿Puede deletrear eso?**
	PWEH-de deh-leh-treh-AHR EH-so
Would you please repeat that?	**¿Puede repetir, por favor?**
	PWEH-deh rreh-peh-TEER pohr fah-VOHR
Would you point that out in this dictionary?	**¿Puede señalarlo en este diccionario?**
	PWEH-deh seh-nyah-LAHR-loh ehn EHS-deh deek-syoh-NAHR-yoh

THE KEY QUESTIONS

With the right hand gestures, you can get a lot of mileage from the following list of single-word questions and answers.

Who?	**¿Quién? ¿Quiénes?**
	KYEHN? KYEH-nehs?
What?	**¿Qué?**
	keh
When?	**¿Cuándo?**
	KWAHN-doh
Where?	**¿Dónde?**
	DOHN-deh
To where?	**¿Adónde?**
	ah-DOHN-deh
Why?	**¿Por qué?**
	pohr-KEH
How?	**¿Cómo?**
	KOH-moh
Which?	**¿Cuál?**
	KWAHL
How many? / How much?	**¿Cuánto? ¿Cuántos?**
	KWAHN-toh, KWAHN-tohs

THE ANSWERS: WHO

For full coverage of pronouns, see p21.

I	**yo**
	yoh
you	**usted / tú**
	oos-TEHD, too
him	**él**
	ehl
her	**ella**
	EH-yah
us	**nosotros**
	noh-SOH-trohs
them	**ellos / ellas**
	EH-yohs, EH-yahs

THE ANSWERS: WHEN
For full coverage of time, see p12.

now	**ahora**
	ah-OH-rah
later	**después**
	dehs-PWEHS
in a minute	**en un minuto**
	ehn oon mee-NOO-toh
today	**hoy**
	oy
tomorrow	**mañana**
	mah-NYAH-nah
yesterday	**ayer**
	ah-YEHR
in a week	**en una semana**
	ehn OO-nah seh-MAH-nah
next week	**la próxima semana**
	lah PROHK-see-mah seh-MAH-nah
last week	**la semana pasada**
	lah seh-MAH-nah pah-SAH-dah
next month	**el próximo mes**
	ehl PROHK-see-moh MEHS
At ____	**A las ____**
	ah lahs
ten o'clock this morning.	**diez en punto esta mañana.**
	DYEHS ehn POON-toh EHS-tah mah-NYAH-nah
two o'clock this afternoon.	**dos en punto esta tarde.**
	dohs ehn POON-toh EHS-tah TAHR-deh
seven o'clock this evening.	**siete en punto esta noche.**
	SYEH-teh ehn POON-toh EHS-ahOH-cheh

For full coverage of numbers, see p7.

THE ANSWERS: WHERE

here	**aquí / acá**
	ah-KEE, ah-KAH
there	**allá / allí**
	ah-YAH, ah-EE
near	**cerca**
	SEHR-kah
closer	**más cerca**
	mahs SEHR-kah
closest	**lo más cerca**
	loh MAHS SEHR-kah
far	**lejos**
	LEH-hohs
farther	**más lejos**
	mahs LEH-hohs
farthest	**lo más lejos**
	loh MAHS LEH-hohs
across from	**atrás de**
	ah-TRAHS deh
next to	**al lado de**
	ahl LAH-doh deh
behind	**detrás de**
	deh-TRAHS deh
straight ahead	**adelante / siguiente**
	ah-deh-LAHN-teh, see-GYEHN-teh
left	**la izquierda**
	lah ees-KYEHR-dah
right	**la derecha**
	lah deh-REH-chah
up	**arriba**
	ah-RREE-bah
down	**abajo**
	ah-BAH-hoh
lower	**más abajo**
	mahs ah-BAH-hoh
higher	**más arriba**

	mahs ah-RREE-bah
forward	**hacia delante**
	AH-syah deh-LAHN-teh
back	**hacia atrás**
	AH-syah ah-TRAHS
around	**alrededor**
	ahl-reh-deh-DOHR
across the street	**al cruzar la calle**
	ahl kroo-SAHR lah KAH-yeh
down the street	**calle abajo**
	KAH-yeh ah-BAH-hoh
on the corner	**en la esquina**
	ehn lah ehs-KEE-nah
kitty-corner	**la esquina diagonal**
	lah ehs-KEE-nah dee-ah-goh-NAHL
_____ blocks from here	**a _____ cuadras de aquí**
	ah _____ KWAH-drahs deh ah-KEE

For a full list of numbers, see the next page

THE ANSWERS: WHICH

this one	**éste / ésta**
	EH-steh, EH-stah
that (that one, close by)	**ese / esa**
	EH-seh, EH-sah
(that one, in the distance)	**aquel / aquella**
	ah-KEHL, ah-KEH-yah
these	**éstos / éstas**
	EHS-tohs, EHS-tahs
those (those there, close by)	**ésos / ésas**
	EH-sohs, EH-sahs
	ehl heh-REHN-teh

NUMBERS & COUNTING

one	**uno** *OO-noh*	seventeen	**diecisiete** *dyeh-see-SYEH-teh*
two	**dos** *dohs*	eighteen	**dieciocho** *dyeh-SYOH-choh*
three	**tres** *trehs*	nineteen	**diecinueve** *dyeh-see-NWEH-veh*
four	**cuatro** *KWAH-troh*	twenty	**veinte** *VEH-een-teh*
five	**cinco** *SEENG-koh*	twenty-one	**veintiuno** *veh-een-TYOO-noh*
six	**seis** *SEH-ees*	thirty	**treinta** *TREH-een-tah*
seven	**siete** *SYEH-teh*	forty	**cuarenta** *kwah-REN-teh*
eight	**ocho** *OH-cho*	fifty	**cincuenta** *seen-KWEHN-tah*
nine	**nueve** *NWEH-veh*	sixty	**sesenta** *seh-SEHN-tah*
ten	**diez** *dyehs*	seventy	**setenta** *seh-TEHN-tah*
eleven	**once** *OHN-seh*	eighty	**ochenta** *o-CHEHN-tah*
twelve	**doce** *DOH-seh*	ninety	**noventa** *noh-VEHN-tah*
thirteen	**trece** *TREH-seh*	one hundred	**cien** *syehn*
fourteen	**catorce** *kah-TOHR-seh*	two hundred	**doscientos** *doh-SYEHN-tohs*
fifteen	**quince** *KEEN-seh*	one thousand	**mil** *meel*
sixteen	**dieciséis** *dyeh-see-SEH-ees*		

FRACTIONS & DECIMALS

one eighth	**un octavo**
	oon ohk-TAH-voh
one quarter	**un cuarto**
	oon KWAHR-toh
one third	**un tercio**
	oon TEHR-syoh
one half	**medio**
	MEH-dyoh
two thirds	**dos tercios**
	dohs TEHR-syohs
three quarters	**tres cuartos**
	trehs KWAHR-tohs
double	**doble**
	DOH-bleh
triple	**triple**
	TREE-pleh
one tenth	**un décimo**
	oon DEH-see-moh
one hundredth	**un centésimo**
	oon sehn-TEH-see-moh
one thousandth	**un milésimo**
	oon mee-LEH-see-moh

MATH

addition	**la suma**
	SOO-mah
2 +1	**dos más uno**
	dohs mahs OO-noh
subtraction	**la resta**
	RREHS-tah
2 - 1	**dos menos uno**
	dohs MEH-nohs OO-noh

multiplication	**la multiplicación**
	mool-tee-plee-kah-SYOHN
2×3	**dos por tres**
	dohs pohr trehs
division	**la división**
	dee-vee-SYOHN
$6 \div 3$	**Seis dividido entre tres**
	SEH-ees dee-vee-DEE-doh EHN-
	treh TREHS

ORDINAL NUMBERS

first	**primero -a**
	pree-MEH-roh / pree-MEH-rah
second	**segundo -a**
	seh-GOON-doh / seh-GOON-dah
third	**tercero -a**
	tehr-SEH-roh / tehr-SEH-rah
fourth	**cuarto -a**
	KWAHR-toh / KWAHR-tah
fifth	**quinto -a**
	KEEN-toh / KEEN-tah
sixth	**sexto -a**
	SEHK-sto / SEHK-stah
seventh	**séptimo -a**
	SEHP-tee-moh / SEHP-tee-mah
eighth	**octavo -a**
	ohk-TAH-voh / ohk-TAH-vah
ninth	**noveno -a**
	noh-VEH-noh / noh-VEH-nah
tenth	**décimo -a**
	DEH-see-moh / DEH-see-mah
last	**último -a**
	OOL-tee-mo / OOL-tee-mah

MEASUREMENTS

Measurements will usually be metric, though you may need a few
American measurement terms.

inch	**la pulgada**
	pool-GAH-dah
foot	**el pie**
	PYEH
mile	**la milla**
	MEE-yah
millimeter	**el milímetro**
	mee-lee-MEH-troh
centimeter	**el centimetro**
	sehn-tee-MEH-troh
meter	**el metro**
	MEH-troh
kilometer	**el kilómetro**
	kee-LOH-meh-troh
hectare	**la hectárea**
	hehk-TAH-reh-ahs
squared	**cuadrado -a**
	kwah-DRAH-doh / kwah-DRAH-dah
short	**corto -a**
	KOHR-toh / KOHR-tah
long	**largo -a**
	LAHR-goh / LAHR-gah

VOLUME

milliliters	**mililitros**
	mee-lee-LEE-trohs
liter	**litro**
	LEE-troh
kilo	**kilo**
	Kee-loh
ounce	**onza**
	OHN-sah

cup	**taza**
	TAH-sah
pint	**pinta**
	PEEN-tah
quart	**cuarto (de galón)**
	KWAHR-toh deh gah-LOHN
gallon	**galón**
	gah-LOHN

QUANTITY

some	**algún -a / algunos -as**
	ahl-GOON / ahl-GOO-nah /
	ahl-GOO-nohs / ahl-GOO-nahs
none	**nada / ninguno -a / ningunos -as**
	NAH-dah / neeng-GOO-noh /
	neeng-GOO-nah / neeng-GOO-
	nohs / neeng-GOO-nahs
all	**todo -a / todos -as**
	TOH-doh / TOH-dah / TOH-dohs /
	TOH-dahs
many / much	**mucho -a / muchos -as**
	MOO-cho / MOO-cha / MOO-chohs /
	MOO-chas
a little bit (can be used for	**un poco / una poca**
quantity or for time)	*oon POH-koh / oo-nah POH-kah*
dozen	**docena**
	doh-SEH-na

SIZE

small	**pequeño -a**
	peh-KEH-nyoh / peh-KEH-nyah
the smallest (literally "the	**el / la / lo más pequeño -a**
most small")	*ehl / lah / loh mahs peh-KEH-*
	nyoh / peh-KEH-nyah

medium	**mediano -a**
	meh-DYAH-no / meh-DYAH-na
big	**grande**
	GRAHN-deh
fat	**gordo -a**
	GOHR-doh / GOHR-dah
wide	**ancho -a**
	AHN-cho / AHN-cha
narrow	**angosto -a**
	ahng-GOH-stoh / ahng-GOH-stah

TIME

Time in Spanish is referred to, literally, by the hour. What time is it? translates literally as "What hour is it? / What hours are they?" *For full coverage of number terms, see p7.*

HOURS OF THE DAY

What time is it?	**¿Qué hora es?**
	keh OH-ra ehs
At what time?	**¿A qué hora?**
	ah KEH OH-rah
For how long?	**¿Por cuánto tiempo?**
	pohr KWAHN-toh TYEHM-poh
It's one o'clock.	**Es la una en punto.**
	ehs lah OO-nah ehn POON-toh
It's two o'clock.	**Son las dos en punto.**

A little tip

By adding a diminutive suffix -ito / -ita, -ico / -ica, or a combination of the two, you can make anything smaller or shorter. These endings replace the original -o and -a.

| advice, tip | **consejo** (*kohn-SEH-hoh*) |
| a little tip | **consejito** (*kohn-seh-HEE-toh*) |

	sohn lahs DOHS ehn POON-toh
It's two thirty.	**Son las dos y media.**
	sohn lahs DOHS ee MEH-dyah
It's two fifteen.	**Son las dos y cuarto.**
	sohn lahs DOHS ee KWAHR-toh
It's a quarter to three.	**Son las tres menos cuarto**
	sohn las TREHS MEH-nohs KWAHR-toh
	Falta un cuarto para las tres.
	FAHL-tah oon KWAHR-toh pah-rah lahs trehs
It's noon.	**Es mediodía.**
	ehs MEH-dyoh DEE-ah
It's midnight.	**Es medianoche.**
	ehs meh-dyah-NOH-cheh
It's early.	**Es temprano.**
	ehs tehm-PRAH-noh
It's late.	**Es tarde.**
	ehs TAHR-deh
in the morning	**de la mañana**
	deh lah mah-NYAH-nah
in the afternoon	**de la tarde**
	deh lah TAHR-deh
at night	**de la noche**
	deh lah NOH-cheh
dawn	**la madrugada**
	lah mah-droo-GAH-dah

DAYS OF THE WEEK

Sunday	**el domingo** *ehl doh-MEENG-go*
Monday	**el lunes** *ehl LOO-nehs*
Tuesday	**el martes** *ehl MAHR-tehs*
Wednesday	**el miércoles** *ehl MYEHR-koh-lehs*
Thursday	**el jueves** *ehl HWEH-vehs*
Friday	**el viernes** *ehl VYEHR-nehs*
Saturday	**el sábado** *ehl SAH-bah-doh*
today	**hoy** *oy*
tomorrow	**mañana** *mah-NYAH-nah*
yesterday	**ayer** *ah-YEHR*
the day before yesterday	**anteayer** *ahn-teh-ah-YEHR*
one week	**una semana** *OO-nah seh-MAH-nah*
next week	**la próxima semana** *lah PROHK-see-mah seh-MAH-nah*
last week	**la semana pasada** *lah seh-MAH-nah pah-SAH-dah*

MONTHS OF THE YEAR

January	**enero** *eh-NEH-roh*
February	**febrero** *feh-BREH-roh*

March	**marzo**
	MAHR-soh
April	**abril**
	ah-BREEL
May	**mayo**
	MAH-yoh
June	**junio**
	HOO-nee-oh
July	**julio**
	HOO-lee-oh
August	**agosto**
	ah-GOHS-toh
September	**septiembre**
	sehp-TYEHM-breh
October	**octubre**
	ohk-TOO-breh
November	**noviembre**
	noh-VYEHM-breh
December	**diciembre**
	dee-SYEHM-breh
next month	**el mes entrante**
	ehl MEHS ehn-TRAHN-teh
	el próximo mes
	ehl PROHK-see-moh MEHS
last month	**el mes pasado**
	ehl MEHS pah-SAH-doh

SEASONS OF THE YEAR

spring	**la primavera**
	lah pree-mah-VEH-rah
summer	**el verano**
	ehl veh-RAH-noh
autumn	**el otoño**
	ehl oh-TOH-nyoh
winter	**el invierno**
	ehl een-VYEHR-noh

Falsos Amigos

If you try winging it with Spanglish, beware of false cognates, known as falsos amigos, "false friends"—Spanish words that sound like English ones, but with different meanings. Here are some of the most commonly confused terms.

suburbio	slum
barrio	suburb
bomba	pump / tank / bomb
explosivo	bomb
arma	weapon
brazo	arm
constipado -a	congested
estreñido -a	constipated
embarazada	pregnant
avergonzado -a	embarrassed
injuria	insult
herida	injury
parientes	relatives
padres	parents
largo	long
grande	large
actual	now, current
verdadero -a	actual
asistir	to attend
ayudar	to assist
sopa	soup
jabón	soap
ropa	clothing
ropa vieja (lit. old clothes)	delicious Cuban dish of stewed, shredded beef
cuerda	rope

SPANISH GRAMMAR BASICS

Classified as a Romance language, descended from the Latin spoken when Spain was part of the Roman Empire, Spanish is a linguistic amalgamation closely related to Latin, French, Italian, Portuguese, and Romanian. Spanish was strongly affected by the Arabic of Spain's Moorish conquerors, who occupied the country from A.D. 711 to 1492. When Spain conquered what is today Latin America, it imposed its language on millions of Native Americans, from the Caribbean to Tierra del Fuego. But the indigenous languages they spoke, in turn, affected the local spoken Spanish, accounting for some of the rich diversity of the language.

THE ALPHABET

Spanish is a straightforward language with a simple alphabet. If foreign letters (k and w) are counted, the alphabet has 27 letters (ñ, in addition to the English alphabet).

Spanish also has two double letters: ll (elle), pronounced like y in English "yes," and rr (erre), pronounced like an English r trilled by vibrating the end of the tongue against the hard palate, just above the upper teeth. There is also ch, as in chipmunk.

Letter	Name	Pronunciation of Letter Name
a	a	*ah*
b	be	*beh*
c	ce	*seh*
d	de	*deh*
e	e	*eh*
f	efe	*EH-feh*
g	ge	*heh*
h	hache	*AH-cheh*
i	i	*ee*
j	jota	*HOH-tah*
k	ka	*kah*
l	ele	*EH-leh*
m	eme	*EH-meh*
n	ene	*EH-neh*

Letter	Name	Pronunciation of Letter Name
ñ	eñe	*EH-nyeh*
o	o	*oh*
p	pe	*peh*
q	cu	*koo*
r	ere	*EH-reh*
s	ese	*EH-seh*
t	te	*teh*
u	u	*oo*
v	ve, uve	*veh*
w	doble u, ve doble	*DOH-bleh oo, veh DOH-bleh*
x	equis	*EH-kees*
y	i griega	*ee GRYEH-gah*
z	seta	*SEH-tah*

PRONUNCIATION GUIDE

Vowels

a	ah as the a in father: abajo *(ah BAH hoh)*
au	ow as in cow: automático *(ow-to-MAH-tee-koh)*
ay	aye as in "All in favor, say aye": hay *(aye)*
e	eh to rhyme with the e in nestle: espera *(ehs PEH rah)*
i	ee as in feed: pasillo *(pah SEE yoh)*
o	oh as in boat: modismo *(moh DEES moh)*
oy	oy as in boy: hoy *(oy)*
u	oo as in the word coo: buscar *(boos KAHR)*

Consonants

b	as in bean, but softer with less explosion than in English: buscar *(boos-KAHR)*
c	before e and i as English initial s; ce is pronounced as seh: necesito *(neh seh SEE toh)*; ci is pronounced as see: cinco *(SEENG-koh)*; before a, o, u as English k, but softer with less explosion: caballero *(kah bah YEH roh)*; consejo *(kohn SEH hoh)*; Cuba *(KOO bah)*

cu	in combination with a, e, i, o pronounced like the qu in quick: cuándo *(KWAHN doh)*; cuestión *(kwehs TYOHN)*
d	as the d in day, but softer with less explosion than in English. Some final ds can be pronounced as the th in the: usted *(oo STEHTH)*. If you pronounce Spanish d like the English d, you will be understood: ciudad *(see-oo-DAHD)*; de *(deh)*
f	as in fox: favor *(fah-VOHR)*
g	before e and i as English h; ge is pronounced like he in hen: emergencia *(eh-mehr-HEHN-syah)*; gi is pronounced like English he: puerta giratoria *(PWEHR-tah hee-rah-TOHR-yah)*
	before a, o, u as initial hard g in English as in gate: llegar *(yeh GAHR)*; tengo *(TEHN-goh)*; seguridad *(seh-goo-ree-DAHD)*
h	silent; hizo *(EE-soh)*, hasta *(AHS-tah)*; hi before a vowel is pronounced like English y: hielo *(YEH-loh)*
j	as English h in hot: equipaje *(eh-kee-PAH-heh)*
k	as in English: kilómetro *(kee-LOH-meh-troh)*
l	as in English: ala *(AH-lah)*
ll	as the initial y in yeah: llegada *(yeh-GAH-dah)*
m	as in English: aeromozo *(eh-roh-MOH-soh)*
n	as in English: negocios *(neh-GOH-syohs)*
ñ	as ny in canyon: cañón *(kahn-YOHN)*
p	as in English but softer: pasaporte *(pah-sah-POHR-teh)*
q	qu is pronounced as k: máquina *(MAH-kee-nah)*
r	as in English but more clipped: puerta *(PWEHR-tah)*
rr	as a trilled r sound, vibrating the end of the tongue against the area just above the top teeth: perro *(PEH-rroh)*. A single r that starts a word is pronounced like the double r: rayos X *(RRAH-yohs EH-kees)*
s	as in English: salida *(sah-LEE-dah)*

t	as in English but softer: tranvía *(trahn-VEE-ah)*
v	as in English: vuelo *(VWEH-loh)*
w	as in English: waflera *(wah-FLEH-rah)*
x	like English x: próximo *(PROHK-see-moh)*; in some old names and some names of Native American origin, like h: Don Quixote *(dohn kee HOH teh)*, México *(MEH-hee-koh)* spelled with j in Spain; before a consonant, like s: Taxco *(TAHS-koh)*
y	as in English: yo *(yoh)*; by itself, as the ee sound in bead: y *(ee)*
z	like English s: aterrizaje *(ah-teh-rree-SAH-heh)*

WORD PRONUNCIATION

Syllables in words are also accented in a standard pattern. Generally, the last syllable is stressed except when a word ends in a vowel, n, or s; then the stress falls on the second to last syllable. If a word varies from this pattern, an accent mark is shown. Examples:

Ending in r

comer   *koh-MEHR*

Ending in a

comida   *koh-MEE-dah*

Ending in s

comemos   *koh-MEH-mohs*

Ending in n but with an accent mark

comilón   *koh-mee-LOHN*

GENDER, ADJECTIVES, MODIFIERS

Each noun takes a masculine or feminine gender, most often accompanied by a masculine or feminine definite article (el or la). Definite articles ("the"), indefinite articles ("a," "an"), and related adjectives must also be masculine or feminine, singular or plural, depending on the noun they're modifying.

The Definite Article ("The")

	Masculine	Feminine
Singular	*el* perro (the dog)	*la* mesa (the table)
Plural	*los* perros (the dogs)	*las* mesas (the tables)

The Indefinite Article ("A" or "An")

	Masculine	Feminine
Singular	*un* perro (a dog)	*una* mesa (a table)
Plural	*unos* perros (some dogs)	*unas* mesas (some tables)

PERSONAL PRONOUNS

AMAR: "To Love"		
I love.	*Yo* amo.	AH-moh
You (singular familiar) love.	*Tú* amas.	AH-mahs
He / She loves. You (singular, formal) love.	*Él / Ella / Ud.* ama.	AH-mah
We love.	*Nosotros -as* amamos.	ah-MAH-mohs
You (plural, familiar) love.	*Vosotros -as* amáis.	ah-MAH-ees
They / You (plural, formal) love.	*Ellos / Ellas / Uds.* aman.	AH-mahn

Hey, You!

Spanish has two words for "you"—tú, spoken among friends and familiars, and Usted (abbreviated Ud. or Vd.), used among strangers or as a sign of respect toward elders and authority figures. When speaking with a stranger, expect to use Usted, unless you are invited to do otherwise. The second-person familiar plural form (vosotros) is rarely used, and then only in Spain, Argentina, and Chile. Ustedes (abbreviated Uds. or Vds.) is used instead, even among friends, especially in Latin America.

REGULAR VERB CONJUGATIONS

Spanish verb infinitives end in AR (hablar, to speak), ER (comer, to eat), or IR (asistir, to attend). Most verbs (known as "regular verbs") are conjugated according to those endings. To conjugate the present tense of regular verbs, simply drop the AR, ER, or IR and add the following endings:

Present Tense

AR Verbs	HABLAR "To Speak"	
I speak.	Yo hablo.	AH-bloh
You (singular familiar) **speak.**	Tú hablas.	AH-blahs
He / She speaks. **You** (singular formal) **speak.**	Él / Ella / Ud. habla.	AH-blah
We speak.	Nosotros -as hablamos.	ah-BLAH-mohs
You (plural familiar) **speak.**	Vosotros -as habláis.	ah-BLAH-ees
They / You (plural formal) **speak.**	Ellos / Ellas / Uds. hablan.	AH-blahn

ER Verbs **COMER "To Eat"**

I eat.	Yo como.	KOH-moh
You (singular familiar) eat.	Tú comes.	KOH-mehs
He / She eats. You (singular formal) eat.	Él / Ella / Ud. come.	KOH-meh
We eat.	Nosotros -as comemos.	koh-MEH-mohs
You (plural familiar) eat.	Vosotros -as coméis.	koh-MEH-ees
They / You (plural formal) eat.	Ellos / Ellas / Uds. comen.	KOH-mehn

IR Verbs **ASISTIR "To Attend"**

I attend.	Yo asisto.	ah-SEES-toh
You (singular familiar) attend.	Tú asistes.	ah-SEES-tehs
He / She attends. You (singular formal) attend.	Él / Ella / Ud. asiste.	ah-SEES-teh
We attend.	Nosotros -as asistimos.	ah-sees-TEE-mohs
You (plural familiar) attend.	Vosotros -as asistís.	ah-sees-TEES
They / You (plural formal) attend.	Ellos / Ellas / Uds. asisten.	ah-SEES-tehn

Simple Past Tense

These are the simple past tense conjugations for regular verbs.

AR Verbs	HABLAR "To Speak"	
I spoke.	Yo hablé.	ah-BLEH
You (singular familiar) spoke.	Tú hablaste.	ah-BLAHS-teh
He / She/ You (singular formal) spoke.	Él / Ella / Ud. habló.	ah-BLOH
We spoke.	Nosotros -as hablamos.	ah-BLAH-mohs
You (plural familiar) spoke.	Vosotros -as hablasteis.	ah-BLAHS-teh-ees
They / You (plural formal) spoke.	Ellos / Ellas / Uds. hablaron.	ah-BLAH-rohn

ER Verbs	COMER "To Eat"	
I ate.	Yo comí.	koh-MEE
You (singular familiar) ate.	Tú comiste.	koh-MEES-teh
He / She / You singular formal) ate.	Él / Ella / Ud. comió.	koh-mee-OH
We ate.	Nosotros -as comimos.	koh-MEE-mohs
You (plural familiar) ate.	Vosotros -as comisteis.	koh-MEES-teh-ees
They / You (plural formal) ate.	Ellos / Ellas / Uds. comieron.	koh-MYEH-rohn

IR Verbs	ASISTIR "To Attend"	
I attended.	Yo asist*í*.	ah-sees-TEE
You (singular familiar) attended.	Tú asist*iste*.	ah-sees-TEES-teh
He / She / You (singular formal) attended.	Él / Ella / Ud. asist*ió*.	ah-sees-TYOH
We attended.	Nosotros -as asist*imos*.	ah-sees-TEE-mohs
You plural familiar) attended.	Vosotros -as asist*isteis*.	ah-sees-TEES-teh-ees
They / You (plural formal) attended.	Ellos / Ellas / Uds. asist*ieron*.	ah-sees-TYEH-rohn

The Future

For novice Spanish speakers, the easiest way to express the future is to conjugate the irregular verb IR (to go) + a + any infinitive ("I am going to speak," "you are going to speak," etc.).

I am going to speak.	Yo *voy a* hablar.	voy ah ah-BLAHR
You (singular familiar) are going to speak.	Tú *vas a* hablar.	vahs ah ah-BLAHR
He / She is going to speak. You (singular formal) are going to speak.	Él / Ella / Ud. *va a* hablar.	vah ah ah-BLAHR
We are going to speak.	Nosotros -as *vamos a* hablar.	VAH-mohs ah ah-BLAHR

You (plural familiar) **are going to speak.**	Vosotros -as *vais a* hablar.	VAH-ees ah ah-BLAHR
They / You (plural formal) **are going to speak.**	Ellos / Ellas / Uds. *van a* hablar.	vahn ah ah-BLAHR

TO BE OR NOT TO BE (ESTAR & SER)

There are two forms of "being" in Spanish. One is for physical location or temporary conditions (estar), and the other is for fixed qualities or conditions (ser).

I am here.
(temporary, estar)

Yo estoy aquí.

I am from the United States.
(fixed, ser)

Yo soy de los Estados Unidos.

Norman is bored.
(temporary, estar)

Norman está aburrido.

Norman is boring.
(quality, ser)

Norman es aburrido.

The TV is old.
(quality, ser)

La televisión es vieja.

The TV is broken.
(condition, estar)

La televisión está rota.

Present Tense
Estar "To Be" (conditional)

I am.	Yo est*oy*.	ehs-TOY
You (singular, familiar) **are.**	Tú est*ás*.	ehs-TAHS
He / She is. You (singular formal) **are.**	Él / Ella / Ud. est*á*.	ehs-TAH
We are.	Nosotros -as est*amos*.	ehs-TAH-mohs
You (plural familiar) **are.**	Vosotros -as est*áis*.	ehs-TAH-ees
They / You (plural formal) **are.**	Ellos / Ellas / Uds. est*án*.	ehs-TAHN

Simple Past Tense
Estar "To Be" (conditional)

I was.	Yo est*uve*.	ehs-TOO-veh
You were.	Tú est*uviste*.	ehs-too-VEES-teh
He / She was. You (formal) **were.**	Él / Ella / Ud. est*uvo*.	ehs-TOO-voh
We were.	Nosotros -as est*uvimos*.	ehs-too-VEE-mohs
You were.	Vosotros -as est*uvisteis*.	ehs-too-VEES-teh-ees
They / You (plural formal) **were.**	Ellos / Ellas / Uds. est*uvieron*.	ehs-too-VYEH-rohn

Present Tense

	Ser "To be" (permanent)	
I am.	Yo *soy.*	soy
You (singular familiar) **are.**	Tú *eres.*	EH-rehs
He/ She is. **You** (singular formal) **are.**	Él / Ella / Ud. *es.*	ehs
We are.	Nosotros -as *somos.*	SOH-mohs
You (plural familiar) **are.**	Vosotros -as *sois.*	SOH-ees
They / You (plural formal) **are.**	Ellos / Ellas / Uds. *son.*	sohn

Simple Past Tense

	Ser "To be" (permanent)	
I was.	Yo *fui.*	FOO-ee
You (singular familiar) **were.**	Tú *fuiste.*	foo-EES-teh
He/ She was. You (singular formal) **were.**	Él / Ella / Ud. *fue.*	FOO-eh
We were.	Nosotros -as *fuimos.*	foo-EE-mohs
You (plural) familiar) **were.**	Vosotros -as *fuisteis.*	foo-EES-teh-ees
They / You (plural formal) **were.**	Ellos / Ellas / Uds. *fueron*	foo-EH-rohn

IRREGULAR VERBS

Spanish has numerous irregular verbs that stray from the standard AR, ER, and IR conjugations. Rather than bog you down with too much grammar, we're providing the present tense conjugations for the most commonly used irregular verbs.

TENER "To Have" (possess)		
I have.	Yo *tengo*.	TEHNG-goh
You (singular familiar) have.	Tú *tienes*.	TYEH-nehs
He / She has. You (singular formal) have.	Él / Ella / Ud. *tiene*.	TYEH-neh
We have.	Nosotros -as *tenemos*.	TYEH-neh
You (plural familiar) have.	Vosotros -as *tenéis*.	teh-NEH-mohs
They / You (plural formal) have.	Ellos / Ellas / Uds. *tienen*.	TYEH-nehn

Tener

Tener means "to have," but it's also used to describe conditions such as hunger, body pain, and age. For example:
Tengo hambre. I'm hungry.
(Literally: I have hunger.)
Tengo dolor de cabeza. I have a headache.
Tengo diez años. I am ten years old.
(Literally: I have ten years.)

HACER "To Do, To Make"

I make.	Yo ha*go.*	AH-goh
You (singular familiar) **make.**	Tú ha*ces.*	AH-sehs
He / She makes. You (singular formal) **make.**	Él / Ella / Ud. ha*ce.*	AH-seh
We make.	Nosotros -as ha*cemos.*	ah-SEH-mohs
You (plural familiar) **make.**	Vosotros -as ha*céis.*	ah-SEH-ees
They / You (plural formal) **make.**	Ellos / Ellas / Uds. ha*cen.*	AH-sehn

---

Hacer

The verb *hacer* means "to make" or "to do," but it's also used to describe the weather and the passage of time. For example:

Hace calor. It's hot.
(Literally: It makes hot.)
Hace frío. It's cold.
(Literally: It makes cold.)
   OR
Hace tres años que visité España. Three years ago, I visited Spain.
(Literally: It makes three years since I visited Spain.)

QUERER "To Want"

I want.	Yo quiero.	KYEH-roh
You (singular familiar) want.	Tú quieres.	KYEH-rehs
He / She wants. You (singular formal) want.	Él / Ella / Ud. quiere.	KYEH-reh
We want.	Nosotros -as queremos	keh-REH-mohs
You (plural familiar) want.	Vosotros -as queréis.	keh-REH-ees
They / You plural formal want.	Ellos / Ellas / Uds. quieren.	KYEH-rehn

PODER "To Be Able"

I can. (I)	Yo puedo.	PWEH-doh
You (singular familiar) can.	Tú puedes.	PWEH-dehs
He / She can. You singular formal) can.	Él / Ella / Ud. puede.	PWEH-deh
We can.	Nosotros -as podemos.	poh-DEH-mohs
You (plural familiar) can.	Vosotros -as podéis.	poh-DEH-ees
They / You (plural formal) can.	Ellos / Ellas / Uds. pueden.	PWEH-dehn

HABER "To Have" (with past participle)		
I have.	Yo he.	eh
You (singular familiar) **have.**	Tú h*as*.	ahs
He / She has. You (singular formal) **have.**	Él / Ella / Ud. h*a*.	ah
We have.	Nosotros -as h*emos*.	EH-mohs
You (plural familiar) **have.**	Vosotros -as h*abéis*.	ah-BEH-ees
They / You plural formal) **have.**	Ellos / Ellas / Uds. h*an*.	ahn

PEDIR "To Ask"		
I ask.	Yo p*i*do.	PEE-doh
You (singular familiar) **ask.**	Tú p*i*des.	PEE-dehs
He / She asks. You (singular formal) **ask.**	Él / Ella / Ud. p*i*de.	PEE-deh
We ask.	Nosotros -as ped*imos*.	peh-DEE-mohs
You (plural familiar) **ask.**	Vosotros -as ped*ís*.	PEH-dees
They / You (plural formal) **ask.**	Ellos / Ellas / Uds. p*i*den.	PEE-dehn

Note: Verbs that end in **-cer** such as **conocer** change the **c** to **zc** before an ending that begins with **o** or **a**.

CONOCER "To Know" (someone)		
I know.	Yo conozco.	koh-NOHS-koh
You (singular familiar) know.	Tú conoces.	koh-NOH-sehs
He / She knows. You (singular formal) know.	Él / Ella / Ud. conoce.	koh-NOH-seh
We know.	Nosotros -as conocemos.	koh-noh-SEH-mohs
You (plural familiar) know.	Vosotros -as conocéis.	koh-noh-SEH-ees
They / You (plural formal) know.	Ellos / Ellas / Uds. conocen.	koh-NOH-sehn

SABER "to Know" (something)		
I know.	Yo sé.	koh-NOHS-koh
You (singular familiar) know.	Tú sabes.	koh-NOH-sehs
He/ She knows. You (singular formal) know.	Él / Ella / Ud. sabe.	koh-NOH-seh
We know.	Nosotros -as sabemos.	koh-noh-SEH-mohs
You (plural familiar) know.	Vosotros -as sabéis.	koh-noh-SEH-ees
They / You (plural formal) know.	Ellos / Ellas / Uds. saben.	koh-NOH-sehn

Gustar

Spanish doesn't have a verb that literally means "to like." Instead, they use *gustar*, which means to please. So rather than say I like chocolate, you say:

Me gusta el chocolate. I like chocolate.
(Literally: Chocolate is pleasing to me.)

When what is liked is plural, the verb is plural:

Me gustan las tortillas. I like tortillas.
(Literally: Tortillas are pleasing to me.)

The person doing the liking is represented by an indirect object pronoun placed in front of the verb, as illustrated below.

	GUSTAR "To Like"
I like the tortilla.	*Me* **gusta la tortilla.**
You (informal singular) **like the tortilla.**	*Te* **gusta la tortilla.**
He / She likes the tortilla. You (formal singular) **like the tortilla.**	*Le* **gusta la tortilla.**
We like the tortilla.	*Nos* **gusta la tortilla.**
You (informal plural) **like the tortilla.**	*Os* **gusta la tortilla.**
They / You (formal plural) **like the tortilla.**	*Les* **gusta la tortilla.**

REFLEXIVE VERBS

Spanish has many reflexive verbs (when its subject and object both refer to the same person or thing). The following common verbs are used reflexively: vestirse (to get dressed, literally to dress oneself), quedarse (to stay, literally to stay oneself), bañarse (to bathe oneself), and levantarse (to wake up, literally to raise oneself).

VESTIRSE "To Dress"

I get dressed.	Yo me visto.	meh VEES-toh
You (singular familiar) get dressed.	Tú te vistes.	teh VEES-tehs
He / She gets dressed. You (singular formal) get dressed.	Él / Ella / Ud. se viste.	seh VEES-teh
We get dressed.	Nosotros -as nos vestimos.	nohs vehs-TEE-mohs
You (plural familiar) get dressed	Vosotros -as os vestís	ohs vehs-TEES
They / You (plural formal) get dressed.	Ellos / Ellas / Uds. se visten.	seh VEES-tehn

CHAPTER TWO

GETTING THERE & GETTING AROUND

This section deals with every form of transportation. Whether you've just reached your destination by plane or you're renting a car to tour the countryside, you'll find the phrases you need in the next 30 pages.

AT THE AIRPORT

I am looking for ____	**Estoy buscando ____**
	ehs-TOY boos-KAHN-doh
a porter.	**un portero.**
	oon pohr-TEH-roh
the check-in counter.	**el mostrador de registro.**
	ehl mohs-trah-DOHR deh reh-HEES-troh
the ticket counter.	**el mostrador de ventas de boletos.**
	ehl mohs-trah-DOHR deh VEHN-tahs deh boh-LEH-tohs
arrivals.	**las llegadas.**
	lahs yeh-GAH-dahs
departures.	**las salidas.**
	lahs sah-LEE-dahs
gate number ____.	**la puerta de salida ____.**
	lah PWEHR-tah de sah-LEE-dah

For full coverage of numbers, see p7.

the waiting area.	**el área de espera.**
	ehl AH-reh-ah deh ehs-PEH-rah
the men's restroom.	**el baño para caballeros.**
	ehl BAH-nyoh PAH-rah kah-bah-YEH-rohs
the women's restroom.	**el baño para damas.**
	ehl BAH-nyoh PAH-rah DAH-mahs

the police station.	**la estación de policías.**
	lah ehs-tah-SYOHN deh poh-lee-SEE-ahs
a security guard.	**un guardia de seguridad.**
	oon GWAHR-dyah deh seh-goo-ree-DAHD
the smoking area.	**el área de fumar.**
	ehl AH-reh-ah deh foo-MAHR
the information booth.	**el puesto de información.**
	ehl PWEHS-toh deh een-for-mah-SYOHN
a public telephone.	**un teléfono público.**
	oon teh-LEH-foh-noh POO-blee-koh
an ATM.	**un cajero automático.**
	oon kah-HEH-roh ow-toh-MAH-tee-koh
baggage claim.	**el reclamo de equipaje.**
	ehl reh-KLAH-moh de eh-kee-PAH-heh
a luggage cart.	**un carrito para equipaje.**
	oon kah-RREE-toh PAH-rah eh-kee-PAH-heh
a currency exchange.	**un lugar de cambio de moneda.**
	oon loo-GAHR deh KAHM-byoh deh moh-NEH-dah
a café.	**un café.**
	oon kah-FEH
a restaurant.	**un restaurante.**
	oon rehs-tow-RAHN-teh
a bar.	**una cantina.**
	OO-nah kahn-TEE-nah

a bookstore or newsstand.	**una librería o un puesto de periódicos.**
	OO-nah lee-breh-REE-ah oh oon PWEHS-toh deh peh-ree-OH-dee-kohs
a duty-free shop.	**una tienda libre de impuestos.**
	OO-nah TYEHN-dah LEE-breh deh eem-PWEHS-tohs
Is there Internet access here?	**¿Hay acceso al Internet aquí?**
	aye ahk-SEH-soh ahl een-tehr-NEHT ah-KEE
I'd like to page someone.	**Quisiera mandar a llamar a alguien.**
	kee-SYEH-rah mahn-DAHR ah yah-MAHR ah AHLG-yehn
Do you accept credit cards?	**¿Aceptan tarjetas de crédito?**
	ah-SEHP-tahn tahr-HEH-tahs deh KREH-dee-toh

CHECKING IN

I would like a one-way ticket to ____.	**Me gustaría un boleto de ida para ____.**
	meh goos-tah-REE-ah oon boh-LEH-toh deh EE-dah PAH-rah
I would like a round trip ticket to ____.	**Me gustaría un boleto de ida y vuelta para ____.**
	meh goos-tah-REE-ah oon boh-LEH-toh de EE-dah ee VWEHL-tah PAH-rah
How much are the tickets?	**¿Cuánto cuestan los boletos?**
	KWAHN-toh KWEHS-tahn lohs boh-LEH-tohs
Do you have anything less expensive?	**¿Tiene algo más económico?**
	TYEH-neh AHL-goh mahs eh-koh-NOH-mee-koh
How long is the flight?	**¿Cuán largo es el vuelo?**
	kwahn LAHR-goh ehs ehl VWEH-loh

Common Airport Signs

Llegadas	Arrivals
Salidas	Departures
Terminal	Terminal
Puerto de salida	Gate
Boletería	Ticketing
Aduana	Customs
Reclamo de equipaje	Baggage Claim
Empuje	Push
Jale	Pull
No fumar	No Smoking
Entrada	Entrance
Salida	Exit
Caballeros	Men's
Damas	Women's
Autobuses de transporte	Shuttle Buse
Taxis	Taxis

For full coverage of number terms, see p7.
For full coverage of time, see p12.

What time does flight _____ leave?	**¿A qué hora sale el vuelo _____?** *ah keh OH-rah SAH-leh ehl VWEH-loh*
What time does flight _____ arrive?	**¿A qué hora llega el vuelo _____?** *ah keh OH-rah YEH-gah ehl VWEH-loh*
Do I have a connecting flight?	**¿Tengo un vuelo de conexión?** *TEHNG-goh oon VWEH-loh deh koh-nehk-SYOHN*
Do I need to change planes?	**¿Necesito cambiar aviones?** *neh-seh-SEE-toh kahm-BYAHR ah-VYOH-nehs*
My flight leaves at __:__.	**Mi vuelo sale a las ____:____.** *mee VWEH-loh SAH-leh ah lahs*

GETTING THERE

For full coverage of numbers, see p7.

What time will the flight arrive?	**¿A qué hora llega el vuelo?** *ah keh OH-rah YEH-gah ehl VWEH-loh*
Is the flight on time?	**¿El vuelo está a tiempo?** *ehl VWEH-loh ehs-TAH ah TYEHM-poh*
Is the flight delayed?	**¿El vuelo está retrasado?** *ehl VWEH-loh ehs-TAH reh-trah-SAH-doh*
From which terminal is flight _____ leaving?	**¿De cuál terminal sale el vuelo _____?** *deh kwahl tehr-mee-NAHL SAH-leh ehl VWEH-loh*
From which gate is flight _____ leaving?	**¿De cuál puerta de salida sale el vuelo _____?** *deh kwahl PWEHR-tah deh sah-LEE-dah SAH-leh ehl VWEH-loh*
How much time do I need for check-in?	**¿Cuánto tiempo necesito para registrarme?** *KWAHN-toh TYEHM-poh neh-seh-SEE-toh PAH-rah reh-hees-TRAHR-me*

Is there an express check-in line?

¿Hay una fila expresa?
aye OO-nah FEE-lah ehs-PREH-soh

Is there electronic check-in?

¿Hay registro electrónico?
ay reh-HEES-troh eh-lehk-TROH-nee-koh

Seat Preferences

I would like _____ ticket(s) in _____

Quisiera _____ boleto(s) en _____
kee-SYEH-rah _____ boh-LEH-toh(s) ehn

first class.

primera clase.
pree-MEH-rah KLAH-seh

business class.

la clase de negocios.
lah KLAH-seh deh neh-GOH-syohs

economy class.

la clase económica.
lah KLAH-seh eh-koh-NOH-mee-kah

I would like _____

Me gustaría _____
meh goos-tah-REE-ah

Please don't give me _____

Por favor no me dé _____
pohr fah-VOHR noh meh deh

a window seat.

un asiento de ventana.
oon ah-SYEHN-toh deh vehn-TAH-nah

an aisle seat.

un asiento de pasillo.
oon ah-SYEHN-toh deh pah-SEE-yoh

an emergency exit row seat.

un asiento en la fila de emergencia.
oon ah-SYEHN-toh ehn lah FEE-lah deh eh-mehr-HEHN-syah

a bulkhead seat.

un asiento detrás del tabique.
oon ah-SYEHN-toh deh-TRAHS dehl tah-BEE-keh

a seat by the restroom.

un asiento cerca de los baños.
oon ah-SYEHN-toh SEHR-kah deh lohs BAH-nyohs

GETTING THERE

a seat near the front.	**un asiento cerca del frente.** *oon ah-SYEHN-toh SEHR-kah* *dehl FREHN-teh*
a seat near the middle.	**un asiento cerca del centro.** *oon ah-SYEHN-toh SEHR-kah* *dehl SEHN-troh*
a seat near the back.	**un asiento cerca de atrás.** *oon ah-SYEHN-toh SEHR-kah* *deh ah-TRAHS*
Is there a meal on the flight?	**¿Sirven comida en este vuelo?** *SEER-vehn koh-MEE-dah ehn EHS-* *teh VWEH-loh*
I'd like to order ____	**Quisiera ordenar ____** *kee-SYEH-rah ohr-deh-NAHR*
a vegetarian meal.	**una comida vegetariana.** *OO-nah koh-MEE-dah veh-heh-* *tah-RYAH-nah*
a kosher meal.	**una comida kósher.** *OO-nah koh-MEE-dah KOH-shehr*
a diabetic meal.	**una comida para diabéticos.** *OO-nah koh-MEE-dah PAH-rah* *dyah-BEH-tee-kohs*
I am traveling to ____.	**Estoy viajando hacia ____.** *ehs-TOY vyah-HAHN-doh HAH-* *syah*
I am coming from ____.	**Estoy regresando de ____.** *ehs-TOY reh-greh-SAHN-doh de*
I arrived from ____.	**Llegué de ____.** *yeh-GEH deh*

For full coverage of country terms, see English / Spanish dictionary.

I'd like to change / cancel / confirm my reservation.	**Quisiera cambiar / cancelar /** **confirmar mi reservación.** *kee-SYEH-rah kahm-BYAHR /* *kahn-seh-LAHR / kohn-feer-MAHR* *mee reh-sehr-vah-SYOHN*

I have ____ bags to check.	**Tengo ____ bolsas que registrar.** *TEHNG-goh ____ BOHL-sahs keh* *reh-hees-TRAHR*

For full coverage of numbers, see p7.

Passengers with Special Needs

Is that wheelchair accessible?	**¿Eso es accesible para personas con impedimentos?** *EH-soh ehs ahk-seh-SEE-bleh PAH-rah pehr-SOH-nahs kohn eem-peh-dee-MEHN-tohs*
May I have a wheelchair / walker please?	**¿Me puede dar una silla de ruedas / un andador, por favor?** *meh PWEH-deh dahr OO-nah SEE-yah deh RWEH-dahs / oon ahn-dah-DOHR pohr fah-VOHR*
I need some assistance boarding.	**Necesito un poco de ayuda al abordar.** *neh-seh-SEE-toh oon POH-koh deh ah-YOO-dah ahl ah-bohr-DAHR*
I need to bring my service dog.	**Necesito traer a mi perro de servicio.** *neh-seh-SEE-toh trah-EHR ah mee PEH-rroh deh sehr-VEE-syoh*
Do you have services for the hearing impaired?	**¿Tienen servicios para las personas con impedimentos auditivos?** *TYEH-nehn sehr-VEE-syohs PAH-rah lahs pehr-SOH-nahs kohn eem-peh-dee-MEHN-tohs ow-dee-TEE-vohs*
Do you have services for the visually impaired?	**¿Tienen servicios para las personas con impedimentos visuales?** *TYEH-nehn sehr-VEE-syohs pah-rah lahs pehr-SOH-nahs kohn eem-peh-dee-MEHN-tohs vee-soo-AH-lehs*

Trouble at Check-In

How long is the delay?	**¿Cuán largo es el retraso?**
	kwahn LAHR-goh ehs ehl reh-TRAH-soh
My flight was late.	**Mi vuelo estuvo tarde.**
	mee VWEH-loh ehs-TOO-voh TAHR-deh
I missed my flight.	**Perdí mi vuelo.**
	pehr-DEE mee VWEH-loh
When is the next flight?	**¿Cuándo es el próximo vuelo?**
	KWAHN-doh ehs ehl PROHK-see-moh VWEH-loh
May I have a meal voucher?	**¿Me puede dar un vale para comida?**
	meh PWEH-deh dahr oon VAH-leh pah-rah koh-MEE-dah
May I have a room voucher?	**¿Me puede dar un vale para hospedaje?**
	meh PWEH-deh dahr oon VAH-leh pah-rah ohs-peh-DAH-heh

AT CUSTOMS / SECURITY CHECKPOINTS

I'm traveling with a group.	**Estoy viajando con un grupo.**
	ehs-TOY vyah-HAHN-doh kohn oon GROO-poh
I'm on my own.	**Estoy viajando solo -a.**
	ehs-TOY vyah-HAHN-doh SOH-loh -lah
I'm traveling on business.	**Estoy viajando por negocios.**
	ehs-TOY vyah-HAHN-doh pohr neh-GOH-syohs
I'm on vacation.	**Estoy de vacaciones.**
	ehs-TOY deh vah-kah-SYOH-nehs
I have nothing to declare.	**No tengo nada que declarar.**
	noh TEHNG-goh NAH-dah keh deh-klah-RAHR

I would like to declare ____.	**Quisiera declarar ____.**
	kee-SYEH-rah deh-klah-RAHR
I have some liquor.	**Tengo un poco de licor.**
	TEHNG-goh oon POH-koh deh lee-KOHR
I have some cigars.	**Tengo unos cigarros.**
	TENHG-goh oo-nohs see-GAH-rrohs
They are gifts.	**Son regalos.**
	sohn reh-GAH-lohs
They are for personal use.	**Son para uso personal.**
	sohn PAH-rah OO-soh pehr-soh-NAHL
That is my medicine.	**Esa es mi medicina.**
	EH-sah ehs mee meh-dee-SEE-nah
I have my prescription.	**Tengo mi receta.**
	TEHNG-goh mee rreh-SEH-tah
My children are traveling on the same passport.	**Mis niños están viajando bajo el mismo pasaporte.**
	mees NEE-nyohs ehs-TAHN vyah-HAHN-doh BAH-hoh ehl MEES-moh pah-sah-POHR-teh
I'd like a male / female officer to conduct the search.	**Quisiera que un oficial varón / mujer haga el registro.**
	kee-SYEH-rah keh oon oh-fees-YAHL vah-ROHN / moo-HEHR AH-gah ehl reh-HEES-trohx

Trouble at Security

Help me. I've lost ____	**Ayúdeme. Perdí ____**
	ah-YOO-dah-meh pehr-DEE
my passport.	**mi pasaporte.**
	mee pah-sah-POHR-teh
my boarding pass.	**mi boleta de abordaje.**
	mee boh-LEH-tah deh bohr-DAH-heh

Listen Up: Security Lingo

Por favor, quítese los zapatos.	Please remove your shoes.
Quítese la chaqueta / el suéter.	Remove your jacket / sweater.
Quítese las joyas.	Remove your jewelry.
Coloque su equipaje sobre el cinturón.	Place your bags on the conveyor belt.
Por favor hágase a un lado.	Step to the side.
Debemos realizar una inspección manual.	We have to do a hand search.

my identification.	**mi identificación.**
	mee ee-dehn-tee-fee-kah-SYOHN
my wallet.	**mi cartera.**
	mee kahr-TEH-rah
my purse.	**mi bolso.**
	mee BOHL-soh
Someone stole my purse / wallet!	**¡Alguien me robó mi bolso / cartera!**
	ah-YOO-dah AHLG-yehn meh roh-BOH mee BOHL-soh / kahr-TEH-rah

IN-FLIGHT

It's unlikely you'll need much Spanish on the plane, but these phrases will help if a bilingual flight attendant is unavailable or if you need to talk to a Spanish-speaking neighbor.

I think that's my seat.	**Creo que ese es mi asiento.**
	KREH-oh keh EH-seh ehs mee ah-SYEHN-toh
May I have ____	**¿Me puede dar ____**
	meh PWEH-deh dahr
water?	**agua?**
	AH-wah

sparkling water?	**agua carbonatada?**
	AH-wah kahr-boh-nah-TAH-dah
orange juice?	**jugo de naranja?**
	HOO-goh deh nah-RAHN-hah
soda?	**soda / refresco / gaseosa?**
	SOH-dah / reh-FREHS-koh / gah-seh-OH-sah
diet soda?	**soda / refresco / gaseosa de dieta?**
	SOH-dah / reh-FREHS-koh / gah-seh-OH-sah deh DYEH-tah
a beer?	**una cerveza?**
	OO-nah sehr-VEH-sah
wine?	**vino?**
	VEE-noh

For a complete list of drinks, see p88.

a pillow?	**una almohada?**
	OO-nah ahl-moh-AH-dah
a blanket?	**una frazada?**
	OO-nah frah-SAH-dah
a hand wipe?	**una toallita húmeda?**
	OO-nah toh-ah-YEE-tah OO-meh-dah
headphones?	**audífonos?**
	ow-DEE-foh-nohs
a magazine or newspaper?	**una revista o un periódico?**
	OO-nah reh-VEES-tah oh oon pehr-YOH-dee-koh
When will the meal be served?	**¿Cuándo servirán la comida?**
	KWAHN-doh sehr-vee-RAHN lah koh-MEE-dah
How long until we land?	**¿Cuánto falta para llegar?**
	KWAHN-toh FAHL-tah pah-rah yeh-GAHR

May I move to another seat?	**¿Me puedo mover a otro asiento?**
	meh PWEH-doh moh-VEHR ah OH-troh ah-SYEHN-toh
How do I turn the light on / off?	**¿Cómo apago / enciendo la luz?**
	KOH-moh ah-PAH-go / ehn-SYEHN-doh lah loos

Trouble In-Flight

These headphones are broken.	**Estos audífonos están rotos.**
	EHS-tohs ow-DEE-foh-nohs ehs-TAHN ROH-tohs
I spilled.	**Tuve un derrame.**
	TOO-veh oon deh-RRAH-meh
My child spilled.	**Mi niño -a tuvo un derrame.**
	mee NEE-nyoh -nyah TOO-veh oon deh-RRAH-me
My child is sick.	**Mi niño -a está enfermo -a.**
	mee NEE-nyoh -nyah ehs-TAH ehn-FEHR-moh -mah
I need an airsickness bag.	**Necesito una bolsa para mareos.**
	neh-seh-SEE-toh OO-nah BOHL-sah pah-rah mah-REH-ohs
I smell something strange.	**Huelo algo extraño.**
	WEH-loh AHL-goh ehs-TRAH-nyoh
That passenger is behaving suspiciously.	**Ese pasajero se está comportando sospechosamente.**
	EH-seh pah-sah-HEH-roh seh ehs-TAH kohm-pohr-TAHN-doh sohs-peh-choh-sah-MEHN-teh

BAGGAGE CLAIM

Where is baggage claim for flight ____?	**¿Dónde está el reclamo de equipaje para el vuelo ____?**
	DOHN-deh ehs-TAH ehl reh-KLAH-moh deh eh-kee-PAH-heh pah-rah ehl VWEH-loh

Would you please help with my bags?	**¿Me puede ayudar con mis bolsas?** *meh PWEH-deh ah-yoo-DAHR kohn mees BOHL-sahs*
I am missing ____ bags.	**Me faltan ____ bolsas.** *meh FAHL-tahn ____ BOHL-sahs*

For full coverage of numbers, see p7.

My bag is ____	**Mi bolsa ____** *mee BOHL-sah*
lost.	**está perdida.** *ehs-TAH pehr-DEE-dah*
damaged.	**está dañada.** *ehs-TAH dah-NYAH-dah*
stolen.	**fue robada.** *fweh roh-BAH-dah*
a suitcase.	**es una maleta.** *ehs OO-nah mah-LEH-ta*
a briefcase.	**es un maletín.** *ehs oon mah-leh-TEEN*
a carry-on.	**es una maleta de mano.** *ehs OO-nah mah-LEH-tah deh MAH-noh*
a suit bag.	**es una bolsa para trajes.** *ehs OO-nah BOHL-sah PAH-rah TRAH-hehs*
a trunk.	**es un baúl.** *ees oon bah-OOL*
golf clubs.	**son palos de golf.** *sohn PAH-lohs deh gohlf*

For full coverage of color terms, see English / Spanish Dictionary.

hard.	**es dura.** *ehs DOO-rah*
made out of ____	**está hecha de ____** *ehs-TAH EH-chah deh ____*
canvas.	**lona.** *LOH-nah*

vinyl.	**vinilo.**
	vee-NEE-loh
leather.	**cuero.**
	KWEH-roh
hard plastic.	**plástico duro.**
	PLAH-stee-koh DOO-roh
aluminum.	**aluminio.**
	ah-loo-MEE-nyoh

RENTING A VEHICLE

Is there a car rental agency in the airport?	**¿Hay una agencia de alquiler de autos en el aeropuerto?**
	aye OO-nah ah-HEN-syah deh ahl-kee-LEHR deh OW-tohs ehn ehl ah-eh-roh-PWEHR-toh
I have a reservation.	**Tengo una reservación.**
	TEHNG-goh OO-nah reh-sehr-vah-SYOHN

Vehicle Preferences

I would like to rent ____	**Quisiera alquilar ____**
	kee-SYEH-rah ahl-kee-LAHR
an economy car.	**un auto económico.**
	oon OW-toh eh-koh-NOH-mee-koh
a midsize car.	**un auto mediano.**
	oon OW-toh meh-DYAH-noh
a sedan	**un sedán.**
	oon seh-DAHN
a convertible.	**un convertible.**
	oon kohn-vehr-TEE-bleh
a van.	**una furgoneta.**
	OO-nah foor-goh-NEH-tah
a sports car.	**un auto deportivo.**
	oon OW-toh deh-pohr-TEE-voh

a 4-wheel-drive vehicle.

un auto de tracción en las cuatro ruedas.
oon OW-toh deh trahk-SYOHN ehn lahs KWAH-troh RWEH-dahs

a motorcycle.

una motocicleta.
OO-nah moh-toh-see-KLEH-tah

a scooter.

una motoneta.
OO-nah mo-toh-NEH-tah

Do you have one with ____

¿Tiene uno con ____
TYEH-neh OO-noh kohn

air conditioning?

aire acondicionado?
AYEE-reh ah-kohn-dee-syoh-NAH-doh

a sunroof?

techo corredizo?
TEH-choh koh-rreh-DEE-soh

a CD player?

un lector de discos compactos?
oon lehk-TOHR deh DEES-kohs kohm-PAHK-tohs

satellite radio?

radio satélite?
RAH-dyoh sah-TEH-lee-teh

satellite tracking?

navegación por satélite?
nah-veh-gah-SYOHN pohr sah-TEH-lee-teh

an onboard map?

un mapa a bordo?
oon MAH-pah ah-BOHR-doh

a DVD player?

un lector de DVD?
oon lehk-TOHR deh deh-veh-DEH

child seats?

asientos infantiles?
ah-SYEHN-tohs een-fahn-TEE-lehs

Do you have a ____

¿Tiene un auto ____
TYEH-neh oon OW-toh

smaller car?

más pequeño?
mahs peh-KEH-nyoh

bigger car?

más grande?
mahs GRAHN-deh

GETTING THERE

cheaper car?	**más barato?**
	mahs bah-RAH-toh
Do you have a non-smoking car?	**¿Tiene un auto de no fumar?**
	TYEH-neh oon OW-toh deh noh foo-MAHR
I need an automatic transmission.	**Necesito una transmisión automática.**
	neh-seh-SEE-toh OO-nah trahns-mee-SYOHN ow-toh-MAH-tee-kah
A standard transmission is okay.	**Una transmisión manual está bien.**
	OO-nah trahns-mee-SYOHN mah-NWAHL eh-STAH BYEHN
May I have an upgrade?	**¿Puedo recibir una mejora de categoría?**
	PWEH-doh reh-see-BEER OO-nah meh-HO-rah deh kah-teh-goh-REE-ah

Money Matters

What's the daily / weekly / monthly rate?	**¿Cuál es la tarifa diaria / semanal / mensual?**
	kwahl ehs lah tah-REE-fah DYAHR-yah / seh-mah-NAHL / mehn-SWAHL
What is the mileage rate?	**¿Cuál es la tarifa por milla / kilómetro?**
	kwahl ehs lah tah-REE-fah pohr MEE-yah / kee-LOH-meh-troh
How much is insurance?	**¿Cuánto cuesta el seguro?**
	KWAHN-toh KWEHS-tah ehl seh-GOO-roh
Are there other fees?	**¿Hay otros honorarios?**
	aye OH-trohs oh-noh-RAHR-yohs
Is there a weekend rate?	**¿Hay una tarifa de fin de semana?**
	aye OO-nah tah-REE-fah deh feen deh seh-MAH-nah

Technical Questions

What kind of fuel does it take?	**¿Qué tipo de combustible usa?** *keh TEE-poh deh kohm-boos-TEE-bleh OO-sah*
Do you have the manual in English?	**¿Tiene el manual en inglés?** *TYEH-neh ehl mah-NWAHL ehn eeng-GLEHS*
Do you have a booklet in English with the local traffic laws?	**¿Tiene un folleto en inglés con las leyes de tráfico locales?** *TYEH-neh oon foh-YEH-toh ehn eeng-GLEHS kohn lahs LEH-yehs deh TRAH-fee-koh loh-KAH-lehs*

Car Troubles

The _____ doesn't work.	**_____ no funciona.** *noh foon-SYOH-nah*

See diagram on p54 for car parts.

It is already dented.	**Ya está abollado.** *YAH ehs-TAH ah-boh-YAH-doh*
It is scratched.	**Está rayado.** *ehs-TAH rah-YAH-doh*
The windshield is cracked.	**El parabrisas está agrietado.** *ehl pah-rah-BREE-sahs ehs-TAH ahg-ryeh-TAH-doh*
The tires look low.	**Las llantas se ven un poco vacías.** *lahs YAHN-tahs seh vehn oon POH-koh VAH-syahs*
It has a flat tire.	**Tiene una llanta vacía.** *TYEH-neh OO-nah YAHN-tah VAH-syah*
Whom do I call for service?	**¿A quién llamo para servicio?** *ah KYEHN YAH-moh pah-rah sehr-VEE-syoh*
It won't start.	**No enciende.** *noh ehn-SYEHN-deh*

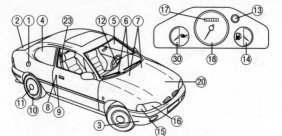

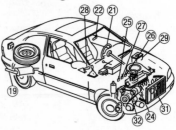

1. la puerta del tanque
   del combustible
2. el portaequipaje
3. los parachoques
4. la ventana
5. el parabrisas
6. el limpiaparabrisas
7. el lavador
   de parabrisas
8. el seguro
9. los seguros
   automáticos
10. las llantas
11. las ruedas
12. la ignición
13. la luz de advertencia
14. el indicador del combustible
15. las luces de giro
16. los focos delanteros

17. el odómetro
18. el velocímetro
19. el silenciador
20. el capó
21. el volante
22. el espejo
23. el cinturón de seguridad
24. el motor
25. el acelarador
26. el embrague
27. los frenos
28. el freno de mano
29. el acumulador
30. el indicador de aceite
31. el radiador
32. la manguera del ventilador

It's out of gas.	**No tiene combustible.** *noh TYEH-neh kohm-boos-TEEB-leh*
The Check Engine light is on.	**La luz de examinar el motor está encendida.** *lah loos dee ehk-sah-mee-NAHR ehl moh-TOHR ehs-TAH ehn-sehn-DEE-dah*
The oil light is on.	**La luz del aceite está encendida.** *lah loos dehl ah-SEH-ee-teh ehs-TAH ehn-sehn-DEE-dah*
The brake light is on.	**La luz del freno está encendida.** *lah loos dehl FREH-noh ehs-TAH ehn-sehn-DEE-dah*
It runs rough.	**Corre un poco áspero.** *KOH-rreh oon POH-koh AHS-peh-roh*
The car is over-heating.	**El auto se sobrecalienta.** *ehl OW-toh seh soh-breh-kah-LYEHN-tah*

Asking for Directions

Excuse me, please.	**Perdóneme.** *pehr-DOH-neh-meh*
How do I get to ____?	**¿Cómo llego a ____?** *KOH-moh YEH-goh ah*
Go straight.	**Siga directo.** *SEE-gah dee-REHK-toh*
Turn left.	**Vire a la izquierda.** *VEE-reh ah lah ees-KYEHR-dah*
Continue right.	**Continúe a mano derecha.** *kohn-tee-NOO-eh ah MAH-noh dee-REH-chah*
It's on the right.	**Está a mano derecha.** *ehs-TAH ah MAH-noh dee-REH-chah*

GETTING THERE

Can you show me on the map?	**¿Puede mostrarme en el mapa?**
	PWEH-deh mohs-TRAHR-meh ehn
	ehl MAH-pah
How far is it from here?	**¿Cuán lejos está de aquí?**
	kwahn LEH-hohs ehs-TAH deh ah-KEE
Is this the right road for ____?	**¿Es ésta la carretera correcta para ____?**
	ehs EHS-tah lah kah-rreh-TEH-rah
	koh-RREHK-tah PAH-rah
I've lost my way.	**Estoy perdido -a.**
	ehs-TOY pehr-DEE-doh -dah
Would you repeat that?	**¿Puede repetir eso?**
	PWEH-deh reh-peh-TEER EH-so
Thanks for your help.	**Gracias por su ayuda.**
	GRAH-syahs pohr soo ah-YOO-dah

For full coverage of direction-related terms, see p5.

Sorry, Officer

What is the speed limit?	**¿Cuál es el límite de velocidad?**
	kwahl ehs ehl LEE-mee-teh deh
	veh-loh-see-DAHD

Road Signs

Límite de velocidad	Speed Limit
Pare	Stop
Ceda el paso	Yield
Peligro	Danger
Calle sin salida	No Exit
Tránsito en una dirección	One Way
No entre	Do Not Enter
Carretera cerrada	Road Closed
Peaje	Toll
Efectivo solamente	Cash Only
No estacione	No Parking
Tarifa de estacionamiento	Parking Fee
Estacionamiento	Parking Garage

I wasn't going that fast.	**Yo no iba tan rápido.**
	yoh noh EE-bah tahn RAH-pee-doh
How much is the fine?	**¿De cuánto es la multa?**
	deh KWAHN-toh ehs lah
	MOOL-tah
Where do I pay the fine?	**¿Dónde pago la multa?**
	DOHN-deh PAH-goh lah MOOL-tah
Do I have to go to court?	**¿Tengo que ir a corte?**
	TEHNG-goh keh eer ah KOHR-teh
I had an accident.	**Tuve un accidente.**
	TOO-veh oon ahk-see-DEHN-teh
The other driver hit me.	**El otro chofer me dio.**
	ehl OH-troh choh-FEHR meh
	DEE-oh
I'm at fault.	**Es mi culpa.**
	ehs mee KOOL-pah

BY TAXI

Where is the taxi stand?	**¿Dónde está el puesto de taxis?**
	DOHN-deh ehs-TAH ehl PWEHS-
	toh deh TAHK-sees
Is there a limo / bus / van for my hotel?	**¿Hay una limosina / un autobús / una furgoneta para mi hotel?**
	ay OO-nah lee-moh-SEE-nah / oon
	ow-toh-BOOS / OO-nah foor-goh-
	NEH-tah PAH-rah mee oh-TEHL

GETTING THERE

Listen Up: Taxi Lingo

¡Súbanse!	Get in!
Deje su equipaje. Lo tengo.	Leave your luggage. I got it.
Sale 100 pesos por cada maleta.	It's 100 pesos for each bag.
¿Cuántos pasajeros?	How many passengers?
¿Tiene prisa?	Are you in a hurry?

I need to get to ____.	**Necesito ir a ____.**
	neh-seh-SEE-toh eer ah
How much will that cost?	**¿Cuánto costará eso?**
	KWAHN-toh kohs-tah-RAH EH-soh
How long will it take?	**¿Cuánto tomará?**
	KWAHN-toh toh-mah-RAH
Can you take me / us to the train / bus station?	**¿Puede llevarme / llevarnos a la estación del tren / autobús?**
	PWEH-deh yeh-VAHR-meh / yeh-VAHR-nohs ah lah ehs-tah-SYOHN dehl trehn / ow-toh-BOOS
I am in a hurry.	**Tengo prisa.**
	TEHNG-goh PREE-sah
Slow down.	**Reduzca la velocidad.**
	rreh-DOOS-kah lah veh-loh-see-DAHD
Am I close enough to walk?	**¿Estoy suficientemente cerca como para caminar?**
	ehs-TOY soo-fee-syehn-teh-MEHN-teh SEHR-kah koh-moh pah-rah kah-mee-NAHR
Let me out here.	**Déjeme salir de aquí.**
	DEH-heh-meh sah-LEER deh ah-KEE
That's not the correct change.	**Ese no es el cambio correcto.**
	EH-seh noh ehs ehl KAM-byoh koh-REHK-toh

BY TRAIN

How do I get to the train station?	**¿Cómo llego a la estación del tren?**
	KOH-moh YEH-goh ah lah ehs-tah-SYOHN dehl trehn
Would you take me to the train station?	**¿Puede llevarme a la estación del tren?**
	PWEH-deh yeh-VAHR-meh ah lah ehs-tah-SYOHN dehl trehn

How long is the trip to ___?	**¿Cuán largo es el viaje a ___?** *kwahn LAHR-goh ehs ehl VYAH-heh ah*
When is the next train?	**¿Cuándo sale el próximo tren?** *KWAHN-doh SAH-leh ehl PROHK-see-moh trehn*
Do you have a schedule / timetable?	**¿Tiene un itinerario?** *TYEH-neh oon ee-tee-neh-RAH-ryoh*
Do I have to change trains?	**¿Tengo que cambiar trenes?** *TEHNG-goh keh kahm-BYAHR TREH-nehs*
a one-way ticket	**un boleto de ida** *oon boh-LEH-toh deh EE-dah*
a round-trip ticket	**un boleto de ida y vuelta** *oon boh-LEH-toh deh EE-dah ee VWEHL-tah*
Which platform does it leave from?	**¿De cuál plataforma sale?** *deh kwahl plah-tah-FOHR-mah SAH-leh*
Is there a bar car?	**¿Hay un vagón cantina?** *aye oon vah-GOHN kahn-TEE-nah*
Is there a dining car?	**¿Hay un vagón para cenar?** *aye oon vah-GOHN pah-rah seh-NAHR*
Which car is my seat in?	**¿En cuál vagón está mi asiento?** *ehn kwahl vah-GOHN ehs-TAH mee ah-SYEHN-toh*
Is this seat taken?	**¿Este asiento está ocupado?** *EHS-teh ah-SYEHN-toh ehs-TAH oh-koo-PAH-doh*
Where is the next stop?	**¿Dónde es la próxima parada?** *DOHN-deh ehs lah PROHK-see-mah pah-RAH-dah*
How many stops to ___?	**¿Cuántas paradas hasta ___?** *KWAHN-tahs pah-RAH-dahs AHS-tah*

| What's the train number and destination? | ¿Cuál es el número del tren y su destino? |
| | *kwahl ehs ehl NOO-meh-roh dehl trehn ee soo dehs-TEE-noh* |

BY BUS

How do I get to the bus station?	¿Cómo llego a la estación de autobuses?
	KOH-moh YEH-go ah lah ehs-tah-SYOHN deh ow-toh-BOO-sehs
Would you take me to the bus station?	¿Me puede llevar a la estación de autobuses?
	meh PWEH-deh yeh-VAHR ah lah ehs-tah-SYOHN deh ow-toh-BOO-sehs
May I have a bus schedule?	¿Me puede dar un itinerario?
	meh PWEH-deh dahr oon ee-tee-neh-RAH-ryoh
Which bus goes to ____?	¿Cuál autobús va para ____?
	kwahl ow-toh-BOOS vah pah-rah
Where does it leave from?	¿De dónde sale?
	deh DOHN-deh SAH-leh
How long does the bus take?	¿Cuánto se tarda el autobús?
	KWAHN-toh seh TAHR-dah ehl ow-toh-BOOS
How much is it?	¿Cuánto cuesta?
	KWAHN-to KWEH-stah
Is there an express bus?	¿Hay un autobús expreso?
	ay oon ow-toh-BOOS ehs-PREH-soh
Does it make local stops?	¿Hace paradas locales?
	AH-seh pah-RAH-dahs loh-KAH-lehs

Does it run at night?	**¿El autobús corre de noche?**
	ehl ow-toh-BOOS KOH-rreh deh NOH-che
When does the next bus leave?	**¿Cuándo parte el próximo autobús?**
	KWAHN-doh PAHR-teh ehl PROHK-see-moh ow-toh-BOOS
a one-way ticket	**un boleto de ida**
	oon boh-LEH-toh deh EE-dah
a round-trip ticket	**un boleto de ida y vuelta**
	oon boh-LEH-toh deh EE-dah ee VWEHL-tah
How long will the bus be stopped?	**¿Por cuánto tiempo estará detenido el autobús?**
	pohr KWAHN-toh TYEHM-poh ehs-tah-RAH deh-teh-NEE-doh ehl ow-toh-BOOS
Is there an air conditioned bus?	**¿Hay un autobús con aire acondicionado?**
	aye oon ow-toh-BOOS kohn AYE-reh ah-kohn-dee-syoh-NAH-doh
Is this seat taken?	**¿Este asiento está ocupado?**
	EHS-teh ah-SYEHN-toh ehs-TAH oh-koo-PAH-doh
Where is the next stop?	**¿Dónde es la próxima parada?**
	DOHN-deh ehs lah PROHK-see-mah pah-RAH-dah

GETTING THERE

Humping the Bus?!

Be very careful with the verb *coger*. In Spain, it means to catch or grab—as in, I'm going to catch the bus. But in much of Latin America, coger is an obscenity—the equivalent of "fuck" in English. If all you want to do is *ride* the bus (in the literal sense), it's best to say **Voy a tomar el autobús** in Latin America.

Please tell me when we reach ____.	**Por favor dígame cuando lleguamos a ____.**
	pohr fah-VOHR DEE-gah-meh KWAHN-doh yeh-GAH-mohs ah
Let me off here.	**Déjeme aquí.**
	DEH-heh-meh ah-KEE

BY BOAT OR SHIP

Would you take me to the port?	**¿Me puede llevar al puerto?**
	meh PWEH-deh yeh-VAHR ahl PWEHR-toh
When does the ship sail?	**¿Cuándo zarpa el barco?**
	KWAHN-doh SAHR-pah ehl BAHR-koh
How long is the trip?	**¿Cuán largo es el viaje?**
	kwahn LAHR-goh ehs ehl VYAH-heh
Where are the life preservers?	**¿Dónde están los salvavidas?**
	DOHN-deh ehs-TAHN lohs sahl-vah-VEE-dahs
I would like a private cabin.	**Quisiera un camarote privado.**
	kee-SYEH-rah oon kah-mah-ROH-teh pree-VAH-doh
Is the trip rough?	**¿El viaje es difícil?**
	ehl VYAH-heh ehs dee-FEE-seel
I feel seasick.	**Me siento mareado -a.**
	meh SYEHN-toh mah-reh-AH-doh -dah
I need some seasick pills.	**Necesito unas píldoras para los mareos.**
	neh-seh-SEE-toh OO-nahs peel-DOH-rahs pah-rah lohs mah-REH-ohs
Where is the bathroom?	**¿Dónde está el baño?**
	DOHN-deh ehs-TAH ehl BAH-nyoh

Does the ship have a casino?

¿El barco tiene un casino?
ehl BAHR-koh TYEH-neh oon kah-SEE-noh

Will the ship stop at ports along the way?

¿El barco se detendrá en puertos a lo largo del camino?
ehl BAHR-koh seh deh-tehnd-RAH ehn PWEHR-tohs ah loh LAHR-goh dehl kah-MEE-noh

BY SUBWAY

Where's the subway station?

¿Dónde está la estación de metro?
DOHN-deh ehs-TAH lah ehs-tah-SYOHN deh MEH-troh

Where can I buy a ticket?

¿Dónde puedo comprar un boleto?
DOHN-deh PWEH-doh kohm-PRAHR oon boh-LEH-toh

GETTING THERE

SUBWAY TICKETS

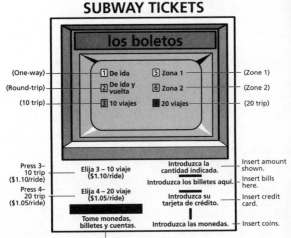

los boletos

(One-way) — 1 De ida
(Round-trip) — 2 De ida y vuelta
(10 trip) — 3 10 viajes
5 Zona 1 — (Zone 1)
6 Zona 2 — (Zone 2)
20 viajes — (20 trip)

Press 3– 10 trip ($1.10/ride) — **Elija 3 – 10 viaje ($1.10/ride)**

Press 4– 20 trip ($1.05/ride) — **Elija 4 – 20 viaje ($1.05/ride)**

Introduzca la cantidad indicada. — Insert amount shown.

Introduzca los billetes aquí. — Insert bills here.

Introduzca su tarjeta de crédito. — Insert credit card.

Tome monedas, billetes y cuentas.

Introduzca las monedas. — Insert coins.

(Take change, tickets, receipt)

Could I have a map of the subway?	**¿Puede darme un mapa del metro?** *PWEH-deh DAHR-meh oon MAH-pah dehl MEH-troh*
Which line should I take for ____?	**¿Cuál línea debo tomar para ____?** *kwahl LEE-neh-ah DEH-boh toh-MAHR PAH-rah*
Is this the right line for ____?	**¿Es ésta la línea correcta para ____?** *ehs EHS-tah lah LEE-neh-ah koh-RREHK-tah PAH-rah*
Which stop is it for ____?	**¿Cuál es la parada para ____?** *kwahl ehs lah pah-RAH-dah PAH-rah*
How many stops is it to ____?	**¿Cuántas paradas faltan para ____?** *KWAHN-tahs pah-RAH-dahs FAHL-tahn PAH-rah*
Is the next stop ____?	**¿La próxima parada es ____?** *lah PROHK-see-mah pah-RAH-dah ehs*
Where are we?	**¿Dónde estamos?** *DOHN-deh ehs-TAH-mohs*
Where do I change to ____?	**¿Adónde me cambio para ____?** *ah-DOHN-deh meh KAHM-byoh PAH-rah*
What time is the last train to ____?	**¿A qué hora pasa el último tren para ____?** *ah keh OH-rah PAH-sah ehl OOL-tee-moh trehn PAH-rah*

CONSIDERATIONS FOR TRAVELERS WITH SPECIAL NEEDS

Do you have wheelchair access?	**¿Tienen acceso para sillas de ruedas?** *TYEH-nehn ahk-SEH-soh PAH-rah SEE-yahs deh RWEH-dahs*
Do you have elevators? Where?	**¿Tienen elevadores? ¿Dónde?** *TYEH-nehn eh-leh-vah-DOH-rehs DOHN-deh*

Do you have ramps?
Where?

¿Tienen rampas? ¿Dónde?
TYEH-nehn RRAHM-pahs DOHN-deh

Are the restrooms
wheelchair accessible?

¿Los baños son accesibles para
sillas de ruedas?
lohs BAH-nyohs sohn ahk-seh-SEE-blehs pah-rah SEE-yahs deh RWEH-dahs

Do you have audio
assistance for the hearing
impaired?

¿Ustedes tienen asistencia
auditiva para las personas con
impedimentos auditivos?
oos-TEH-dehs TYEH-nehn ah-sees-TEHN-syah ow-dee-TEE-vah PAH-rah lahs pehr-SOH-nahs kohn eem-peh-dee-MEHN-tohs ow-dee-TEE-vohs

I am deaf.

Yo tengo impedimentos auditivos.
yoh TEHN-goh eem-peh-dee-MEHN-tohs ow-dee-TEE-vohs

May I bring my service
dog?

¿Puedo traer a mi perro de
servicio?
PWEH-doh trah-EHR ah mee PEH-rroh deh sehr-VEE-syoh

I am blind.

Yo tengo impedimentos visuales.
yoh TEHN-goh eem-peh-dee-MEHN-tohs vee-SWAH-lehs

I need to charge my
power chair.

**Necesito recargar mi silla de
ruedas eléctrica.**
neh-seh-SEE-toh reh-kahr-GAHR mee SEE-yah deh RWEH-dahs eh-LEHK-tree-kah

CHAPTER THREE

LODGING

This chapter will help you find the right accommodations, at the right price, and the amenities you might need during your stay.

ROOM PREFERENCES

Please recommend ____	**Por favor recomiende ____** *pohr fah-VOHR reh-koh-MYEHN-deh*
a clean hostel.	**una hospedería limpia.** *OO-nah ohs-peh-deh-REE-ah LEEM-pyah*
a moderately priced hotel.	**un hotel de precio módico.** *oon oh-TEHL deh PREH-syoh MOH-dee-koh*
a moderately priced B&B.	**una hospedería con cama y desayuno de precio módico.** *OO-nah ohs-peh-deh-REE-ah kohn KAH-mah ee deh-sah-YOO-noh deh PREH-syoh MOH-dee-ko*
a good hotel / motel.	**un buen hotel / motel.** *oon bwehn oh-TEHL / moh-TEHL*
Does the hotel have ____	**¿El hotel tiene ____** *ehl oh-TEHL TYEH-neh*
a pool?	**una piscina?** *OO-nah pee-SEE-nah*
a casino?	**un casino?** *oon kah-SEE-noh*
suites?	**suites?** *soo-EE-tehs*
a balcony?	**un balcón?** *oon bahl-KOHN*
a fitness center?	**un centro de gimnasia?** *oon SEHN-troh deh heem-NAH-syah*

a spa?	**un balneario?**
	oon bahl-neh-AH-ryoh
a private beach?	**una playa privada?**
	OO-nah PLAH-yah pree-VAH-dah
a tennis court?	**una cancha de tenis?**
	OO-nah KAHN-chah deh
	TEH-nees
I would like a room for ____.	**Quisiera una habitación para**
	____.
	kee-SYEH-rah OO-nah ah-bee-tah-
	SYOHN pah-rah

For full coverage of number terms, see p7.

I would like ____	**Quisiera ____**
	kee-SYEH-rah
a king-sized bed.	**una cama king.**
	OO-nah KAH-mah keeng
a double bed.	**una cama doble.**
	OO-nah KAH-mah DOH-bleh
twin beds.	**dos camas individuales.**
	dohs KAH-mahs een-dee-vee-
	DWAHL-ehs
adjoining rooms.	**habitaciones adjuntas.**
	ah-bee-tah-SYOH-nehs ad-
	HOON-tahs
a smoking room.	**una habitación de fumar.**
	OO-nah ah-bee-tah-SYOHN deh
	foo-MAHR

LODGING

Listen Up: Reservations Lingo

No tenemos vacantes.	We have no vacancies.
¿Hasta cuándo se queda?	How long will you be staying?
¿Sección de fumar o de no fumar?	Smoking or non smoking?

a non-smoking room.	**una habitación de no fumar.** *OO-nah ah-bee-tah-SYOHN deh noh foo-MAHR*
a private bathroom.	**un baño privado.** *oon BAH-nyoh pree-VAH-doh*
a shower.	**una ducha.** *OO-nah DOO-cha*
a bathtub.	**una bañera.** *OO-nah bah-NYEH-rah*
air conditioning.	**aire acondicionado.** *AYE-reh ah-cohn-dee-syoh-NAH-doh.*
televisión.	**un televisor.** *oon teh-leh-vee-SOHR*
cable.	**televisión por cable.** *teh-leh-vee-SYOHN pohr KAH-bleh*
satellite TV.	**televisión por satélite.** *teh-leh-vee-SYOHN pohr sah-TEH-lee-teh*
a telephone.	**un teléfono.** *oon teh-LEH-foh-noh*
Internet access.	**acceso al Internet.** *ahk-SEH-soh ahl een-tehr-NEHT*
high-speed Internet access.	**acceso al Internet de alta velocidad.** *ahk-SEH-soh ahl een-tehr-NEHT deh AHL-tah veh-loh-see-DAHD*
a refrigerator.	**un refrigerador.** *oon reh-free-heh-rah-DOHR*
a beach view.	**vista a la playa.** *VEES-tah ah lah PLAH-yah*
a city view.	**vista a la ciudad.** *VEES-tah ah lah see-oo-DAHD*

a kitchenette.	**una cocina pequeña.**
	OO-nah koh-SEE-nah
	peh-KEH-nyah
a balcony.	**un balcón.**
	oon bahl-KOHN
a suite.	**una suite.**
	OO-nah SWEE-teh
a penthouse.	**un ático de lujo.**
	oon AH-tee-koh deh LOO-ho
I would like a room ____	**Quisiera una habitación ____**
	kee-SYEH-rah OO-nah ah-bee-
	tah-SYOHN
on the ground floor.	**en el primer piso.**
	ehn ehl pree-MEHR PEE-soh
near the elevator.	**cerca del elevador.**
	SEHR-kah dehl eh-leh-vah-DOHR
near the stairs.	**cerca de las escaleras.**
	SEHR-kah deh lahs ehs-kah-
	LEH-rahs
near the pool.	**cerca de la piscina.**
	SEHR-kah deh lah pee-SEE-nah
away from the street.	**lejos de la calle.**
	LEH-hohs deh lah KAH-yeh
I would like a corner room.	**Quisiera una habitación de**
	esquina.
	kee-SYEH-rah OO-na ah-bee-tah-
	SYOHN deh ehs-KEE-nah
Do you have ____	**¿Tiene ____**
	TYEH-neh
a crib?	**una cuna?**
	OO-nah KOO-nah
a foldout bed?	**una cama desplegable?**
	OO-nah KAH-mah dehs-pleh-
	GAH-bleh

FOR GUESTS WITH SPECIAL NEEDS

I need a room with ____	**Necesito una habitación con ____** *neh-seh-SEE-toh OO-nah ah-bee-tah-SYOHN kohn*
wheelchair access.	**acceso para silla de ruedas.** *ahk-SEH-soh pah-rah SEE-yah deh RWEH-dahs*
services for the visually impaired.	**servicios para las personas con impedimentos visuales.** *sehr-VEE-syohs pah-rah lahs pehr-SOH-nahs kohn eem-peh-dee-MEHN-tohs vee-SWAH-lehs*
services for the hearing impaired.	**servicios para las personas con impedimentos auditivos.** *sehr-VEE-syohs pah-rah lahs pehr-SOH-nahs kohn eem-peh-dee-MEHN-tohs ow-dee-TEE-vohs*
I am traveling with a service dog.	**Estoy viajando con un perro de servicio.** *ehs-TOY vyah-HAHN-doh kohn oon PEH-rroh deh sehr-VEE-syoh*

MONEY MATTERS

I would like to make a reservation.	**Quisiera hacer una reservación.** *kee-SYEH-rah ah-SEHR OO-nah reh-sehr-vah-SYOHN*
How much per night?	**¿Cuánto cuesta por noche?** *KWAHN-toh KWEHS-tah pohr NOH-cheh*
Do you have a ____	**¿Tiene una tarifa _____?** *TYEH-neh OO-nah tah-REE-fah*
weekly / monthly rate?	**semanal / mensual?** *seh-mah-NAHL / mehn-SWAHL*
a weekend rate?	**una tarifa de fin de semana?** *OO-nah tah-REE-fah deh feen deh seh-MAH-nah*

We will be staying for ____ days / weeks.

¿Nos quedaremos por ____ días / semanas.
nohs keh-dah-REH-mohs pohr ____ DEE-ahs / seh-MAH-nahs.

For full coverage of number terms, see p7.

When is checkout time?

¿Cuál es la hora de salida?
kwahl ehs lah OH-rah deh sah-LEE-dah

For full coverage of time-related terms, see p12.

Do you accept credit cards / travelers checks?

¿Aceptan tarjetas de crédito / cheques de viajero?
ah-SEHP-tahn tahr-HEH-tahs deh KREH-dee-toh / CHEH-kehs deh vyah-HEH-roh

May I see a room?

¿Puedo ver una habitación?
PWEH-doh vehr OO-nah ah-bee-tah-SYOHN

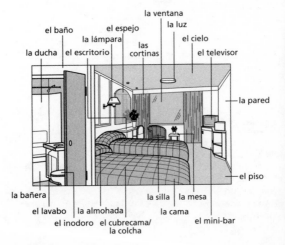

la ventana
el baño
el espejo
la lámpara
la ducha   el escritorio
las cortinas
la luz
el cielo
el televisor
la pared
el piso
la bañera
el lavabo   la almohada
el inodoro   el cubrecama/
la colcha
la silla   la mesa
la cama
el mini-bar

How much are taxes?	¿Cuántos son los impuestos?
	KWAHN-tohs sohn lohs eem-PWEHS-tohs
Is there a service charge?	¿Hay un cargo por servicio?
	aye oon KAHR-goh pohr sehr-VEE-syoh
I'd like to speak with the manager.	Quisiera hablar con el gerente.
	kee-SYEH-rah ah-BLAHR kohn ehl heh-REHN-teh

IN-ROOM AMENITIES

I'd like _____	Quisiera _____
	kee-SYEH-rah
to place an international call.	hacer una llamada internacional.
	ah-SEHR OO-nah yah-MAH-dah een-tehr-nah-syoh-NAHL
to place a long-distance call.	hacer una llamada de larga distancia.
	ah-SEHR OO-nah yah-MAH-dah deh LAHR-gah dees-TAHN-syah
directory assistance in English.	asistencia en inglés.
	ah-sees-TEHN-syah ehn een-GLEHS

Instructions for dialing the hotel phone

Para llamar a otra habitación, marque el número de la habitación.	To call another room, dial the room number.
Para llamadas locales, marque primero el 9.	To make a local call, first dial 9.
Para la operadora, marque el 0.	To call the operator, dial 0.

room service.	**servicio de habitaciones.**
	sehr-VEE-syoh deh ah-bee-tah-
	SYOH-nehs
maid service.	**servicio de camarera.**
	sehr-VEE-syoh deh kah-mah-
	REH-rah
the front desk ATT operator.	**la operadora de ATT de la recepción.**
	lah oh-peh-rah-DOH-rah deh ah
	teh tee deh lah reh-
	sehp-SYOHN
Do you have room service?	**¿Tienen servicio de habitaciones?**
	TYEH-nehn sehr-VEE-syoh deh
	ah-bee-tah-SYOH-nehs
When is the kitchen open?	**¿Cuándo abre la cocina?**
	KWAHN-doh AH-breh lah
	koh-SEE-nah
When is breakfast served?	**¿Cuándo se servirá el desayuno?**
	KWAHN-doh seh sehr-vee-RAH
	ehl deh-sah-YOO-noh

For full coverage of time-related terms, see p12.

Do you offer massages?	**¿Ustedes ofrecen masajes?**
	oo-STEH-dehs oh-FREH-sehn mah-
	SAH-hehs
Do you have a lounge?	**¿Tienen un salón público?**
	TYEH-nehn oon sah-LOHN POO-
	blee-koh
Do you have a business center?	**¿Tienen un centro de negocios?**
	TYEH-nehn oon SEHN-troh deh
	neh-GOH-syohs
Do you serve breakfast?	**¿Sirven desayuno?**
	SEER-vehn deh-sah-YOO-noh
Do you have Wi-Fi?	**¿Ustedes ofrecen red inalámbrica?**
	oos-TEH-dehs oh-FREH-sehn rehd
	ee-nah-LAHM-bree-kah

May I have a newspaper in the morning?	**¿Puedo recibir un periódico en la mañana?** *PWEH-deh reh-see-BEER oon pehr-YOH-dee-koh ehn lah mah-NYAH-nah*
Do you offer a tailor service?	**¿Ustedes ofrecen un servicio de sastre?** *oos-TEH-dehs oh-FREH-sehn oon sehr-VEE-syoh deh SAHS-treh*
Do you offer laundry service?	**¿Ustedes ofrecen servicio de lavandería?** *oos-TEH-dehs oh-FREH-sehn sehr-VEE-syoh deh lah-vahn-deh-REE-ah*
Do you offer dry cleaning?	**¿Ustedes ofrecen servicio de limpieza en seco?** *oos-TEH-dehs oh-FREH-sehn sehr-VEE-syoh deh leem-PYEH-sah ehn SEH-koh*
May we have ____	**¿Podemos tener ____** *poh-DEH-mohs teh-NEHR*
clean sheets today?	**sábanas limpias hoy?** *SAH-bah-nahs LEEM-pee-ahs oy*
more towels?	**más toallas?** *mahs toh-AH-yahs*
more toilet paper?	**más papel sanitario?** *mahs pah-PEHL sah-nee-TAH-ryoh*
extra pillows?	**almohadas adicionales?** *ahl-moh-AH-dahs ah-dees-yoh-NAH-lehs*
Do you have an ice machine?	**¿Tienen una máquina de hielo?** *TYEH-nehn OO-nah MAH-kee-nah deh YEH-loh*

Did I receive any ____

  messages?

  mail?

  faxes?

A spare key, please.

More hangers please.

I am allergic to down pillows

I'd like a wake up call.

¿Recibí ____
reh-see-BEE
  algún mensaje?
  ahl-GOON mehn-SAH-heh
  alguna correspondencia?
  ahl-GOO-nah koh-rrehs-pohn-
  DEHN-syah
  algún fax?
  ahl-GOON fahks

Una llave adicional, por favor.
OO-nah YAH-veh ah-dees-yoh-
NAHL, pohr fah-VOHR

Más perchas por favor.
mahs PEHR-chahs pohr fah-VOHR

Soy alérgico -a a las almohadas de plumas.
soy ah-LEHR-hee-koh I-kah ah lahs ahl-moh-AH-dahs deh PLOO-mahs

Quisiera una llamada para despertar.
kee-SYEH-rah OO-nah yah-MAH-dah pah-rah dehs-pehr-TAHR

For full coverage of how to tell time, see p12.

Do you have alarm clocks?

Is there a safe in the room?

Does the room have a hair dryer?

¿Tiene relojes despertadores?
TYEH-neh reh-LOH-hehs dehs-pehr-tah-DOH-rehs

¿Hay una caja fuerte en la habitación?
aye OO-nah KAH-hah FWEHR-teh ehn lah ah-bee-tah-SYOHN

¿La habitación tiene un secador de pelo?
lah ah-bee-tah-SYOHN TYEH-neh oon seh-kah-DOHR deh PEH-loh

LODGING

HOTEL ROOM TROUBLE

May I speak with the manager?	**¿Puedo hablar con el gerente?** *PWEH-doh ah-BLAHR kohn ehl heh-REHN-teh*
The ___ does not work.	**___ no funciona.** *noh foon-SYOH-nah*
television	**El televisor** *ehl teh-leh-vee-SOHR*
telephone	**El teléfono** *ehl teh-LEH-foh-noh*
air conditioning	**El aire acondicionado** *ehl AYE-reh ah-kohn-dee-syoh-NAH-doh*
Internet access	**El acceso al Internet** *ehl ahk-SEH-soh ahl een-tehr-NET*
cable TV	**El servicio de cable TV** *ehl sehr-VEE-syoh deh KAH-bleh teh VEH*
There is no hot water.	**No hay agua caliente.** *noh ay AH-wah kah-LYEHN-teh*
The toilet is over-flowing!	**¡El inodoro se está desbordando!** *ehl ee-noh-DOH-roh seh ehs-TAH dehs-bohr-DAHN-doh*

This room is ____	**Esta habitación ____**
	EHS-tah ah-bee-tah-SYOHN
too noisy.	**es muy ruidosa.**
	ehs MOO-ee roo-ee-DOH-sah
too cold.	**está muy fría.**
	ehs-TAH MOO-ee FREE-ah
too warm.	**está muy cálida.**
	ehs-TAH MOO-ee KAH-lee-dah
This room has ____	**Esta habitación tiene ____**
	EHS-tah ah-bee-tah-SYOHN
	TYEH-neh
bugs.	**insectos.**
	een-SEHK-tohs
mice.	**ratones.**
	rah-TOH-nehs
I'd like a different room.	**Quisiera una habitación diferente.**
	kee-SYEH-rah OO-nah ah-bee-tah-
	SYOHN dee-feh-REHN-teh
Do you have a bigger room?	**¿Tiene una habitación más grande?**
	TYEH-neh OO-nah ah-bee-tah-
	SYOHN mahs GRAHN-deh
I locked myself out of my room.	**Me quedé fuera de mi habitación.**
	meh keh-DEH FWEH-rah deh mee
	ah-bee-tah-SYOHN
Do you have any fans?	**¿Tiene abanicos?**
	TYEH-ne ah-bah-NEE-kohs
The sheets are not clean.	**Las sábanas no están limpias.**
	lahs SAH-bah-nahs noh ehs-TAHN
	LEEM-pyahs
The towels are not clean.	**Las toallas no están limpias.**
	lahs to-AH-yahs noh ehs-TAHN
	LEEM-pyahs
The room is not clean.	**La habitación no está limpia.**
	lah ah-bee-tah-SYOHN noh ehs-
	TAH LEEM-pyah

LODGING

The guests next door / above / below are being very loud.	**Los huéspedes al lado / arriba / abajo son muy ruidosos.** *lohs WEHS-peh-dehs ahl LAH-doh / ah-RREE-bah / ah-BAH-hoh sohn MOO-ee roo-ee-DOH-sohs*

CHECKING OUT

I think this charge is a mistake.	**Creo que este cargo es un error.** *KREH-oh keh EHS-teh KAHR-goh ehs oon eh-RROHR*
Please explain this charge to me.	**Por favor explíqueme este cargo.** *pohr fah-VOHR ehs-PLEE-keh-meh EHS-teh KAHR-goh*
Thank you, we enjoyed our stay.	**Gracias, disfrutamos nuestra estadía.** *GRAH-syahs dees-froo-TAH-mohs NWEHS-trah ehs-tah-DEE-ah*
The service was excellent.	**El servicio fue excelente.** *ehl sehr-VEE-syoh fweh ehk-seh-LEHN-teh*
The staff is very professional and courteous.	**El personal es muy profesional y cortés.** *ehl pehr-soh-NAHL ehs MOO-ee proh-feh-syoh-NAHL ee kohr-TEHS*
Please call a cab for me.	**Por favor, llame a un taxi para mí.** *pohr fah-VOHR YAH-meh ah oon TAHK-see PAH-rah mee*
Would someone please get my bags?	**¿Alguien puede ayudarme con mis bolsas?** *AHLG-yehn PWEH-deh ah-yoo-DAHR-meh kohn mees BOHL-sahs*

HAPPY CAMPING

I'd like a site for ____

Quisiera un lugar para ____
kee-SYEH-rah oon loo-GAHR pah-rah

 a tent.

  una tienda de campaña.
  OO-nah TYEHN-dah deh kahm-PAH-nyah

 a camper.

  un carro de acampar.
  oon KAH-rroh deh ah-kahm-PAHR

Are there ____

¿Hay ____
ay

 bathrooms?

  baños?
  BAH-nyohs

 showers?

  duchas?
  DOOH-chahs

Is there running water?

¿Hay agua de llave?
ay AH-wah deh YAH-veh

Is the water drinkable?

¿El agua es potable?
ehl AH-wah ehs poh-TAH-bleh

Where is the electrical hookup?

¿Dónde está la conexión eléctrica?
DOHN-deh ehs-TAH lah koh-nehk-SYOHN eh-LEHK-tree-kah

CHAPTER FOUR

DINING

This chapter includes a menu reader and the language you need to communicate in a range of dining establishments and food markets.

FINDING A RESTAURANT

Would you recommend a good ____ restaurant?

¿**Podría recomendar un buen restaurante** ____
poh-DREE-ah reh-koh-mehn-DAHR oon bwehn reh-stow-RAHN-teh

local	**local?** *loh-KAHL*
Italian	**italiano?** *ee-tah-LYAH-noh*
French	**francés?** *frahn-SEHS*
German	**alemán?** *ah-leh-MAHN*
Spanish	**español?** *ehs-pah-NYOHL*
Chinese	**chino?** *CHEE-noh*
Japanese	**japonés?** *hah-poh-NEHS*
Asian	**asiático?** *ah-SYAH-tee-koh*
pizza	**de pizza?** *deh PEET-sah*
steakhouse	**de parrilla?** *deh pah-RREE-yah*
family	**familiar?** *fah-mee-LYAHR*

seafood	**de mariscos?**
	deh mah-REES-kohs
vegetarian	**vegetariano?**
	veh-heh-tah-RYAH-noh
buffet-style	**estilo buffet?**
	ehs-TEE-loh boo-FEH
Greek	**griego?**
	GRYEH-goh
budget	**económico?**
	eh-koh-NOH-mee-koh
Which is the best restaurant in town?	**¿Cuál es el mejor restaurante en el pueblo?**
	kwahl ehs ehl meh-HOHR reh-stoh-RAHN-teh ehn ehl PWEH-bloh
Is there a late-night restaurant nearby?	**¿Hay un restaurante cercano abierto hasta tarde en la noche?**
	aye oon reh-stoh-RAHN-teh SEHR-kah-noh ah-BYEHR-toh AHS-tah TAHR-deh ehn lah NOH-cheh
Is there a restaurant that serves breakfast nearby?	**¿Hay un restaurante cercano que sirva desayuno?**
	aye oon reh-stoh-RAHN-teh SEHR-ka-noh keh SEER-vah deh-sah-YOO-noh
Is it very expensive?	**¿Es muy caro?**
	ehs MOO-ee KAH-roh
Do I need a reservation?	**¿Necesito una reservación?**
	neh-seh-SEE-toh OO-nah reh-sehr-vah-SYOHN
Do I have to dress up?	**¿Necesito vestirme elegante-mente?**
	neh-seh-SEE-toh veh-STEER-meh eh-leh-gahn-teh-MEHN-teh

Do they serve lunch?	**¿Sirven almuerzo?**
	SEER-vehn ahl-MWEHR-soh
What time do they open for dinner?	**¿A qué hora abren para la cena?**
	ah KEH OH-rah AHB-rehn PAH-rah lah SEH-nah
For lunch?	**¿Para almuerzo?**
	PAH-rah ahl-MWEHR-soh
What time do they close?	**¿A qué hora cierran?**
	ah KEH OH-rah SYEH-rrahn
Do you have a take out menu?	**¿Tienen un menú para llevar?**
	TYEH-nehn oon meh-NOO PAH-rah yeh-VAHR
Do you have a bar?	**¿Tienen un bar?**
	TYEH-nehn oon bahr
Is there a café nearby?	**¿Hay un café cerca?**
	aye oon kah-FEH SEHR-kah

GETTING SEATED

Are you still serving?	**¿Todavía están sirviendo?**
	toh-dah-VEE-ah ehs-TAHN seer-VYEHN-doh
How long is the wait?	**¿Cuán larga es la espera?**
	kwahn LAHR-gah ehs lah ehs-PEH-rah
Do you have a no-smoking section?	**¿Tienen una sección de no fumar?**
	TYEH-nehn OO-nah sehk-SYOHN deh noh foo-MAHR
A table for ____, please.	**Una mesa para ____, por favor.**
	OO-nah MEH-sah PAH-rah ____, pohr fah-VOHR

For a full list of numbers, see p7.

Do you have a quiet, table?	**¿Tienen una mesa tranquila?**
	TYEH-nehn OO-nah MEH-sah trahn-KEE-lah

Listen Up: Restaurant Lingo

¿**Sección de fumar o de no fumar?**
*sehk-SYOHN deh foo-MAHR
oh deh noh foo-MAHR*

Smoking or
nonsmoking?

Necesita una corbata y
una chaqueta.
*neh-seh-SEE-tah OO-nah kohr-
BAH-tah ee OO-na chah-KEH-tah*

You'll need a tie and
jacket.

Lo siento, no se permite
pantalones cortos.
*loh SYEHN-toh noh seh pehr-MEE-
tehn pahn-tah-LOH-nehs KOHR-tohs*

I'm sorry, no shorts are
allowed.

¿**Le puedo traer algo de tomar?**
*leh PWEH-doh trah-EHR
AHL-goh deh toh-MAHR*

May I bring you
something to drink?

¿**Le gustaría ver una**
lista de vinos?
*leh goos-tah-REE-ah vehr OO-
nah LEES-tah deh VEE-nohs*

Would you like to see
a wine list?

¿**Le gustaría saber**
cuáles son nuestros
platos especiales?
*leh goos-tah-REE-ah sah-BEHR
KWAH-lehs sohn NWEHS-trohs
PLAH-tohs ehs-peh-SYAH-lehs*

Would you like to hear
our specials?

¿**Está listo para ordenar?**
*ehs-TAH LEES-toh PAH-rah
ohr-deh-NAHR*

Are you ready to order?

Lo siento señor. Su
tarjeta de crédito ha sido
rechazada.
*loh SYEHN-toh seh-NYOHR
soo tahr-HEH-tah deh
KREH-dee-toh hah SEE-doh
reh-chah-SAH-dah*

I'm sorry, sir, your credit
card was declined.

May we sit outside / inside please?	**¿Podemos sentarnos afuera / adentro por favor?** *poh-DEH-mohs sehn-TAHR-nohs ah-FWEH-rah / ah-DEHN-troh pohr fah-VOHR*
May we sit at the counter?	**¿Podemos sentarnos en el mostrador?** *poh-DEH-mohs sehn-TAHR-nohs ehn ehl mohs-trah-DOHR*
A menu please?	**¿Un menú por favor?** *oon meh-NOO pohr fah-VOHR*

ORDERING

Do you have a special tonight?	**¿Tienen un especial esta noche?** *TYEH-nehn oon ehs-peh-SYAHL EHS-tah NOH-cheh*
What do you recommend?	**¿Qué recomienda usted?** *KEH reh-koh-MYEHN-dah oos-TEHD*
May I see a wine list?	**¿Puedo ver una lista de vinos?** *PWEH-doh vehr OO-nah LEES-tah deh VEE-nohs*
Do you serve wine by the glass?	**¿Ustedes sirven vino por la copa?** *oos-TEH-dehs SEER-vehn VEE-noh pohr lah KOH-pah*
May I see a drink list?	**¿Puedo ver una lista de bebidas?** *PWEH-doh vehr OO-nah LEES-tah deh beh-BEE-dahs*
I would like it cooked ____	**Me gustaría ____** *meh goos-tah-REE-ah*
rare.	**crudo.** *KROO-doh*
medium rare.	**a medio cocer.** *ah MEH-dyoh koh-SEHR*
medium.	**término medio.** *TEHR-mee-noh MEH-dyoh*

medium well.	**medio bien cocido.**
	MEH-dyoh byehn koh-SEE-doh
well.	**bien cocido.**
	byehn koh-SEE-doh
charred.	**achicharrado.**
	ah-chee-chah-RRAH-doh
Do you have a ____ menu?	**¿Tiene un menú ____**
	TYEH-neh oon meh-NOO
diabetic	**diabético?**
	dee-ah-BEH-tee-koh
kosher	**kósher?**
	KOH-shehr
vegetarian	**vegetariano?**
	veh-heh-tah-RYAH-noh
children's	**para niños?**
	PAH-rah NEE-nyohs
What is in this dish?	**¿Qué hay en este plato?**
	keh aye ehn EHS-teh PLAH-toh
How is it prepared?	**¿Cómo está preparado?**
	KOH-moh eh-STAH preh-PAH-
	rah-do
What kind of oil is that cooked in?	**¿En qué tipo de aceite está cocido?**
	ehn keh TEE-poh deh ah-SEH-ee-teh eh-STAH koh-SEE-doh
Do you have any low-salt dishes?	**¿Tiene platos bajos en sal?**
	TYEH-neh PLAH-tohs BAH-hohs ehn sahl
On the side, please.	**Al lado, por favor.**
	ahl LAH-doh pohr fah-VOHR
May I make a substitution?	**¿Puedo hacer una sustitución?**
	PWEH-doh ah-SEHR OO-nah soos-tee-too-SYOHN

I'd like to try that.	**Me gustaría probar eso.** *meh goos-tah-REE-ah proh-BAHR EH-soh*
Is that fresh?	**¿Eso es fresco?** *EH-so ehs FREHS-koh*
Waiter!	**¡Mozo! ¡Mesero!** (Colombia) *MOH-soh / meh-SEH-roh*
Extra butter, please.	**Mantequilla adicional, por favor.** *mahn-teh-KEE-yah ah-dee-syoh- NAHL pohr fah-VOHR*
No butter, thanks.	**Sin mantequilla, por favor.** *seen mahn-teh-KEE-yah pohr fah- VOHR*
No cream, thanks.	**Sin crema, por favor.** *seen KREH-mah pohr fah-VOHR*
Dressing on the side, please.	**El aderezo por el lado, por favor.** *ehl ah-deh-REH-soh pohr ehl LAH- doh, pohr fah-VOHR*
No salt, please.	**Sin sal, por favor.** *seen sahl pohr fah-VOHR*
May I have some oil, please?	**¿Me puede dar un poco de aceite, por favor?** *meh PWEH-deh dahr oon POH-koh deh ah-SEH-ee-teh pohr fah-VOHR*
More bread, please.	**Más pan, por favor.** *mahs pahn pohr fah-VOHR*
I am lactose intolerant.	**Soy intolerante a la lactosa.** *soy een-toh-loh-RAHN-teh ah lah lahk-TOH-sah*
Would you recommend something without milk?	**¿Podría recomendar algo sin leche?** *poh-DREE-ah reh-koh-mehn-DAHR AHL-goh seen LEH-cheh*

I am allergic to ____	**Soy alérgico -a a ____** *soy ah-LEHR-hee-koh -kah ah*
seafood.	**los mariscos.** *lohs mah-REES-kohs*
shellfish.	**los crustáceos.** *lohs kroos-TAH-seh-ohs*
nuts.	**las nueces.** *lahs-NWEH-sehs*
peanuts.	**los cacahuates, los manís (Puerto Rico, S.Am.)** *lohs kah-kah-WAH-tehs, lohs mah-NEES*
Water ____, please.	**Agua ____, por favor.** *AH-wah ____ pohr fah-VOHR*
with ice	**con hielo** *kohn YEH-loh*
without ice	**sin hielo** *seen YEH-loh*
I'm sorry, I don't think this is what I ordered.	**Lo siento, no creo que esto sea lo que ordené.** *loh SYEHN-toh noh KREH-oh keh EHS-toh SEH-ah loh keh ohr-deh-NEH*
My meat is a little over / under cooked.	**Mi carne está un poco recocida / cruda.** *mee KAHR-neh ehs-TAH oon POH-koh reh-koh-SEE-dah / KROO-dah*
My vegetables are a little over / under cooked.	**Mis vegetales están un poco recocidos / crudos.** *mees veh-he-TAH-lehs ehs-TAHN oon POH-koh reh-koh-SEE-dohs / KROO-dohs*
There's a bug in my food!	**¡Hay un insecto en mi comida!** *aye oon een-SEHK-toh ehn mee koh-MEE-dah*

May I have a refill?	**¿Puede rellenar mi bebida?** *PWEH-deh reh-yeh-NAHR mee* *beh-BEE-dah*
A dessert menu, please.	**Un menú de postres, por favor.** *oon meh-NOO deh POHS-trehs* *pohr fah-VOHR*

DRINKS

alcoholic	**con alcohol** *kohn ahl-koh-OHL*
neat / straight	**sencillo** *sehn-SEE-yoh*
on the rocks	**en las rocas** *ehn lahs ROH-kahs*
with (seltzer or soda) water	**con agua (de seltzer o de soda)** *kohn AH-wah (deh sehlt-SEHR oh* *deh SOH-dah)*
beer	**cerveza** *sehr-VEH-sah*
wine	**vino** *VEE-noh*
house wine	**vino de la casa** *VEE-noh deh lah KAH-sah*
sweet wine	**vino dulce** *VEE-noh DOOL-seh*
dry white wine	**vino blanco seco** *VEE-noh BLAHN-koh SEH-koh*
rosé	**vino rosado** *VEE-noh roh-SAH-doh*
light-bodied wine	**vino de cuerpo liviano** *VEE-noh deh KWEHR-poh lee-* *VYAH-noh*
red wine	**vino tinto** *VEE-noh TEEN-toh*

How Do You Take It?

Tomar means to take. But if a bartender asks, *¿Quiere tomar algo?*, he's not inviting you to steal his fancy corkscrew. He's asking what you'd like to drink.

full-bodied wine	**vino de cuerpo entero** *VEE-noh deh KWEHR-poh ehn-TEH-roh*
sparkling sweet wine	**vino dulce burbujeante** *VEE-noh DOOL-seh boor-boo-heh-AHN-teh*
liqueur	**licor** *lee-KOHR*
brandy	**brandy** *BRAHN-dee*
cognac	**coñac** *koh-NYAHK*
gin	**ginebra** *hee-NEH-brah*
vodka	**vodka** *VOHD-kah*
rum	**ron** *rohn*
nonalcoholic	**sin alcohol** *seen ahl-koh-OHL*
hot chocolate	**chocolate caliente** *cho-koh-LAH-teh kah-LYEHN-teh*
lemonade	**limonada** *lee-moh-NAH-dah*
milkshake	**batido de leche** *bah-TEE-doh deh LEH-cheh*

milk	**leche**
	LEH-cheh
tea	**té**
	teh
coffee	**café**
	kah-FEH
cappuccino	**cappuccino**
	kah-poo-CHEE-noh
espresso	**café expreso**
	kah-FEH ehs-PREH-soh
iced coffee	**café helado**
	kah-FEH heh-LAH-doh
fruit juice	**jugo de fruta**
	HOO-goh deh FROO-tah

For a full list of fruits, see p103.

SETTLING UP

I'm stuffed.	**Estoy lleno -a.**
	ehs-TOY YEH-noh -nah
The meal was excellent.	**La comida estuvo excelente.**
	lah koh-MEE-dah ehs-TOO-voh
	ehk-seh-LEHN-teh
There's a problem with my bill.	**Hay un problema con mi factura.**
	aye oon proh-BLEH-mah kohn mee
	fahk-TOO-rah
Is the tip included?	**¿La propina está incluida?**
	lah proh-PEE-nah ehs-TAH
	een-kloo-EE-dah
My compliments to the chef!	**¡Mis felicitaciones para el chef!**
	mees feh-lee-see-tah-SYOH-nehs
	PAH-rah ehl chef
Check, please.	**El cheque, por favor.**
	ehl CHEH-keh pohr fah-VOHR

MENU READER

Latin American cuisine varies broadly from region to region, but we've tried to make our list of classic dishes as encompassing as possible.

APPETIZERS / TAPAS

aceitunas: olives
ah-seh-ee-TOO-nahs

albóndigas: meatballs in sauce
ahl-BOHN-dee-gahs

bacalao: dried salt cod
bah-kah-LAH-oh

conejo: braised rabbit
koh-NEH-ho

croquetas: croquettes
kroh-KEH-tahs

gambas: broiled shrimp with garlic
GAHM-bahs

jamón: ham
hah-MOHN

  jamón de bellota: free-range, acorn-fed ham
  hah-MOHN deh beh-YOH-tah

  jamón ibérico: aged Iberian ham
  hah-MOHN ee-BEH-ree-koh

  jamón serrano: dry-cured serrano ham
  hah-MOHN seh-RRAH-noh

pescados fritos: fried fish
pehs-KAH-dohs FREE-tohs

quesos: cheeses
KEH-sohs

  de leche de cabra: goat's milk
  deh LEH-cheh deh KAH-brah

  mozzarella: mozzarella
  moht-sah-REH-yah

  parmesano: Parmesan
  pahr-meh-SAH-noh

rallado: grated
rah-YAH-doh

requesón: cottage
reh-keh-SOHN

suave: mild
soo-AH-veh

tortilla española: omelet with potato
tohr-TEE-yah ehs-pah-NYOH-lah

SALADS

chonta: hearts-of-palm salad
CHOHN-tah

ensalada mixta: salad with lettuce, tomatoes, olives, tuna
ehn-sah-LAH-dah MEES-tah

ensalada de verduras: green salad
ehn-sah-LAH-dah deh vehr-DOO-rahs

ensalada de espinacas: spinach salad
ehn-sah-LAH-dah deh ehs-pee-NAH-kahs

ensalada de arúgula: arugula salad
ehn-sah-LAH-dah deh ah-ROO-goo-lah

ensalada de tomates: tomato salad
ehn-sah-LAH-dah deh toh-MAH-tehs

ensalada de berro: watercress salad
ehn-sah-LAH-dah deh BEH-rroh

ensalada de lechuga romaine: romaine salad
ehn-sah-LAH-dah deh leh-CHOO-gah rroh-MEHN

SAUCES / SEASONING BASES

adobo: mixture of crushed peppercorns, salt, oregano, garlic,
  olive oil, and lime juice or vinegar
ah-DOH-boh

mole: sauce of unsweetened chocolate, chiles, and spices
MOH-leh

romesco: tomato / almond sauce with olive oil and garlic
rroh-MEHS-koh

sofrito: mixture of onions, cilantro, garlic, and chiles
soh-FREE-tohs

SOUPS AND STEWS

asopao: Puerto Rican gumbo made with chicken or shellfish
ah-soh-PAH-oh

buseca: stew with sausages
boo-SEH-kah

caldo gallego: soup with salt pork, white beans, chorizo, ham,
   and turnip / collard greens
KAHL-doh gah-YEH-goh

gazpacho: cold vegetable soup
gahs-PAH-cho

locro de papas: creamy potato soup
LOH-kroh deh PAH-pahs

manchamantel: chicken or pork stew with mixed vegetables
   and fruit
mahn-chah-mahn-TEHL

menudo: tripe stew
meh-NOO-doh

mondongo: beef tripe and vegetable soup
mohn-DOHN-goh

sancocho, sancochado: thick soup with meats, vegetables, and
   corn on the cob, served with rice
sahn-KOH-choh, sahn-koh-CHAH-doh

sancocho de gallina: chicken soup
sahn-KOH-choh deh gah-YEE-nah

sopa de ajo: garlic soup
SOH-pah deh AH-hoh

sopa de chiles poblanos: green chili soup
SOH-pah deh CHEE-lehs poh-BLAH-nohs

sopa negra / frijoles negros: black bean soup
SOH-pah NEH-grah / free-HOH-lehs NEH-grohs

RICE DISHES

arroz con gandules: yellow rice with pigeon peas
ah-RROHS kohn gahn-DOO-lehs

arroz negro: rice stew with octopus in its own ink
ah-RROHS NEH-groh

paella: festive seafood / meat rice stew with vegetables, seasoned with saffron
pah-EH-yah

SIDE / VEGETABLE DISHES

aguacate relleno, palta rellena (S.Am): stuffed avocado
ah-wah-KAH-teh rreh-YEH-noh

calabacitas en crema: squash in cream sauce
kah-lah-bah-SEE-tahs ehn KREH-mah

chiles rellenos: poblano peppers stuffed with cheese or ground meat, battered and fried
CHEE-lehs rreh-YEH-nohs

patacones, chifles (Peru, Ecuador): fried plantains
pah-tah-KOH-nehs, CHEE-flehs

pristinos: pumpkin fritters
prees-TEE-nohs

rocoto relleno: stuffed pepper
rroh-KOH-toh rreh-YEH-noh

tostones: fried breadfruit or plantain slices
tohs-TOH-nehs

yuca frita: fried yucca
YOO-kah FREE-tah

For a full list of vegetables, see p105.

SAUSAGES

butifarra: spiced pork breakfast sausage
boo-tee-FAH-rrah

chorizo: spicy pork sausage
cho-REE-soh

morcilla: black pudding
mohr-SEE-yah

salchichón: Puerto Rican salami-style sausage
sahl-chee-CHOHN

BEEF

bife de lomo: filet mignon
BEE-feh deh LOH-moh

carne en polvo: seasoned ground beef
KAHR-neh ehn POHL-voh

carne mechada: Cuban-style stuffed beef
KAHR-neh meh-CHAH-dah

locro criollo: beef stew with potatoes
LOH-kroh kree-OH-yoh

lomo fino: beef tenderloin in port sauce
LOH-moh FEE-noh

lomo salteado, loma saltado (S.Am): beef strips with mixed
  vegetables and rice
LOH-moh sahl-teh-AH-doh, LOH-moh sahl-TAH-do

olla de carne: beef stew with yucca, squash, and pumpkin
OH-yah deh KAHR-neh

ropa vieja: stewed shredded beef
ROH-pah VYEH-hah

ORGAN MEATS

menudo: tripe stew
meh-NOO-doh

pastelón de menudencias: tripe pie
pahs-teh-LOHN deh meh-noo-DEHN-syahs

riñoncitos al vino: chicken kidneys stewed in a wine sauce.
rreh-nyohn-SEE-tohs ahl VEE-noh

guisado de riñones: kidney stew
gee-SAH-doh deh ree-NYOH-nehs

GOAT

cabrito asado: oven-roasted kid
kah-BREE-toh ah-SAH-doh

seco de chivo: goat stew in wine sauce
SEH-koh deh CHEE-voh

PORK

carnitas: slow-cooked pork served with corn tortillas
kahr-NEE-tahs

chicharrón: deep-fried pork skin
chee-chah-RROHN

cochinillo / lechón asado: roast suckling pig
koh-chee-NEE-yoh / leh-CHOHN ah-SAH-doh
costillas: pork ribs
kohs-TEE-yahs
puerco en adobo: pork in chili sauce
PWEHR-koh ehn ah-DOH-boh
seco de chancho: pork stew
SEH-koh deh CHAHN-cho

POULTRY

ají de gallina: creamed chicken with green chilis
ah-HEE deh gah-YEE-nah
arroz con pollo: rice with chicken and vegetables
ah-RROHS kohn POH-yoh
chilaquiles: chicken / cheese / tortilla casserole
chee-lah-KEE-lehs
mole poblano: chicken with bitter chocolate / chile sauce
MOH-leh poh-BLAH-noh
pollo a la brasa: spit-roasted chicken
POH-yoh ah lah BRAH-sah
pollo al jerez: chicken in sherry
POH-yoh ahl heh-REHS
pollo frito: fried chicken
POH-yoh FREE-toh
empanadas de pavo: turkey individual meat pies
ehm-pah-NAH-dahs deh PAH-voh
patas de pavo rellenas: stuffed turkey legs
PAH-tahs deh PAH-voh reh-YEH-nahs
sopa de pavo: turkey soup
SOH-pah deh PAH-voh

FISH AND SEAFOOD

ceviche: seafood marinated with lemon or lime, along with
  cilantro, garlic, red pepper, and onion; served cold
seh-VEE-cheh

escabeche: spicy fish stew
ehs-kah-BEH-cheh

zarzuela: mixed fish and seafood soup with tomatoes, saffron, garlic, and wine served over bread
sahr-SWEH-lah

jueyes hervidos: boiled crab
HWEH-yehs ehr-VEE-dohs

camarones en cerveza: shrimp in beer
kah-mah-ROH-nehs ehn sehr-VEH-sah

bacalao guisado: cod marinated in herbs
bah-kah-LAH-oh gee-SAH-doh

camarones al ajillo: garlic shrimp stew
kah-mah-ROH-nehs ahl ah-HEE-yoh

chupin de camarones: spicy shrimp stew
CHOO-peen deh kah-mah-ROH-nehs

salmorejo de jueyes: crab in tomato and garlic sauce.
sahl-moh-REH-hoh deh HWEH-yehs

taquitos de pescado: grilled shark in tomato sauce on tacos.
tah-KEE-tohs deh pehs-KAH-doh

guiso de róbalo: Cuban style sea bass stew.
GEE-soh deh ROH-bah-loh

For a full list of fish, see p102.

DESSERTS

arroz con leche / arroz con dulce: rice pudding
ah-RROHS kohn LEH-cheh / ah-RROHS kohn DOOL-seh

buñuelos: round, thin fritters dipped in sugar (may also be savory)
boon-yoo-EH-lohs

dulce de plátano: ripe yellow plantains cooked in wine and spices
DOOL-seh deh PLAH-tah-noh

flan: custard
flahn

helado: ice cream
eh-LAH-doh

panqueques: dessert crepes with caramel and whipped cream
pahn-KEH-kehs

sopapillas: puffed up crisps of a pie crust like dough, drizzled
with honey and sprinkled with powdered sugar
soh-pah-PEE-yahs

tembleque: coconut milk custard
tehm-BLEH-keh

pastel tres leches: three-milk cake
pahs-TEHL trehs LEH-chehs

STREET FOOD

arepas: savory stuffed cornmeal patties
ah-REH-pahs

caña: raw sugar cane
KAH-nyah

chalupas: corn tortillas filled with meat and cheese
chah-LOO-pahs

chicha: juice, punch
CHEE-chah

chorreados: corn pancakes with sour cream
choh-rreh-AH-dohs

churros: breakfast / dessert fritters
CHOO-rrohs

coco verde: green coconut
KOH-koh VEHR-deh

cuchifrito: deep-fried pork pieces (ears, tail, etc.)
koo-chee-FREE-toh

Eating out of Pocket

Street food is generally inexpensive. Keep a supply of
small-denomination bills and change on you because
treat vendors generally won't be able to change large
bills.

empañadas / empanadas: turnovers filled with meat and / or
  cheese, beans, potatoes
ehm-pah-NYAH-dahs / ehm-pah-NAH-dahs

empanadas chilenas: turnovers filled with meat, boiled onion
  and raisins, an olive, and part of a hard-boiled egg
ehm-pah-NAH-dahs chee-LEH-nahs

enchiladas: pastries stuffed with cheese, meat, or potatoes
ehn-chee-LAH-dahs

gorditas: thick, fried corn tortillas stuffed with cheese, beans,
  and / or meat
gohr-DEE-tahs

juanes: rice tamales with chicken or fish
HWAH-nehs

piraguas, raspadillas (Peru): shaved ice with fruit syrup
pee-RAH-wahs, rahs-pad-DEE-yahs

pupusas: corn pancakes with cheese
poo-POO-sahs

quesadillas: tortillas with cheese
keh-sah-DEE-yahs

rellenos: bits of meat or cheese breaded with yucca or potato
  paste and deep fried
rreh-YEH-nohs

salteñas (aka empanadas chilenas): chicken or beef with onions
  and raisins wrapped in pastry
sahl-TEH-nyahs

tacos: traditional Mexican are made with ground tongue
TAH-kohs

tamales: chicken, pork, or potatoes with chiles in cornmeal
  steamed inside a banana leaf or corn husk
tah-MAH-lehs

tortas: sandwiches with meat and/or cheese, garnished with
  vegetables (frosted cake in S.Am)
TOHR-tahs

BUYING GROCERIES

In most Latin American countries, groceries can be bought at open-air "farmers' markets," neighborhood stores, or large supermarkets.

AT THE SUPERMARKET

Which aisle has ____	**¿En cuál pasillo se encuentran ___** *ehn kwahl pah-SEE-yoh seh ehn-KWEHN-trahn*
spices?	**las especias?** *lahs ehs-PEH-syahs*
toiletries?	**los artículos de tocador?** *lohs ahr-TEE-koo-lohs deh toh-kah-DOHR*
paper plates and napkins?	**los platos de papel y las servilletas?** *lohs PLAH-tohs deh pah-PEHL ee lahs sehr-vee-YEH-tahs*
canned goods?	**los artículos enlatados?** *lohs ahr-TEE-koo-lohs ehn-lah-TAH-dohs*
snack food?	**los bocadillos?** *lohs boh-kah-DEE-yohs*
baby food?	**la comida de bebés?** *lah koh-MEE-dah deh beh-BEHS*
water?	**el agua?** *ehl AH-wah*
juice?	**el jugo?** *ehl HOO-goh*
bread?	**el pan?** *ehl pahn*
cheese?	**el queso?** *ehl KEH-soh*

fruit?	**las frutas?**
	lahs FROO-tahs
cookies?	**las galletas?**
	lahs gah-YEH-tahs

AT THE BUTCHER SHOP

Is the meat fresh?	**¿La carne es fresca?**
	lah KAHR-neh ehs FREHS-kah
Do you sell fresh ____	**¿Ustedes venden ____**
	oos-TEH-dehs VEHN-dehn
beef?	**carne de res fresca?**
	KAHR-neh deh rrehs FREHS-cah
pork?	**cerdo fresco?**
	SEHR-doh FREHS-koh
lamb?	**cordero fresco?**
	kohr-DEH-roh FREHS-koh
goat?	**cabra fresca?**
	KAH-brah FREHS-kah
I would like a cut of ____	**Quisiera un corte de ____**
	kee-SYEH-rah oon KOHR-teh deh
tenderloin.	**lomo / filete.**
	LOH-moh / fee-LEH-teh
T-bone.	**chuletón.**
	choo-leh-TOHN
brisket.	**pecho.**
	PEH-cho
rump roast.	**cuadril / solomillo.**
	kwah-DREEL / soh-loh-MEE-yoh
chops.	**chuletas.**
	choo-LEH-tahs
filet.	**filete.**
	fee-LEH-teh
Thick / Thin cuts please.	**Cortes finos / gruesos por favor.**
	KOHR-tehs FEE-nohs / GRWEH-sohs pohr fah-VOHR

Please trim the fat.	**Por favor, córtele la grasa.**
	pohr fah-VOHR KOHR-teh-leh lah
	GRAH-sah
Do you have any sausage?	**¿Tiene salchichas?**
	TYEH-neh sahl-CHEE-chas
Is the ____ fresh?	**¿Es / Son fresco -a -os -as ____**
	ehs / sohn FREHS-koh -kah -kohs
	-kahs
fish	**el pescado?**
	ehl pehs-KAH-doh
seafood	**los mariscos?**
	lohs mah-REES-kohs
shrimp	**los camarones?**
	lohs kah-mah-ROH-nehs
octopus	**el pulpo?**
	ehl POOL-poh
squid	**el calamar?**
	ehl kahl-ah-MAHR
sea bass	**el róbalo?**
	ehl ROH-bah-loh
flounder	**la platija?**
	lah plah-TEE-hah
clams	**las almejas?**
	lahs ahl-MEH-hahs
oysters	**las ostras?**
	lahs OHS-trahs
shark	**el tiburón?**
	ehl tee-boo-ROHN
turtle	**la tortuga?**
	lah tohr-TOO-gah
May I smell it?	**¿Puedo olerlo -a?**
	PWEH-doh oh-LEHR-loh -lah

Would you please ____	**¿Por favor, puede ____**
	pohr fah-VOHR PWEH-deh
filet it?	**cortarlo -a en filetes?**
	kohr-TAHR-loh -lah ehn
	fee-LEH-tehs
debone it?	**deshuesarlo -a?**
	dehs-weh-SAHR-loh -lah
remove the head and	**quitarle la cabeza y la cola?**
tail?	*kee-TAHR-leh lah*
	kah-BEH-sah ee lah KOH-lah

AT THE PRODUCE STAND / MARKET

Fruits

banana	**plátano, banana**
	PLAH-tah-noh, bah-NAH-nah
apple	**manzana**
	mahn-ZAH-nah
grapes (green, red)	**uvas (verdes, rojas)**
	OO-vahs (VEHR-dehs, RROH-hahs)
orange	**naranja**
	nah-RAHN-hah
lime	**lima, limoncillo,**
	limón verde (Mexico)
	LEE-mah, lee-mohn-SEE-yoh,
	lee-mohn VEHR-de
lemon	**limón, limón amarillo (Mexico)**
	lee-MOHN, lee-MOHN ah-mah-
	REE-yoh
mango	**mango**
	MAHNG-goh
melon	**melón**
	meh-LOHN
cantaloupe	**cantalupo, melón**
	kahn-tah-LOO-poh, meh-LOHN

watermelon	**sandía, melón de agua** *sahn-DEE-ah, meh-LOHN deh AH-wah*
honeydew	**melón** *meh-LOHN*
cranberry	**arándano rojo** *ah-RAHN-dah-noh ROH-hoh*
cherry	**cereza** *seh-REH-sah*
peach	**melocotón, durazno** *meh-loh-koh-TOHN, doo-RAHS-noh*
apricot	**albaricoque** *ahl-bah-ree-KOH-keh*
strawberry	**fresa, frutilla (Chile)** *FREH-sah, froo-TEE-yah*
blueberry	**arándano azul, mora azul** *ah-RAHN-dah-noh ah-SOOL, MOH-rah ah-SOOL*
kiwi	**kiwi** *KEE-wee*
pineapple	**piña** *PEE-nyah*
blackberries	**zarzamora, mora negra** *sahr-sah-MOH-rah, MOH-rah NEH-grah*
carambola, star fruit	**carambola** *kah-rahm-BOH-lah*
citron	**cidra** *SEE-drah*
coconut	**coco** *KOH-koh*
grapefruit	**toronja** *toh-ROHN-hah*

guava	**guayaba**
	wah-YAH-bah
gooseberry	**grosella**
	groh-SEH-yah
papaya	**papaya**
	pah-PAH-yah
palm fruit	**fruta de palma**
	FROO-tah deh PAHL-mah
breadfruit	**fruta de pan, panapén, pana**
	FROO-tah deh pahn, pah-nah-
	PEHN, PAH-nah
soursop (spiny, yellow-green fruit with tart pulp)	**guanábana**
	wah-NAH-bah-nah
tamarind	**tamarindo**
	tah-mah-REEN-doh
tangerine	**mandarina**
	mahn-dah-REE-nah
plum	**ciruela**
	seer-WEH-lah
pear	**pera**
	PEH-rah

Vegetables

plantain	**plátano verde, plantaina, llantén**
	PLAH-tah-noh VEHR-deh, plahn-
	TAHEE-nah, yahn-TEHN
regular	**regular**
	reh-goo-LAHR
ripe	**maduro**
	mah-DOO-roh
lettuce	**lechuga**
	leh-CHOO-gah
spinach	**espinaca**
	ehs-pee-NAH-kah

avocado	**aguacate, palta (S.Am)**
	ah-wah-KAH-teh, PAHL-tah
artichoke	**alcachofa**
	ahl-kah-CHOH-fah
olives	**aceitunas**
	ah-sehee-TOO-nahs
beans	**frijoles**
	free-HOH-lehs
green beans	**frijoles verdes, vainitas (S.Am)**
	free-HOH-lehs VEHR-dehs, vahee-NEE-tahs
tomato	**tomate, jitomate (Mexico)**
	toh-MAH-teh, hee-toh-MAH-teh
potato	**papa, patata**
	PAH-pah, pah-TAH-tah
peppers	**pimiento, chile**
	pee-MYEHN-toh, CHEE-leh
hot	**picante**
	pee-KAHN-teh
mild	**suave**
	soo-AH-veh
poblano	**poblano**
	poh-BLAH-noh
jalapeno	**jalapeño**
	hah-lah-PEH-nyoh
habanero	**habanero, habañero**
	ah-bah-NEH-roh, ah-bah-NYEH-roh
chipotle	**chipotle**
	chee-POHT-leh
cayenne	**pimienta de Cayena**
	pee-MYEHN-tah deh kah-YEH-nah
cascabeles	**cascabeles**
	kahs-kah-BEH-lehs

onion	**cebolla**
	seh-BOH-yah
celery	**apio**
	AH-pyoh
broccoli	**brócoli**
	BROH-koh-lee
cauliflower	**coliflor**
	koh-lee-FLOHR
carrot	**zanahoria**
	sah-nah-OH-ryah
corn	**maíz**
	mah-EES
cucumber	**pepino**
	peh-PEE-noh
bean sprouts	**brotes de soja**
	BROH-tehs deh SOH-ha
okra	**quimbombo**
	keem-BOHM-boh
bamboo shoots	**retoños de bambú**
	reh-TOH-nyohs deh bahm-BOO
breadnut	**panapén**
	pah-nah-PEHN
sweet corn	**maíz dulce**
	mah-EES DOOL-seh
eggplant	**berenjena**
	beh-rehn-HEH-nah
sorrel	**acedera**
	ah-seh-DEH-rah
yam	**batata, camote (S.Am)**
	bah-TAH-tah, kah-MOH-teh
squash	**zapallo**
	sah-PAH-yoh
ñame (white yam)	**ñame (batata blanca)**
	NYAH-meh (bah-TAH-tah BLAHN-kah)

Fresh herbs and spices

cilantro	**cilantro**	*see-LAHN-troh*
coriander	**culantro**	*kooh-LAHN-troh*
black pepper	**pimienta negra**	*pee-MYEHN-tah NEH-grah*
salt	**sal**	*sahl*
basil	**albahaca**	*ahl-bah-AH-kah*
parsley	**perejil**	*peh-reh-HEEL*
oregano	**orégano**	*oh-REH-gah-noh*
sage	**salvia**	*SAHL-vyah*
thyme	**tomillo**	*toh-MEE-yoh*
cumin	**comino**	*koh-MEE-noh*
paprika	**paprika**	*pah-PREE-kah*
garlic	**ajo**	*AH-hoh*
clove	**clavo**	*KLAH-voh*
allspice	**pimienta inglesa**	*pee-MYEHN-tah eeng-GLEH-sah*
saffron	**azafrán**	*ah-sah-FRAHN*
rosemary	**romero**	*rroh-MEH-roh*
anise	**anís**	*AH-nees*

sugar	**azúcar**
	ah-SOO-kahr
marjoram	**mejorana**
	meh-hoh-RAH-nah
dill	**eneldo**
	eh-NEHL-doh
caraway	**alcaravea**
	ahl-kah-rah-VEH-ah
bay leaf	**hoja de laurel seca**
	OH-hah deh low-REHL SEH-kah
cacao	**cacao**
	kah-KAH-oh
dried	**seco**
	SEH-koh
fresh	**fresco**
	FREHS-koh
seed	**en semilla**
	ehn seh-MEE-yah

AT THE DELI

What kind of salad is that?	**¿Qué tipo de ensalada es ésa?**
	keh TEE-poh deh ehn-sah-LAH-dah ehs EH-sah
What type of cheese is that?	**¿Qué tipo de queso es ese?**
	keh TEE-poh deh KEH-soh ehs EH-seh
What type of bread is that?	**¿Qué tipo de pan es ese?**
	keh TEE-poh deh pahn ehs EH-seh
Some of that, please.	**Un poco de eso, por favor.**
	oon POH-koh deh EH-soh pohr fah-VOHR
Is the salad fresh?	**¿La ensalada está fresca?**
	lah ehn-sah-LAH-dah ehs-TAH FREHS-kah

DINING

I'd like _____

Quisiera _____
kee-SYEH-rah

a sandwich.

un sándwich.
oon SAHND-weech

a salad.

una ensalada.
OO-nah ehn-sah-LAH-dah

tuna salad.

ensalada de atún.
ehn-sah-LAH-dah deh ah-TOON

chicken salad.

ensalada de pollo.
ehn-sah-LAH-dah deh POH-yoh

roast beef.

asado de res.
ah-SAH-doh deh rehs

ham.

jamón.
hah-MOHN

that cheese.

ese queso.
EH-seh KEH-soh

cole slaw.

ensalada de col.
ehn-sah-LAH-dah deh KOHL

a package of tofu.

un paquete de tofu.
oon pah-KEH-teh deh TOH-foo

mustard.

mostaza.
mohs-TAH-sah

mayonaisse.

mayonesa.
mah-yoh-NEH-sah

a pickle.

un pepinillo.
oon peh-pee-NEE-yoh

Is that smoked?

¿Eso es ahumado?
EH-soh ehs ah-oo-MAH-doh

a pound (in kgs)

una libra (0.454 kg)
OO-nah LEE-brah

a quarter-pound (in kgs)

un cuarto de libra (0.113 kg)
ooh KWAHR-toh deh LEE-brah

a half-pound (in kgs)

media libra (0.227 kg)
MEH-dyah LEE-brah

CHAPTER FIVE

SOCIALIZING

Whether you're meeting people in a bar or a park, you'll find the language you need, in this chapter, to make new friends.

GREETINGS

Hello.	**Hola.** *OH-lah*
How are you?	**¿Cómo estás?** *KOH-moh ehs-TAHS*
Fine, thanks.	**Bien, gracias.** *byehn GRAH-syahs*
And you?	**¿Y usted?** *ee oos-TEHD*
I'm exhausted from the trip.	**Estoy cansado -a del viaje.** *ehs-TOY kahn-SAH-doh -dah dehl VYAH-heh*
I have a headache.	**Tengo dolor de cabeza.** *TEHNG-goh doh-LOHR deh kah-BEH-sah*
I'm terrible.	**Estoy terrible.** *ehs-TOY teh-RREE-bleh*
I have a cold.	**Tengo un resfriado.** *TEHNG-goh oon rehs-free-AH-doh*
Good morning.	**Buenos días.** *BWEH-nohs DEE-ahs*
Good evening.	**Buenas noches.** *BWEH-nahs NOH-chehs*
Good afternoon.	**Buenas tardes.** *BWEH-nahs TAHR-dehs*
Good night.	**Buenas noches.** *BWEH-nahs NOH-chehs*

Listen Up: Common Greetings

Es un placer. *ehs oon plah-SEHR*	It's a pleasure.
Mucho gusto. *MOO-choh GOOS-toh*	Delighted.
A la orden. *ah lah OHR-dehn*	At your service. / As you wish.
Encantado -a. *ehn-kahn-TAH-do -dah*	Charmed.
Buenas. *BWEH-nahs*	Good day. (shortened)
Hola. *OH-lah*	Hello.
¿Qué tal? *keh TAHL*	How's it going?
¿Cómo anda? *KOH-moh AHN-dah*	How's it going?
¿Qué hubo? *keh OO-boh*	What's up?
¿Qué pasa? *keh PAH-sah*	What's going on?
¡Venga! *VEHN-gah*	Bye! (Spain)
Adiós. *ah-DYOHS*	Goodbye.
Nos vemos. *nohs VEH-mohs*	See you later.

THE LANGUAGE BARRIER

I don't understand.	**No entiendo.** *noh ehn-TYEHN-doh*
Please speak more slowly.	**Por favor hable más lento.** *pohr fah-VOHR AH-bleh mahs LEHN-toh*

Please speak louder.	**Por favor hable más alto.**
	pohr fah-VOHR AH-bleh mahs AHL-toh
Do you speak English?	**¿Usted habla inglés?**
	oos-TEHD AH-blah eeng-GLEHS
I speak ____ better than Spanish.	**Yo hablo ____ mejor que español.**
	yoh AH-bloh ____ meh-HOHR keh ehs-pah-NYOHL

Curse Words

ere are some common c rse ords sed across atin merica and pain

mierda / cagada	shit
MYEHR-dah / kah-GAH-dah	
hijo de puta	son of a bitch (literally, son of a whore)
EE-hoh deh POO-tah	
huevón	jerk
weh-VOHN	
carajo	damn
kah-RAH-hoh	
culón	ass
koo-LOHN	
jodido / jodienda	screwed up
hoh-DEE-doh / hoh-DYEHN-dah	
cabrón	bastard
kah-BROHN	
chingada	fucked up (Mexican)
cheeng-GAH-dah	
follar / coger / joder	to fuck
foh-YAHR / koh-HEHR / hoh-DEHR	
See p22, 23 for conjugation.	

SOCIALIZING

Please spell that.	**Por favor deletree eso.**
	pohr fah-VOHR deh-leh-TREH-eh
	EH-soh
Please repeat that?	**¿Por favor repita eso?**
	pohr fah-VOHR reh-PEE-tah
	EH-soh
How do you say ____?	**¿Cómo usted dice ____?**
	KOH-moh oos-TEHD DEE-seh
Would you show me that in this dictionary?	**¿Me puede mostrar eso en este diccionario?**
	meh PWEH-deh mohs-TRAHR EH-soh ehn EHS-teh deek-syoh-NAH-ryoh

GETTING PERSONAL

People in Latin America are generally friendly, but more formal than Americans or Europeans. Remember to use the *usted* form of address, until given permission to employ the more familiar *tú*.

INTRODUCTIONS

What is your name?	**¿Cuál es su nombre?**
	kwahl ehs soo NOHM-breh
My name is ____.	**Me llamo ____.**
	meh YAH-moh
I'm very pleased to meet you.	**Es un placer conocerle.**
	ehs oon plah-SEHR koh-noh-SEHR-leh
May I introduce my ____	**¿Puedo presentarle a mi ____ ?**
	PWEH-doh preh-sehn-TAHR-leh ah mee
How is your ____	**¿Cómo está su / están sus ____**
	KOH-moh ehs-TAH soo / ehs-TAHN soos
wife?	**esposa?**
	ehs-POH-sah
husband?	**esposo?**
	ehs-POH-soh

child?	**hijo -a?**
	EE-hoh -hah
friends?	**amigos?**
	ah-MEE-gohs
boyfriend / girlfriend?	**novio -a?**
	NOH-vyoh -vyah
family?	**familia?**
	fah-MEE-lyah
mother?	**madre?**
	MAH-dreh?
father?	**padre?**
	PAH-dreh
brother / sister?	**hermano -a?**
	ehr-MAH-noh -nah
friend?	**amigo -a?**
	ah-MEE-goh -gah
neighbor?	**vecino?**
	veh-SEE-noh
boss?	**jefe?**
	HEH-feh
cousin?	**primo -a?**
	PREE-moh -mah?
aunt / uncle?	**tía -o?**
	TEE-ah -oh
boyfriend / girlfriend?	**novio -a?**
	NOH-vyoh -vyah
fiancée / fiancé?	**prometido -a?**
	proh-meh-TEE-doh -dah
partner?	**socio -a?**
	SOH-syoh -syah
niece/nephew?	**sobrino -a?**
	soh-BREE-noh -nah
parents?	**padres?**
	PAH-drehs
grandparents?	**abuelos?**
	ah-BWEH-lohs

Dos and Don'ts

Don't refer to your parents as *los parientes*, which means relatives. Do call them *los padres* (even though *el padre* means father).

Are you married / single?	**¿Usted es casado -a / soltero -a?**
	oos-TEHD ehs kah-SAH-doh -dah / sohl-TEH-roh -rah
I'm married.	**Soy casado -a.**
	soy kah-SAH-doh -dah
I'm single.	**Soy soltero -a.**
	soy sohl-TEH-roh -rah
I'm divorced.	**Soy divorciado -a.**
	soy dee-vohr-SYAH-doh -dah
I'm a widow / widower.	**Soy viudo -a.**
	soy VYOO-doh -dah
We're separated.	**Estamos separados.**
	ehs-TAH-mohs seh-pah-RAH-dohs
I live with my boyfriend / girlfriend.	**Vivo con mi novio -a.**
	VEE-voh kohn mee NOH-vyoh -vyah
How old are you?	**¿Qué edad usted tiene?**
	keh eh-DAHD oo-STEHD TYEH-neh
How old are your children?	**¿Qué edad tienen sus hijos?**
	keh eh-DAHD TYEH-nehn soos EE-hos
Wow! That's very young.	**¡Caramba! Eso es muy joven.**
	kah-RAHM-bah EH-soh ehs MOO-ee HOH-vehn
No you're not! You're much younger.	**¡No lo es! Usted es mucho más joven.**
	noh loh ehs oos-TEHD ehs MOO-choh mahs HOH-vehn

Your wife / daughter is beautiful.	**Su esposa / hija es bella.** *soo ehs-POH-sah / EE-hah ehs BEH-yah*
Your husband / son is handsome.	**Su esposo / hijo es guapo.** *soo ehs-POH-soh / EE-hoh ehs WAH-poh*
What a beautiful baby!	**¡Que bebé tan lindo!** *keh beh-BEH tahn LEEN-doh*
Are you here on business?	**¿Usted está aquí por negocios?** *oos-TEHD ehs-TAH ah-KEE pohr neh-GOH-syohs*
I am vacationing.	**Estoy de vacaciones.** *ehs-TOY deh vah-kah-SYOH-nehs*
I'm attending a conference.	**Estoy asistiendo a una conferencia.** *ehs-TOY ah-sees-TYEHN-doh ah OO-nah kohn-feh-REHN-syah*
How long are you staying?	**¿Por cuánto tiempo se va a quedar?** *pohr KWAHN-toh TYEHM-poh seh vah ah keh-DAHR*
What are you studying?	**¿Qué estudia?** *keh ehs-TOO-dyah*
I'm a student.	**Soy estudiante.** *soy ehs-too-DYAHN-teh*
Where are you from?	**¿De dónde es?** *deh DOHN-deh ehs*

PERSONAL DESCRIPTIONS

blond(e)	**rubio -a** *ROO-byoh -byah*
brunette	**moreno -a** *moh-REH-noh -nah*
redhead	**pelirrojo -a** *peh-lee-RRO-hoh -hah*

el frente
el pelo
las cejas
las sienes
los ojos
los oídos
el nariz
las mejillas
los dientes
los labios
la boca
la barbilla

straight hair	**pelo lacio**
	PEH-loh LAH-syoh
curly hair	**pelo rizo / crespo**
	PEH-loh REE-soh / KREH-spoh
kinky hair	**pelo rizo**
	PEH-loh REE-soh
long hair	**pelo largo**
	PEH-loh LAHR-goh
short hair	**pelo corto**
	PEH-loh KOHR-toh
tanned	**bronceado -a**
	brohn-seh-AH-doh -dah
pale	**pálido -a**
	PAH-lee-doh
mocha-skinned	**moreno -a**
	moh-REH-noh -nah
black	**negro -a**
	NEH-groh -grah
white	**blanco -a**
	BLAHN-koh -kah
Asian	**Asiático -a**
	ah-see-AH-tee-koh -kah

African-American	**Africano-americano -a**
	ah-free-KAH-noh-ah-meh-ree-KAH-noh -nah
caucasian	**caucásico -a**
	kow-KAH-see-koh -kah
biracial	**birracial**
	bee-rrah-SYAHL
tall	**alto -a**
	AHL-toh -tah
short	**bajo -a**
	BAH-hoh -hah
thin	**delgado -a**
	dehl-GAH-doh -dah
fat	**gordo -a**
	GOHR-doh -dah
blue eyes	**los ojos azules**
	lohs OH-hohs ah-SOO-lehs
brown eyes	**los ojos marrones**
	lohs OH-hohs mah-RROH-nehs
green eyes	**los ojos verdes**
	lohs OH-hohs VEHR-dehs
hazel eyes	**los ojos cafés**
	OH-hohs kah-FEHS
eyebrows	**las cejas**
	lahs SEH-hahs
eyelashes	**las pestañas**
	lahs pehs-TAH-nyahs
freckles	**las pecas**
	lahs PEH-kahs
moles	**los lunares**
	lohs looh-NAH-rehs
face	**la cara**
	lah KAH-rah

Listen Up: Nationalities

Soy alemán -a.   I'm German.
soy ah-leh-MAHN -nah
Soy argentino -a.   I'm Argentinean.
soy ahr-hehn-TEE-noh -nah
Soy boliviano -a.   I'm Bolivian.
soy boh-lee-VYAH-noh -nah
Soy brazileño -a.   I'm Brazilian.
soy brah-see-LEH-nyoh -nyah
Soy chino -a.   I'm Chinese.
soy CHEE-noh -nah
Soy colombiano -a.   I'm Colombian.
soy koh-lohm-BYAH-noh -nah
Soy costarricense.   I'm Costa Rican.
soy kohs-tah-rree-SEHN-seh
Soy ecuatoriano -a.   I'm Ecuadorian.
soy eh-kwah-toh-RYAH-noh -nah
Soy español -a.   I'm Spanish.
soy ehs-pah-NYOHL -lah
Soy francés.   I'm French.
soy frahn-SEHS
Soy guatemalteco -a.   I'm Guatemalan.
soy wah-teh-mahl-TEH-koh -kah
Soy hindú.   I'm Hindu.
soy een-DOO
Soy hondureño -a.   I'm Honduran
soy ohn-doo-REH-nyoh -nyah
Soy italiano -a.   I'm Italian.
soy ee-tah-LYAH-noh -nah
Soy japonés / japonesa.   I'm Japanese.
soy hah-poh-NEHS -NEH-sah
Soy mexicano -a.   I'm Mexican.
soy meh-hee-KAH-noh -nah
Soy nicaragüense.   I'm Nicaraguan.
soy nee-kah-rah-WEHN-seh

Soy panameño -a.	I'm Panamanian.
soy pah-nah-MEH-nyoh -nyah	
Soy paraguayo -a.	I'm Paraguayan.
soy pah-rah-WAH-yoh -yah	
Soy peruano -a.	I'm Peruvian.
soy peh-roo-AH-noh -nah	
Soy puertorriqueño -a.	I'm Puerto Rican.
soy pwehr-toh-rree-KEH-nyoh -nyah	
Soy ruso -a.	I'm Russian.
soy ROO-soh -sah	
Soy salvadoreño -a.	I'm Salvadorian.
soy sahl-vah-doh-REH-nyoh -nyah	
Soy uruguayo -a.	I'm Uruguayan.
soy oo-roo-WAH-yoh -yah	
Soy venezolano -a.	I'm Venezuelan.
soy veh-neh-soh-LAH-noh -nah	

For a full list of nationalities, see English / Spanish dictionary..

DISPOSITIONS AND MOODS

sad	**triste**
	TREES-teh
happy	**feliz / alegre**
	feh-LEES / ah-LEH-greh
angry	**enojado -a**
	eh-noh-HAH-doh -dah
tired	**cansado -a**
	kahn-SAH-doh -dah
depressed	**deprimido -a**
	deh-pree-MEE-doh -dah
stressed	**estresado -a**
	ehs-treh-SAH-doh -dah
anxious	**ansioso -a**
	ahn-SYOH-soh -sah
confused	**confundido -a**
	kohn-foon-DEE-doh -dah
enthusiastic	**entusiasmado -a**
	ehn-too-syahs-MAH-doh -dah

PROFESSIONS

What do you do for a living?

¿En qué trabaja usted?
ehn keh trah-BAH-hah oo-STEHD

Here is my business card.

Aquí tiene mi tarjeta de presentación.
ah-KEE TYEH-neh mee tahr-HEH-tah deh preh-sehn-tah-SYOHN

I am _____

Soy _____
soy

a doctor.

doctor.
dohk-TOHR

an engineer.

ingeniero -a.
een-heh-NYEH-roh -rah

a lawyer.

abogado -a.
ah-boh-GAH-doh -dah

a salesperson.

vendedor -a.
vehn-deh-DOHR -DOH-rah

a writer.

escritor -a.
ehs-kree-TOHR -TOH-rah

an editor.

editor -a.
eh-dee-TOHR -TOH-rah

a designer.

diseñador -a.
dee-seh-nyah-DOHR -DOH-rah

an educator.

educador
eh-doo-kah-DOHR

an artist.

artista.
ahr-TEES-tah

a craftsperson.

artesano -a.
ahr-teh-SAH-noh -nah

a homemaker.

ama de casa.
AH-mah deh KAH-sah

an accountant.

contable.
kohn-TAH-bleh

a nurse.	**enfermero -a** *ehn-fehr-MEH-roh -rah*
a musician.	**músico -a.** *MOO-see-koh -kah*
a military professional.	**profesional militar.** *proh-feh-syoh-NAHL mee-lee-TAHR*
a government employee.	**empleado gubernamental.** *ehm-pleh-AH-doh goo-behr-nah-mehn-TAHL*

DOING BUSINESS

I'd like an appointment.	**Quisiera hacer una cita.** *kee-SYEH-rah ah-SEHR OO-nah SEE-tah*
I'm here to see ____.	**Estoy aquí para ver a ____.** *ehs-TOY ah-KEE pa-rah vehr ah*
May I photocopy this?	**¿Puedo fotocopiar esto?** *PWEH-doh foh-toh-koh-PYAHR EHS-toh*
May I use a computer here?	**¿Puedo usar la computadora aquí?** *PWEH-doh oo-SAHR lah kohm-poo-tah-DOH-rah ah-KEE*
What's the password?	**¿Cuál es la contraseña?** *kwahl ehs lah kohn-trah-SEH-nyah*
May I access the Internet?	**¿Puedo acceder el Internet?** *PWEH-doh ahk-seh-DEHR ahl een-tehr-NEHT*
May I send a fax?	**¿Puedo enviar un fax?** *PWEH-doh ehn-vee-AHR oon fahks*
May I use the phone?	**¿Puedo usar el teléfono?** *PWEH-doh oo-SAHR ehl teh-LEH-foh-noh*

PARTING WAYS

Keep in touch.	**Manténgase en contacto.**
	mahn-TEHNG-gah-seh ehn kohn-TAHK-toh
Please write or email.	**Por favor escríbame o envíeme un e-mail.**
	pohr fah-VOHR ehs-KREE-bah-meh oh ehn-VEE-eh-meh oon EE-mehl
Here's my phone number. Call me.	**Aquí tiene mi número de teléfono. Llámeme.**
	ah-KEE TYEH-neh mee NOO-meh-roh deh teh-LEH-foh-noh. YAH-meh-meh
May I have your phone number / e-mail please?	**¿Me puede dar su número de teléfono / dirección de e-mail, por favor?**
	meh PWEH-deh dahr soo NOO-meh-roh deh teh-LEH-foh-noh / dee-rehk-SYOHN deh EE-mehl pohr fah-VOHR
May I have your card?	**¿Me puede dar su tarjeta?**
	meh PWEH-deh dahr soo tahr-HEH-tah
Give me your address and I'll write you.	**Déme su dirección y le escribiré.**
	DEH-meh soo dee-rehk-SYOHN ee leh ehs-kree-bee-REH

TOPICS OF CONVERSATION

As in the United States or Europe, the weather and current affairs are common conversation topics.

THE WEATHER

It's so ____	**Es tan ____**
	Ehs tahn

Is it always so _____ ?	**¿Siempre es tan _____ ?**
	SYEHM-preh ehs tahn
sunny.	**soleado.**
	soh-leh-AH-doh
rainy.	**lluvioso.**
	yoo-vee-OH-soh
cloudy.	**nublado.**
	noo-BLAH-doh
humid.	**húmedo.**
	OO-meh-doh
warm.	**caliente.**
	kah-LYEHN-teh
cool.	**frío.**
	FREE-oh
windy.	**ventoso.**
	vehn-TOH-soh
Do you know the weather forecast for tomorrow?	**¿Usted sabe el pronóstico del tiempo para mañana?**
	oo-STEHD SAH-beh ehl proh-NOHS-tee-koh dehl TYEHM-poh PAH-rah mah-NYAH-nah

THE ISSUES

What do you think about _____	**¿Qué usted opina de _____**
	keh oos-TEHD oh-PEE-nah deh
democracy?	**la democracia?**
	lah deh-moh-KRAH-syah
socialism?	**el socialismo?**
	ehl soh-syah-LEES-moh
American Democrats?	**los americanos demócratas?**
	lohs ah-meh-ree-KAH-nohs deh MOH-krah-tahs
American Republicans?	**los americanos republicanos?**
	lohs ah-meh-ree-KAH-nohs reh-poo-blee-KAH-nohs

the environment?	**el medio ambiente?** *ehl MEH-dyoh ahm-BYEHN-teh*
women's rights?	**los derechos de las mujeres?** *lohs deh-REH-chohs deh lahs* *moo-HEH-rehs*
gay rights?	**los derechos de los homo-** **sexuales?** *lohs deh-reh-chos deh lohs oh-* *moh-sehk-SWAH-lehs*
the economy?	**la economía?** *lah eh-koh-noh-MEE-ah*
What political party do you belong to?	**¿A qué partido político usted pertenece?** *ah keh pahr-TEE-doh poh-LEE-* *tee-koh oos-TEHD pehr-teh-* *NEH-seh*
What did you think of the American election?	**¿Qué usted opina de las elecciones americanas?** *keh oos-TEHD oh-PEE-nah deh* *lahs eh-lehk-SYOH-nehs ah-meh-* *ree-KAH-nahs*
What do you think of the war in ____?	**¿Qué usted opina de la guerra en ____?** *keh oos-TEHD oh-PEE-nah deh lah* *GEH-rrah ehn*

RELIGION

Do you go to church / temple / mosque?	**¿Usted asiste a una iglesia / un templo / una mezquita?** *oos-TEHD ah-SEES-teh ah OO-nah* *ee-GLEH-syah / oon TEHM-ploh /* *OO-nah mehs-KEE-tah*
Are you religious?	**¿Usted es religioso?** *ooh-STEHD ehs reh-lee-HYOH-soh*

I'm ____ / I was raised ____ **Soy ____ / Fui criado ____**
soy / FOO-ee kree-AH-doh

Protestant. **protestante.**
proh-tehs-TAHN-teh

Catholic. **católico.**
kah-TOH-lee-koh

Jewish. **judío.**
hoo-DEE-oh

Muslim. **musulmán.**
moo-sool-MAHN

Buddhist. **budista.**
boo-DEES-tah

Greek Orthodox. **ortodoxo griego.**
orh-toh-DOHK-soh GRYEH-goh

Hindu. **hindú.**
een-DOO

agnostic. **agnóstico.**
ahg-NOHS-tee-koh

atheist. **ateo -a.**
ah-TEH-oh -ah

I'm spiritual but I don't attend services. **Soy espiritual pero no asisto a los servicios.**
soy ehs-pee-ree-TWAHL peh-roh noh ah-SEES-toh ah lohs sehr-VEE-syohs

I don't believe in that. **Yo no creo en eso.**
yoh noh KREH-oh ehn EH-soh

That's against my beliefs. **Eso va en contra de mis creencias.**
EH-soh vah ehn KOHN-trah deh mees kreh-EHN-syahs

I'd rather not talk about it. **Preferiría no hablar de ello.**
preh-feh-ree-REE-ah noh ah-BLAHR deh EH-yoh

GETTING TO KNOW SOMEONE

Following are some conversation starters.

MUSICAL TASTES

What kind of music do you like?	**¿Qué tipo de música le gusta?** *keh TEE-poh deh MOO-see-kah leh GOOS-tah*
I like _____	**Me gusta _____** *meh GOOS-tah*
rock 'n' roll.	**el rock and roll.** *ehl rroh-kahnd-ROHL*
hip hop.	**el hip hop, el jip jop.** *ehl eep ohp, ehl heep HOHP*
techno.	**el techno.** *ehl TEHK-noh*
disco.	**el disco.** *ehl DEES-koh*
classical.	**la música clásica.** *lah MOO-see-kah KLAH-see-kah*
jazz.	**el jazz.** *ehl jahs*
country and western.	**la música country.** *lah MOO-see-kah KOHN-tree*
reggae.	**el reggae.** *ehl REH-geh*
calypso.	**el calipso.** *ehl kah-LEEP-soh*
opera.	**la ópera.** *lah OH-peh-rah*
show-tunes / musicals.	**los musicales.** *lohs moo-see-KAH-lehs*
New Age.	**la nueva era.** *lah NWEH-vah EH-rah*
pop.	**la música pop.** *lah MOO-see-kah pohp*

HOBBIES

What do you like to do in your spare time?	¿Qué hace usted en su tiempo libre? *keh AH-seh oos-TEHD ehn soo TYEHM-poh LEE-breh*
I like ____	Me gusta ____ *meh GOOS-tah*
playing guitar.	tocar la guitarra. *toh-KAHR lah gee-TAH-rrah*
piano.	el piano. *ehl PYAH-noh*

For other instruments, see the English / Spanish dictionary.

painting.	pintar. *peen-TAHR*
drawing.	dibujar. *dee-boo-HAHR*
dancing.	bailar. *bah-ee-LAHR*
reading.	leer. *leh-EHR*
watching TV.	ver televisión. *vehr teh-leh-vee-SYOHN*
shopping.	ir de comprar. *eer deh kohm-PRAHR*
going to the movies.	ir al cine. *eer ahl SEE-neh*
hiking.	excursionismo. *ehs-koor-syoh-NEES-moh*
camping.	acampar. *ah-kahm-PAHR*
hanging out.	pasar el rato. *pah-SAHR ehl RAH-toh*
traveling.	viajar. *vyah-HAR*
eating out.	comer fuera. *koh-MEHR FWEH-rah*

cooking.	**cocinar.**
	koh-see-NAHR
sewing.	**coser.**
	koh-SEHR
sports.	**los deportes.**
	lohs deh-POHR-tehs
Do you like to dance?	**¿A usted le gusta bailar?**
	ah oos-TEHD leh GOOS-tah bah-ee-LAHR
Would you like to go out?	**¿Le gustaría salir?**
	leh goos-tah-REE-ah sah-LEER
May I buy you dinner sometime?	**¿Le puedo invitar a cenar alguna vez?**
	leh PWEH-doh een-vee-TAHR ah SEH-nahr ahl-GOO-nah vehs
What kind of food do you like?	**¿Qué tipo de comida le gusta?**
	keh TEE-poh deh koh-MEE-dah leh GOOS-tah

For a full list of food types, see Dining in Chapter 4.

Would you like to go _____	**¿Le gustaría ir _____**
	leh goos-tah-REE-ah eer
to a movie?	**al cine?**
	ahl SEE neh
to a concert?	**a un concierto?**
	ah oon kohn-SYEHR-toh
to the zoo?	**al zoológico?**
	ahl soh-oh-LOH-hee-koh
to the beach?	**a la playa?**
	ah lah PLAH-yah
to a museum?	**al museo?**
	ahl moo-SEH-oh
for a walk in the park?	**a caminar en el parque?**
	ah kah-mee-NAHR ehn ehl PAHR-keh

dancing?	**a bailar?**
	ah bah-ee-LAHR
Would you like to get _____	**¿Le gustaría ir _____**
	leh goos-tah-REE-ah eer
lunch?	**a almorzar?**
	ah ahl-mohr-SAHR
coffee?	**a tomar café?**
	ah toh-MAHR kah-FEH
dinner?	**a cenar?**
	ah seh-NAHR
What kind of books do you like to read?	**¿Qué tipo de libros le gusta leer?**
	keh TEE-poh deh LEE-brohs leh GOOS-tah leh-EHR
I like _____	**Me gusta / gustan _____**
	meh GOOS-tah / GOOS-tahn
mysteries.	**los misterios.**
	lohs mees-TEHR-yohs
Westerns.	**de vaqueros.**
	deh vah-KEH-rohs
dramas.	**los dramas.**
	lohs DRAH-mahs
novels.	**las novelas.**
	lahs noh-VEH-lahs
biographies.	**las biografías.**
	lahs bee-oh-grah-FEE-ahs
auto-biographies.	**las autobiografías.**
	lahs ow-toh-bee-oh-grah-FEE-ahs
romance.	**los romances.**
	lohs roh-MAHN-sehs
history.	**la historia.**
	lah ees-TOH-ryah

For dating terms, see Nightlife in Chaper 10.

CHAPTER SIX

MONEY & COMMUNICATIONS

This chapter covers money, the mail, phone, Internet service, and other tools you need to connect with the outside world.

MONEY

Do you accept _____

¿Aceptan _____
ah-SEHP-tahn

Visa / MasterCard / Discover / American Express / Diners' Club?

Visa / MasterCard / Discover / American Express / Diners' Club?
Pronounced as in english

credit cards?

tarjetas de crédito?
tahr-HEH-tahs deh KREH-dee-toh

bills?

billetes?
bee-YEH-tehs

coins?

monedas?
moh-NEH-dahs

checks?

cheques?
CHEH-kehs

travelers checks?

cheques de viajero?
CHEH-kehs deh vyah-HEH-roh

money transfer?

transferencia de dinero?
trahns-feh-REHN-syah deh dee NEH-roh

May I wire transfer funds here?

¿Puedo hacer una transferencia de dinero aquí?
PWEH-doh ah-SEHR OO-nah trahns-feh-REHN-syah deh dee-NEH-roh ah-KEE

Would you please tell me where to find _____

Por favor, ¿puede decirme dónde puedo encontrar _____
pohr fah-VOHR PWEH-deh deh-SEER-meh DOHN-deh PWEH-doh ehn-kohn-TRAHR

a bank?	**un banco?** *oon BAHN-koh*
a credit bureau?	**una agencia de crédito?** *OO-nah ah-HEHN-syah deh KREH-dee-toh*
an ATM?	**un cajero automático?** *oon kah-HEH-roh ow-toh-MAH-tee-koh*
a currency exchange?	**un lugar de cambio de moneda?** *oon loo-HAHR deh KAHM-byoh deh moh-NEH-dah*
A receipt, please.	**Un recibo, por favor.** *oon reh-SEE-boh pohr fah-VOHR*
Would you tell me ____	**Me puede decir ____** *meh PWEH-deh deh-SEER*
today's interest rate?	**la tasa de interés de hoy?** *lah TAH-sah deh een-teh-REHS deh oy*
the exchange rate for dollars to ____?	**la tasa de cambio de dólares a ____?** *lah TAH-sah deh KAHM-byoh deh DOH-lah-rehs ah*
Is there a service charge?	**¿Hay un cargo por servicio?** *ay oon KAHR-goh pohr sehr-VEES-yoh*
May I have a cash advance on my credit card?	**¿Puedo obtener un adelanto en efectivo de mi tarjeta de crédito?** *PWEH-doh ohb-teh-NEHR oon ah-deh-LAHN-toh ehn eh-fehk-TEE-voh deh mee tahr-HEH-tah deh KREH-dee-toh*
Will you accept a credit card?	**¿Aceptarían una tarjeta de crédito?** *ah-sehp-tah-REE-ahn OO-nah tahr-HEH-tah deh KREH-dee-toh*

Listen Up: Bank Lingo

Por favor, firme aquí.
*pohr fah-VOHR FEER-meh
ah-KEE*

Please sign here.

Aquí está su recibo.
*ah-KEE ehs-TAH soo reh-
SEE-boh*

Here is your receipt.

**Por favor, ¿puedo ver
su identificacion?**
*pohr fah-VOHR PWEH-doh
vehr soo ee-dehn-tee-fee-
kah-SYOHN*

May I see your ID, please?

**Aceptamos cheques
de viajero.**
*ah-sehp-TAH-mohs CHEH-
kehs deh vyah-HEH-roh*

We accept travelers checks.

Solo en efectivo.
*SOH-loh ehn eh-fehk-
TEE-voh*

Cash only.

May I have smaller
bills, please.

**Me puede dar billetes más
pequeños, por favor.**
*meh PWEH-deh dahr bee-YEH-tehs
mahs peh-KEH-nyohs pohr
fah-VOHR*

Can you make change?

¿Puede hacer cambio?
PWEH-deh ah-SEHR KAHM-byoh

I only have bills.

Sólo tengo billetes.
SOH-loh TEHNG-goh bee-YEH-tehs

Some coins, please.

Unas monedas por favor.
*OO-nahs moh-NEH-dahs pohr
fah-VOHR*

ATM Machine

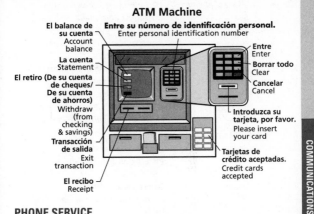

Entre su número de identificación personal.
Enter personal identification number

El balance de su cuenta
Account balance

La cuenta
Statement

El retiro (De su cuenta de cheques/ De su cuenta de ahorros)
Withdraw (from checking & savings)

Transacción de salida
Exit transaction

El recibo
Receipt

Entre
Enter

Borrar todo
Clear

Cancelar
Cancel

Introduzca su tarjeta, por favor.
Please insert your card

Tarjetas de crédito aceptadas.
Credit cards accepted

PHONE SERVICE

Where can I buy or rent a cell phone?

¿Dónde puedo comprar o alquilar un teléfono celular?
DOHN-deh PWEH-doh kohm-PRAHR oh ahl-kee-LAHR oon teh-LEH-foh-noh seh-loo-LAHR

What rate plans do you have?

¿Qué planes de tarifas tienen?
keh PLAH-nehs deh tah-REE-fahs TYEH-nehn

Is this good throughout the country?

¿Ésto es bueno en todo el país?
EHS-teh ehs BWEH-noh ehn TOH-doh ehl pah-EES

May I have a prepaid phone?

¿Me puede dar un teléfono pre-pagado?
meh PWEH-deh dahr oon teh-LEH-foh-noh preh-pah-GAH-doh

Where can I buy a phone card?	**¿Dónde puedo comprar una tarjeta de llamadas?** *DOHN-deh PWEH-doh kohm-PRAHR OO-nah tahr-HEH-tah deh yah-MAH-dahs*
May I add more minutes to my phone card?	**¿Puedo añadirle más minutos a mi tarjeta de llamadas?** *PWEH-doh ah-nyah-DEER-leh mahs mee-NOO-tohs ah me tahr-HEH-tah deh yah-MAH-dahs*

MAKING A CALL

May I dial direct?	**¿Puedo marcar directo?** *PWEH-doh MAHR-kahr dee-REHK-toh*
Operator please.	**Operadora, por favor.** *oh-peh-rah-DOH-rah pohr fah-VOHR*
I'd like to make an international call.	**Quisiera hacer una llamada internacional.** *kee-SYEH-rah ah-SEHR OO-nah yah-MAH-dah een-tehr-nah-syoh-NAHL*

Fuera de Servicio

Before you stick your coins or bills in a vending machine, watch out for the little sign that says *Fuera de Servicio* (Out of Service).

Listen Up: Telephone Lingo

¿Diga? / ¿Bueno? / ¿Hola?	Hello?
DEE-gah, BWEH-noh, OH-lah	
¿A qué número?	What number?
ah keh NOO-meh-roh	
Lo siento, la línea está ocupada.	I'm sorry, the line is busy.
loh SYEHN-toh lah LEE-neh-ah ehs-TAH oh-koo-PAH-dah	
Por favor, cuelgue el teléfono y marque el número de nuevo.	Please, hang up and redial.
pohr fah-VOHR KWEHL-geh ehl teh-LEH-foh-noh ee MAHR-keh ehl NOO-meh-roh deh NWEH-voh	
Lo siento. Nadie responde.	I'm sorry, nobody is answering.
loh SYEHN-toh NAH-dyeh rehs-POHN-deh	
Su tarjeta tiene diez minutos.	Your card has ten minutes left.
soo tahr-HEH-tah TYEH-neh dyehs mee-NOO-tohs	

I'd like to make a collect call.	**Quisiera hacer una llamada a cobro revertido.** *kee-SYEH-rah ah-SEHR OO-nah yah-MAH-dah ah KOH-broh reh-vehr-TEE-doh*
I'd like to use a calling card.	**Quisiera usar una tarjeta de llamadas.** *kee-SYEH-rah oo-SAHR OO-nah tahr-HEH-tah deh yah-MAH-dahs*
Bill my credit card.	**Cargue a mi tarjeta de crédito.** *KAHR-geh ah mee tahr-HEH-tah deh KREH-dee-toh*
May I bill the charges to my room?	**¿Puedo cargar los cargos a mi habitación?** *PWEH-doh kahr-GAHR lohs KAHR-gohs ah mee ah-bee-tah-SYOHN*
May I bill the charges to my home phone?	**¿Puedo cargar los cargos a mi teléfono residencial?** *PWEH-doh kahr-GAHR lohs KAHR-gohs ah mee teh-LEH-foh-noh reh-see-dehn-SYAHL*
Information, please.	**Información, por favor.** *een-fohr-mah-SYOHN pohr fah-VOHR*
I'd like the number for ____.	**Quisiera el número para ____.** *kee-SYEH-rah ehl NOO-meh-roh PAH-rah*
I just got disconnected.	**Me acaba de desconectar.** *meh ah-KAH-bah deh dehs-koh-nehk-TAHR*
The line is busy.	**La línea está ocupada.** *lah LEE-neh-ah ehs-TAH oh-koo-PAH-dah*
I lost the connection.	**Perdí la conexión.** *pehr-DEE lah koh-nehk-SYOHN*

INTERNET ACCESS

Where is an Internet café?	**¿Dónde hay un café con acceso al Internet?** *DOHN-deh aye oon kah-FEH kohn ahk-SEH-soh ahl een-tehr-NET*
Is there a wireless hub nearby?	**¿Hay un nodo de conexión inalámbrica cerca?** *aye oon NOH-doh deh koh-nehk-SYOHN ee-nah-LAHM-bree-kah SEHR-kah*
How much do you charge per minute / hour?	**¿Cuánto cobra por minuto / hora?** *KWAHN-toh KOH-brah pohr mee-NOO-toh / OH-rah*
Can I print here?	**¿Puedo imprimir aquí?** *PWEH-doh eem-pree-MEER ah-KEE*
Can I burn a CD?	**¿Puedo quemar un CD?** *PWEH-doh keh-MAHR oon seh-DEH*
Would you please help me change the language preference to English?	**¿Me puede ayudar a cambiar la opción de idioma al inglés?** *meh PWEH-deh ah-yoo-DAHR ah kahm-BYAHR lah ohp-SYOHN deh ee-DYOH-mah ahl eeng-GLEHS*

May I scan something?	**¿Puedo escanear algo?** *PWEH-doh ehs-kah-neh-AHR* *AHL-goh*
Can I upload photos?	**¿Puedo cargar mis fotos?** *PWEH-doh kahr-GAHR mees* *FOH-tohs*
Do you have a USB port so I can download music?	**¿Tiene un puerto de USB para poder descargar música?** *TYEH-neh oon PWEHR-toh deh oo-* *EH-seh-BEH PAH-rah poh-DEHR* *dehs-kahr-GAHR MOO-see-kah*
Do you have a machine compatible with iTunes?	**¿Tiene una máquina compatible con iTunes?** *TYEH-neh OO-nah MAH-kee-nah* *kohm-pah-TEE-bleh kohn ay-* *TOONS*
Do you have a Mac?	**¿Tiene una computadora Macintosh?** *TYEH-neh OO-nah kohm-poo-tah-* *DOH-rah ah mah-keen-TOHSH*
Do you have a PC?	**¿Tiene una computadora PC?** *TYEH-neh OO-nah kohm-poo-tah-* *DOH-rah peh-SEH*
Do you have a newer version of this software?	**¿Tiene la versión más nueva de este software?** *TYEH-neh lah vehr-SYOHN mahs* *NWEH-vah deh EHS-teh SOHFT-* *wehr*
Do you have broadband?	**¿Tiene conexión de Internet de alta velocidad?** *TYEH-neh koh-nehk-SYOHN deh* *een-tehr-NEHT deh AHL-tah veh-* *loh-see-DAHD*
How fast is your connection speed here?	**¿Cuán rápida es su conexión aquí?** *kwahn RAH-pee-dah ehs soo koh-* *nehk-SYOHN ah-KEE*

GETTING MAIL

Where is the post office?	**¿Dónde está el correo?**
	DOHN-deh ehs-TAH ehl koh-RREH-oh
May I send an international package?	**¿Puedo enviar un paquete internacional?**
	PWEH-doh ehn-vee-AHR oon pah-KEH-teh een-tehr-nah-syoh-NAHL
Do I need a customs form?	**¿Necesito un formulario de aduanas?**
	neh-seh-SEE-toh oon fohr-moo-LAHR-yoh deh ah-DWAH-nahs
Do you sell insurance for packages?	**¿Vende seguros para paquetes?**
	VEHN-deh seh-GOO-rohs PAH-rah pah-KEH-tehs
Please, mark it fragile.	**Por favor, márquelo como frágil.**
	pohr fah-VOHR MAHR-keh-loh koh-moh FRAH-heel
Please, handle with care.	**Por favor, manéjelo con cuidado.**
	pohr fah-VOHR mah-NEH-heh-loh kohn koo-ee-DAH-doh
Do you have twine?	**¿Tiene cuerda?**
	TYEH-neh KWEHR-dah
Where is a DHL office?	**¿Dónde hay una oficina de DHL?**
	DOHN-deh aye OO-nah oh-fee-SEE-nah deh deh AH-cheh EH-leh
Do you sell stamps?	**¿Vende sellos?**
	VEHN-deh SEH-yohs
Do you sell postcards?	**¿Vende postales?**
	VEHN-deh pohs-TAH-lehs
May I send that first class?	**¿Puedo enviar esto por primera clase?**
	PWEH-doh ehn-VEE-ahr EHS-toh pohr pree-MEH-rah KLAH-seh

COMMUNICATIONS

Listen Up: Postal Lingo

¡Próximo!	Next!
PROHK-see-moh	
Por favor, póngalo aquí.	Please, set it here.
pohr fah-VOHR POHNG-	
gah-loh ah-KEE	
¿Qué clase?	Which class?
keh KLAH-seh	
¿Qué tipo de servicio	What kind of service would
quiere?	you like?
keh TEE-poh deh sehr-	
VEE-syoh KYEH-reh	
¿En qué puedo servirle?	How can I help you?
ehn keh PWEH-doh sehr-	
VEER-leh	
ventanilla de entregas	dropoff window
vehn-tah-NEE-yah deh ehn-	
TREH-gahs	
ventanilla de recogidos	pickup window
vehn-tah-NEE-yah deh reh-	
koh-HEE-dohs	

How much to send that express / air mail?	**¿Cuánto cuesta enviar esto por correo urgente / correo aéreo?** *KWAHN-toh KWEHS-tah ehn-VEE-ahr EHS-toh pohr koh-RREH-oh oor-HEHN-teh / koh-RREH-oh ah-EH-reh-oh*
Do you offer overnight delivery?	**¿Ofrece entrega de un día para otro?** *oh-FREH-seh ehn-TREH-gah deh oon DEE-ah PAH-rah OH-troh*

How long will it take to reach the United States?	**¿Cuánto tardará en llegar a los Estados Unidos?** *KWAHN-toh tahr-dah-RAH ehn yeh-GAHR ah lohs ehs-TAH-dohs oo-NEE-dohs*
I'd like to buy an envelope.	**Quisiera comprar un sobre.** *kee-SYEH-rah kohm-PRAHR oon SOH-breh*
May I send it airmail?	**¿Puedo enviarlo por correo aéreo?** *PWEH-doh ehn-VYAHR-loh pohr koh-RREH-oh ah-EH-reh-oh*
I'd like to send it certified / registered mail.	**Quisiera enviarlo por correo certificado.** *kee-SYEH-rah ehn-VYAHR-loh pohr koh-RREH-oh sehr-tee-fee-KAH-doh*

COMMUNICATIONS

CHAPTER SEVEN

CULTURE

CINEMA

Is there a movie theater nearby?	**¿Hay un cine cerca?** *aye oon SEE-neh SEHR-kah*
What's playing tonight?	**¿Qué están dando esta noche?** *keh ehs-TAHN DAHN-doh ehs-TAH NOH-cheh*
Is that in English or Spanish?	**¿Es en inglés o español?** *ehs ehn eeng-GLEHS oh ehs-pah-NYOHL*
Are there English subtitles?	**¿Hay subtítulos en inglés?** *aye soob-TEE-too-lohs ehn eeng-GLEHS*
Is the theater air conditioned?	**¿El teatro tiene aire acondicionado?** *ehl teh-AH-troh TYEH-neh AYE-reh ah-kohn-dee-syoh-NAH-doh*
How much is a ticket?	**¿Cuánto cuesta un boleto?** *KWAHN-toh KWEH-stah oon boh-LEH-toh*
Do you have a ____ discount?	**¿Ofrecen un descuento para ____** *oh-FREH-sehn oon dehs-KWEHN-toh PAH-rah*
senior	**personas mayores de edad?** *pehr-SOH-nahs mah-YOH-rehs deh eh-DAHD?*
student	**estudiantes?** *ehs-too-DYAHN-tehs*
children's	**niños?** *NEE-nyohs*

What time is the movie showing?	**¿A qué hora muestran la película?** *ah keh OH-rah MWEHS-trahn lah peh-LEE-koo-lah*
How long is the movie?	**¿Cuán larga es la película?** *kwahn LAHR-gah ehs lah peh-LEE-koo-lah*
May I buy tickets in advance?	**¿Puedo comprar los boletos por adelantado?** *PWEH-doh kohm-PRAHR lohs boh-LEH-tohs pohr ah-deh-lahn-TAH-doh*
Is it sold out?	**¿Está todo vendido?** *ehs-TAH TOH-doh vehn-DEE-doh*
When does it begin?	**¿A qué hora comienza?** *ah keh OH-rah koh-MYEHN-sah*

PERFORMANCES

Do you have ballroom dancing?	**¿Tienen un salón de bailes?** *TYEH-nehn oon sah-LOHN deh bah-EE-lehs*
Are there any plays showing right now?	**¿Hay alguna obra en escena ahora mismo?** *aye ahl-GOO-nah OH-brah ehn eh-SEH-nah ah-OH-rah MEES-moh*
Is there a dinner theater?	**¿Hay teatro de cena?** *aye teh-AH-troh deh SEH-nah*
Where can I buy tickets?	**¿Dónde puedo comprar boletos?** *DOHN-deh PWEH-doh kohm-PRAHR boh-LEH-tohs*
Are there student discounts?	**¿Ofrecen descuentos para estudiantes?** *oh-FREH-sehn dehs-KWEHN-tohs PAH-rah ehs-too-DYAHN-tehs*
I need ____ seats.	**Quisiera ____ asientos.** *kee-SYEH-rah ____ ah-SYEHN-tohs*

For a full list of numbers, see p7.

For a full list of numbers, see p7.

CULTURE

Listen Up: Box Office Lingo

¿Qué le gustaría ver?
keh leh goos-tah-REE-ah vehr

What would you like to see?

¿Cuántos?
KWAHN-tohs

How many?

¿Para dos adultos?
PAH-rah dohs ah-DOOL-tohs

For two adults?

¿Con mantequilla? ¿Sal?
kohn mahn-teh-KEE-yah sahl

With butter? Salt?

¿Algo más?
AHL-goh mahs

Would you like anything else?

An aisle seat.	**Un asiento de pasillo.** *oon ah-SYEHN-toh deh pah-SEE-yoh*
Orchestra seat, please.	**Un asiento a nivel de orquesta, por favor.** *oon ah-SYEHN-toh ah nee-VEHL deh ohr-KEHS-tah pohr fah-VOHR*
What time does the play start?	**¿A qué hora comienza la obra?** *ah keh OH-rah koh-MYEHN-sah lah OH-brah*
Is there an intermission?	**¿Hay un interludio?** *aye oon een-tehr-LOO-dyoh*
Do you have an opera house?	**¿Tienen un teatro de la ópera?** *TYEH-nehn oon teh-AH-troh deh lah OH-peh-rah*
Is there a local symphony?	**¿Hay una sinfonía local?** *aye OO-nah seen-foh-NEE-ah loh-KAHL*

May I purchase tickets over the phone?	**¿Puedo comprar boletos por teléfono?**
	PWEH-doh kohm-PRAHR boh-LEH-tohs pohr teh-LEH-foh-noh
What time is the box office open?	**¿A qué hora abre la boletería?**
	ah keh OH-rah AH-breh lah boh-leh-teh-REE-ah
I need space for a wheelchair, please.	**Necesito espacio para una silla de ruedas, por favor.**
	neh-seh-SEE-toh ehs-PAH-syoh PAH-rah OO-nah SEE-yah deh RWEH-dahs pohr fah-VOHR
Do you have private boxes available?	**¿Tiene asientos de palco privados disponibles?**
	TYEH-neh ah-SYEHN-tohs deh PAHL-koh pree-VAH-dohs dees-poh-NEE-blehs
Is there a church that gives concerts?	**¿Hay una iglesia que ofrece conciertos?**
	aye OO-nah ee-GLEH-syah keh oh-FREH-seh kohn-SYEHR-tohs
A program, please.	**Un programa, por favor.**
	oon proh-GRAH-mah pohr fah-VOHR
Please show us to our seats.	**Por favor llévenos a nuestros asientos.**
	pohr fah-VOHR YEH-veh-nohs ah NWEHS-trohs ah-SYEHN-tohs

CULTURE

MUSEUMS, GALLERIES, AND SIGHTS

Do you have a museum guide?	**¿Tiene un guía del museo?** *TYEH-neh oon GEE-ah dehl moo-SEH-oh*
Do you have guided tours?	**¿Ofrecen una excursión guiada?** *oh-FREH-sehn OO-nah ehs-koor-SYOHN gee-AH-dah*
What are the museum hours?	**¿Cuál es el horario del museo?** *kwahl ehs ehl oh-RAH-ryoh dehl moo-SEH-oh*
Do I need an appointment?	**¿Necesito una cita?** *neh-seh-SEE-toh OO-nah SEE-tah*
What is the admission fee?	**¿Cuánto es la tarifa de admisión?** *KWAHN-toh ehs lah tah-REE-fah deh ahd-mee-SYOHN*
Do you have ____	**¿Ofrecen ____** *oh-FREH-sehn*
student discounts?	**descuentos para estudiantes?** *dehs-KWEHN-tohs PAH-rah ehs-too-DYAHN-tehs*
senior discounts?	**descuentos para personas mayores / ancianos?** *dehs-KWEHN-tohs PAH-rah pehr-SOH-nahs mah-YOH-rehs / ahn-SYAH-nohs*
Do you have services for the hearing impaired?	**¿Tienen servicios para las personas con impedimentos auditivos?** *TYEH-nehn sehr-VEE-syohs PAH-rah lahs pehr-SOH-nahs kohn eem-peh-dee-MEHN-tohs ow-dee-TEE-vohs*
Do you have audio tours in English?	**¿Ofrecen excursiones por audio en inglés?** *oh-FREH-sehn ehs-koor-SYOH-nehs pohr OW-dyoh ehn eeng-GLEHS*

CHAPTER EIGHT

SHOPPING

This chapter covers the phrases you'll need to shop in a variety of settings, from the mall to the town square artisan market. We also threw in the terminology you'll need to visit the barber or hairdresser.

For coverage of food and grocery shopping, see p100.

GENERAL SHOPPING TERMS

Please tell me ____	**¿Me puede decir ____**
	meh PWEH-deh deh-SEER
how to get to a mall?	**cómo llego a un centro comercial?**
	KOH-moh YEH-goh ah oon SEHN-troh koh-mehr-SYAHL
the best place for shopping?	**el mejor lugar para ir de compras?**
	ehl meh-HOHR loo-GAHR pah-rah EER deh KOHM-prahs
how to get downtown?	**cómo llego al centro de la ciudad?**
	KOH-moh YEH-goh ahl SEHN-troh deh lah see-oo-DAHD

Contrabandistas

Beware of unscrupulous vendors who attempt to sell you illegal, contraband, or fake goods. Most Latin American countries do not allow exportation of pre-Columbian artifacts. (In other words, the ones sold by street vendors aren't real.)

Where can I find a ____	**¿Dónde puedo encontrar una ____**
	DOHN-deh PWEH-doh ehn-kohn-
	TRAHR OO-nah
shoe store?	**tienda de zapatos?**
	TYEHN-dah deh sah-PAH-tohs
men's / women's / children's clothing store?	**tienda de ropa para hombres / mujeres / niños?**
	TYEHN-dah deh RROH-pah PAH-rah HOM-brehs / moo-HEH-rehs / NEE-nyohs
designer fashion shop?	**tienda de moda de diseñador?**
	TYEHN-dah deh MOH-dah deh dee-seh-nyah-DOHR
vintage clothing store?	**tienda de ropa antigua?**
	TYEHN-dah deh RROH-pah ahn-TEE-wah
jewelry store?	**joyería?**
	hoh-yeh-REE-yah
bookstore?	**librería?**
	ee-breh-REE-ah
toy store?	**juguetería?**
	hoo-geh-teh-REE-ah
stationery store?	**tienda de útiles de escritura?**
	TYEHN-dah deh OO-tee-lehs deh ehs-kree-TOO-rah

Cuban Cigars

In Latin America, many shops purport to carry Cuban cigars, but it's just a line. Real Cuban cigars are sold only at stores certified by the Cuban government. Certification will be posted, with an anticounterfeiting hologram on the box. When in doubt: if it's cheap, it's fake. That said, most of the "Cubans" on the market, though they're actually from Honduras or the Dominican Republic, are excellent for the price.

antique shop?	**tienda de antigüedades?**
	TYEHN-dah deh ahn-tee-gweh-DAH-dehs
cigar shop?	**tienda de cigarros?**
	TYEHN-dah deh see-GAH-rrohs
souvenir shop?	**tienda de recuerdos?**
	TYEHN-dah deh reh-KWEHR-dohs
Where can I find a flea market?	**¿Dónde puedo encontrar un pulguero?**
	DOHN-deh PWEH-doh ehn-kohn-TRAHR oon pool-GEH-roh

CLOTHES SHOPPING

I'd like to buy ____	**Quisiera comprar ____**
	kee-SYEH-rah kohm-PRAHR
men's shirts.	**camisas para hombres.**
	kah-MEE-sahs PAH-rah OHM-brehs
women's shoes.	**zapatos para mujeres.**
	sah-PAH-tohs PAH-rah moo-HEH-rehs
children's clothes.	**ropa para niños.**
	RROH-pah PAH-rah NEE-nyohs
toys.	**juguetes.**
	hoo-GEH-tehs

For a full list of numbers, see p7.

I'm looking for a size ____	**Busco una talla ____**
	BOOS-koh OO-nah TAH-yah
small.	**pequeño.**
	peh-KEH-nyoh
medium.	**mediano.**
	meh-DYAH-noh
large.	**grande.**
	GRAHN-deh
extra-large.	**extra grande.**
	EHS-trah GRAHN-deh

los aretes
el collar

el vestido
el reloj

la camisa
la corbata
la chaqueta

el cinturón

los pantalones

los zapatos

I'm looking for ____	**Busco** ____
	BOOS-koh
a silk blouse.	**una blusa de seda.**
	OO-nah BLOO-sah deh SEH-dah
cotton pants.	**pantalones de algodón.**
	pahn-tah-LOH-nehs deh ahl-goh-DOHN
a hat.	**un sombrero.**
	oon sohm-BREH-roh
sunglasses.	**gafas de sol.**
	GAH-fahs deh sohl
underwear.	**ropa interior.**
	RROH-pah een-teh-RYOHR
cashmere.	**cachemir.**
	kah-che-MEER
socks.	**medias.**
	MEH-dyahs
sweaters.	**suéteres.**
	soo-EH-teh-rehs

—las gafas

—la camiseta

—los jeans

—los tennis

a coat.	**un abrigo.** *oon ah-BREE-goh*
a swimsuit.	**un traje de baño.** *oon TRAH-heh deh BAH-nyoh*
May I try it on?	**¿Puedo medírmelo?** *PWEH-doh meh-DEER-meh-loh*
Do you have fitting rooms?	**¿Tiene probadores?** *TYEH-neh proh-bah-DOH-rehs*
This is ____	**Esto me queda ____** *EHS-toh meh KEH-dah*
too tight.	**muy apretado.** *MOO-ee ah-preh-TAH-doh*
too loose.	**muy suelto.** *MOO-ee SWEHL-toh*
too long.	**muy largo.** *MOO-ee LAHR-goh*
too short.	**muy corto.** *MOO-ee KOHR-toh*
This fits great!	**¡Esto me queda bien!** *EHS-toh meh KEH-dah byehn*

Thanks, I'll take it.	**Gracias, me lo llevo.**
	GRAH-syahs meh loh YEH-voh
Do you have that in ____	**¿Tiene eso en ____**
	TYEH-neh EH-soh ehn
a smaller / larger size?	**una talla más pequeña / grande?**
	OO-nah TAH-yah mahs peh-KEH-nyah / GRAHN-deh
a different color?	**un color diferente?**
	oon koh-LOHR dee-feh-REHN-teh
How much is it?	**¿Cuánto es?**
	KWAHN-toh ehs

ARTISAN MARKET SHOPPING

Is there a craft / artisan market?	**¿Hay un mercado de artesanías?**
	aye oon mehr-KAH-doh deh ahr-teh-SAH-nee-ahs
That's beautiful. May I look at it?	**¡Eso es hermoso! ¿Puedo verlo?**
	EH-soh ehs ehr-MOH-soh PWEH-doh VEHR-loh
When is the farmers' market open?	**¿Cuándo está abierto el mercado de granjeros?**
	KWAHN-doh ehs-TAH ah-BYEHR-toh ehl mehr-KAH-doh deh grahn-HEH-rohs
Is that open every day of the week?	**¿Eso está abierto todos los días de la semana?**
	EH-soh ehs-TAH ah-BYEHR-toh TOH-doh lohs DEE-ahs deh lah seh-MAH-nah
How much does that cost?	**¿Cuánto cuesta eso?**
	KWAHN-toh KWEHS-tah EH-soh
That's too expensive.	**Eso es muy caro.**
	EH-soh ehs MOO-ee KAH-roh
How much for two?	**¿Cuánto por los / las dos?**
	KWAHN-doh pohr lohs / lahs dohs

Listen Up: Market Lingo

Por favor pida que le asistan, antes de manejar la mercadería. *pohr fah-VOHR PEE-dah keh leh ah-sees-TAHN ahn-TEHS deh mah-neh-HAHR lah mehr-kah-deh-REE-ah*	Please ask for help before handling goods.
Aquí tengo su cambio. *ah-KEE TEHNG-goh soo KAHM-byoh*	Here is your change.
Dos por cuarenta, señor. *dohs pohr kwah-REHN-tah sehn-YOHR*	Two for forty, sir.

Do I get a discount if I buy two or more?	**¿Me da un descuento si compro dos o más?** *meh dah oon dehs-KWEHN-toh see KOHM-proh dohs oh mahs*
Do I get a discount if I pay in cash?	**¿Me da un descuento si pago en efectivo?** *meh dah oon desh-KWEHN-toh see PAH-goh ehn eh-FEHK-tee-voh*
No thanks, maybe I'll come back.	**No gracias, quizás regreso más tarde.** *noh GRAH-syahs kee-SAHS reh-GREH-soh mahs TAHR-deh*
Would you take $____?	**¿Aceptaría $____?** *ah-SEHP-tah-REE-ah ____ DOH-lah-rehs*

For a full list of numbers, see p7.

That's a deal!	**¡Trato hecho!**
	TRAH-toh EH-choh
Do you have a less expensive one?	**¿Tiene uno -a menos caro -a?**
	TYEH-neh oon / OO-nah MEH-nohs KAH-roh / KAH-rah
Is there tax?	**¿Hay un impuesto?**
	aye oon eem-PWEHS-toh
May I have the VAT forms? (Europe only)	**¿Me puede dar los formularios IVA?**
	meh PWEH-deh dahr lohs fohr-moo-LAHR-yohs ee-veh-AH

BOOKSTORE / NEWSSTAND SHOPPING

Is there a ____ nearby?	**¿Hay ____ cerca?**
	aye ____ SEHR-kah
a bookstore	**una librería**
	OO-nah lee-breh-REE-ah
a newsstand	**un puesto de periódicos**
	oon PWEHS-toh deh pehr-YOH-dee-kohs
Do you have ____ in English?	**¿Tiene ____ en inglés?**
	TYEH-neh ____ ehn eeng-GLEHS
books	**libros**
	LEE-brohs
newspapers	**periódicos**
	pehr-YOH-dee-kohs
magazines	**revistas**
	reh-VEES-tahs
books about local history	**libros acerca de la historia local**
	LEE-brohs ah-SEHR-kah deh lah ees-TOHR-yah loh-KAHL
picture books	**libros de fotos**
	LEE-brohs deh FOH-tohs

SHOPPING FOR ELECTRONICS

With some exceptions, shopping for electronic goods in Latin America or Spain is generally not recommended. Many DVDs, CDs, and other products contain different signal coding from that used in the United States or Canada, to help deter piracy. Radios, as well as older videos and cassette tapes, are probably the biggest exception though, and lots of U.S. market goods are available. Note: Electronic formats are the same for the United States and Canada.

Can I play this in the United States?	**¿Puedo tocar esto en Estados Unidos?**
	PWEH-doh toh-KAHR EHS-toh ehn ehs-TAH-dohs oo-NEE-dohs?
Will this game work on my game console in the United States?	**¿Este juego funcionará en mi consola de juegos en los Estados Unidos?**
	EHS-teh HWEH-goh foon-syoh-nah-RAH ehn mee kohn-SOH-lah deh HWEH-gohs ehn lohs ehs-TAH-dohs oo-NEE-dohs
Do you have this in a U.S. market format?	**¿Tiene esto en un formato para el mercado de los Estados Unidos?**
	TYEH-neh EHS-toh ehn oon fohr-MAH-toh PAH-rah ehl mehr-KAH-doh deh lohs ehs-TAH-dohs oo-NEE-dohs
Can you convert this to a U.S. market format?	**¿Puede convertir esto a un formato para el mercado de los Estados Unidos?**
	PWEH-deh kohn-vehr-TEER EHS-toh ah oon fohr-MAH-toh PAH-rah ehl mehr-KAH-doh deh lohs ehs-TAH-dohs oo-NEE-dohs

Will this work with a 110 VAC adapter?	**¿Esto funcionará con un adaptador de 110 VAC?** *EHS-toh foon-syoh-nah-RAH kohn oon ah-dahp-tah-DOHR deh SYEHN-toh ee dyehs VOHL-tyohs deh koh-RRYEHN-teh ahl-TEHR-nah*
Do you have an adapter plug for 110 to 220?	**¿Tiene un enchufe adaptador de 110 a 220?** *TYEH-neh oon ehn-CHOO-feh ah-dahp-tah-DOHR deh SYEHN-toh ee dyehs ah doh-SYEHN-tohs ee VEH-een-teh*
Do you sell electronics adapters here?	**¿Vende adaptadores electrónicos aquí?** *VEHN-deh ah-dahp-tah-DOH-rehs eh-lehk-TROH-nee-kohs ah-KEE*
Is it safe to use my laptop with this adapter?	**¿Es seguro usar mi computadora portátil con este adaptador?** *ehs seh-GOO-roh oo-SAHR mee kohm-poo-tah-DOH-rah pohr-TAH-teel kohn EHS-teh ah-dahp-tah-DOHR*
If it doesn't work, may I return it?	**¿Si no funciona, puedo devolverlo?** *see noh foon-SYOH-nah PWEH-doh deh-vohl-VEHR-loh*
May I try it here in the store?	**¿Puedo probarlo aquí en la tienda?** *PWEH-doh proh-BAHR-loh ah-KEE ehn lah TYEHN-dah*

AT THE BARBER / HAIRDRESSER

Do you have a style guide?	**¿Tiene una guía de estilo?** *TYEH-neh OO-nah GEE-ah deh eh-STEE-loh*
A trim, please.	**Un recorte, por favor.** *oon rreh-KOHR-teh pohr fah-VOHR*

I'd like it bleached.

Me gustaría el pelo descolorado.
meh goos-tah-REE-ah ehl PEH-loh dehs-koh-loh-RAH-doh

Would you change the color ____

¿Usted le cambiaría el color ____
oos-TEHD leh kahm-byah-REE-ah ehl koh-LOHR

darker?

más oscuro?
mahs oh-SKOO-roh

lighter?

más claro?
mahs KLAH-roh

Would you just touch it up a little?

¿Lo puede retocar un poco?
loh PWEH-deh reh-toh-KAHR oon POH-koh

I'd like it curled.

Me gustaría rizado.
meh goos-tah-REE-ah ree-SAH-doh

Do I need an appointment?

¿Necesito una cita?
neh-seh-SEE-toh OO-nah SEE-tah

Wash, dry, and set.

Lavado, secado y peinado.
lah-VAH-doh seh-KAH-doh ee peh-ee-NAH-doh

Do you do permanents?

¿Hacen permanentes?
AH-sehn pehr-mah-NEHN-tehs

May I make an appointment?

¿Puedo hacer una cita?
PWEH-doh ah-SEHR OO-nah SEE-tah

Please use low heat.

Por favor use poco calor.
pohr fah-VOHR OO-seh POH-koh kah-LOHR

Please don't blow dry it.

Por favor no lo seque con secadora.
pohr fah-VOHR noh loh SEH-keh kohn seh-kah-DOH-rah

Please dry it curly / straight.

Por favor séquelo rizado / lacio.
pohr fah-VOHR SEH-keh-loh kohn ree-SAH-doh / LAH-syoh

Would you fix my braids?	**¿Puede arreglar mis trenzas?**
	PWEH-deh ah-rreh-GLAHR mees
	TREHN-sahs
Would you fix my highlights?	**¿Puede arreglar mis destellos?**
	PWEH-deh ah-rreh-GLAHR mees
	dehs-TEH-yohs
Do you wax?	**¿Hacen depilación con cera?**
	AH-sehn deh-pee-lah-SYOHN kohn
	SEH-rah
Please wax my _____	**Por favor, depile mis _____**
	pohr fah-VOHR deh-PEE-leh mees
legs.	**piernas.**
	PYEHR-nahs
bikini line.	**área del bikini.**
	AH-reh-ah dehl bee-KEE-nee
eyebrows.	**cejas.**
	SEH-hahs
under my nose.	**debajo de mi nariz.**
	deh-BAH-hoh deh mee nah-REES
Please trim my beard.	**Por favor recorte mi barba.**
	pohr fah-VOHR reh-KOHR-teh mee
	BAHR-bah
A shave, please.	**Una afeitada, por favor.**
	OO-nah ah-feh-ee-TAH-dah pohr
	fah-VOHR
Use a fresh blade please.	**Una navaja nueva por favor.**
	OO-nah nah-VAH-hah NWEH-vah
	pohr fah-VOHR
Sure, cut it all off.	**Seguro, córtelo todo.**
	seh-GOO-roh KOHR-teh-loh
	TOH-doh

CHAPTER NINE
SPORTS & FITNESS

GETTING FIT

Is there a gym nearby?

¿Hay un gimnasio cerca?
aye oon heem-NAH-syoh SEHR-kah

Do you have free weights?

¿Tienen pesas de mano?
TYEH-nehn PEH-sahs deh MAH-noh

I'd like to go for a swim.

Me gustaría nadar.
meh goos-tah-REE-ah nah-DAHR

Do I have to be a member?

¿Tengo que ser miembro?
TEHNG-goh keh sehr MYEHM-broh

May I come here for one day?

¿Puedo venir por un día, nada más?
PWEH-doh veh-NEER pohr oon DEE-ah NAH-dah mahs

How much does a membership cost?

¿Cuánto cuesta la membresía?
KWAHN-toh KWEHS-tah lah mehm-breh-SEE-ah

I need to get a locker please.

Necesito un casillero.
neh-seh-SEE-toh oon kah-see-YEH-roh

161

Do you have a lock?	**¿Tiene un candado?**
	TYEH-neh oon kahn-DAH-doh
Do you have a treadmill?	**¿Tiene una caminadora?**
	TYEH-neh OO-nah kah-mee-nah-DOH-rah
Do you have a stationary bike?	**¿Tiene una bicicleta estacionaria?**
	TYEH-neh OO-nah bee-see-KLEH-tah ehs-tah-syoh-NAH-ryah
Do you have handball / squash courts?	**¿Tiene canchas de balonmano / squash?**
	TYEH-neh KAHN-chahs deh bah-lohn-MAH-noh / skwahsh?
Are they indoors?	**¿Son bajo techo?**
	sohn BAH-hoh TEH-cho
I'd like to play tennis.	**Me gustaría jugar tenis.**
	meh goos-tah-REE-ah hoo-GAHR TEH-nees
Would you like to play?	**¿Le gustaría jugar?**
	leh goos-tah-REE-ah hoo-GAHR
I'd like to rent a racquet.	**Quisiera alquilar una raqueta.**
	kee-SYEH-roh ahl-kee-LAHR OO-nah rrah-KEH-tah
I need to buy some ____	**Necesito comprar ____**
	neh-seh-SEE-toh kohm-PRAHR
new balls.	**bolas nuevas.**
	BOH-lahs NWEH-vahs
safety glasses.	**gafas de protección.**
	GAH-fahs deh proh-tehk-SYOHN
May I rent a court for tomorrow?	**¿Puedo alquilar una cancha para mañana?**
	PWEH-doh ahl-kee-LAHR OO-nah KAHN-chah PAH-rah mah-NYAH-nah
May I have clean towels?	**¿Me puede dar toallas limpias?**
	meh PWEH-deh dahr toh-AH-yahs LEEM-pyahs

Where are the showers / locker-rooms?	**¿Dónde están las duchas / los vestuarios?** *DOHN-deh ehs-TAHN lahs DOO-chas / lohs vehs-TWAHR-yohs*
Do you have a workout room for women only?	**¿Tienen un cuarto de entrenamiento para mujeres solamente?** *TYEH-nehn oon KWAHR-toh deh ehn-treh-nah-MYEHN-toh PAH-rah moo-HEH-rehs soh-lah-MEHN-teh*
Do you have aerobics classes?	**¿Tienen clases de aeróbicos?** *TYEH-nehn KLAH-sehs deh ah-eh-ROH-bee-kohs*
Do you have a women's pool?	**¿Tienen una piscina para mujeres?** *TYEH-nehn OO-nah pee-SEE-nah PAH-rah moo-HEH-rehs*
Let's go for a jog.	**Vamos a trotar.** *VAH-mohs ah troh-TAHR*
That was a great workout.	**Fue un tremendo entrenamiento.** *fweh oon treh-MEHN-doh ehn-treh-nah-MYEHN-toh*

CATCHING A GAME

Where is the stadium?	**¿Dónde es el estadio?** *DOHN-deh ehs ehl ehs-TAH-dyoh*

Where can I see a cockfight?	**¿Dónde puedo ver una pelea de gallos?**
	DOHN-deh PWEH-doh vehr OO-nah peh-LEH-ah deh GAH-yohs
Do you have a bullfight?	**¿Tienen una corrida de toros?**
	TYEH-nehn OO-nah koh-RREE-dah deh TOH-rohs
Who is your favorite toreador / matador?	**¿Quién es su toreador / matador favorito?**
	kyehn ehs soo toh-reh-ah-DOHR / mah-tah-DOHR fah-voh-REE-toh
Who is the best goalie?	**¿Quién es el mejor portero?**
	kyehn ehs ehl meh-HOHR pohr-TEH-roh
Are there any women's teams?	**¿Hay equipos de mujeres?**
	aye eh-KEE-pohs deh moo-HEH-rehs
Do you have any amateur / professional teams?	**¿Tienen algún equipo aficionado / profesional?**
	TYEH-nehn ahl-GOON eh-KEE-poh ah-fee-syoh-NAH-doh / proh-feh-syoh-NAHL
Is there a game I could play in?	**¿Hay algún juego en el que yo puedo jugar?**
	aye ahl-GOON HWEH-goh ehn ehl keh yoh PWEH-doh hoo-GAHR
Which is the best team?	**¿Cuál es el mejor equipo?**
	kwahl ehs ehl meh-HOHR eh-KEE-poh
Will the game be on television?	**¿El juego será televisado?**
	ehl HWEH-goh seh-RAH teh-leh-vee-SAH-dah
Where can I buy tickets?	**¿Dónde puedo comprar boletos?**
	DOHN-deh PWEH-doh kohm-PRAHR boh-LEH-tohs

The best seats, please.	**Los mejores asientos, por favor.** *lohs meh-HOH-rehs ah-SYEHN-tohs pohr fah-VOHR*
The cheapest seats, please.	**Los asientos más baratos, por favor.** *lohs ah-SYEHN-tohs mahs bah-RAH-tohs pohr fah-VOHR*
How close are these seats?	**¿Cuán cerca están estos asientos?** *kwahn SEHR-kah ehs-TAHN EHS-tohs ah-SYEHN-tohs*
May I have box seats?	**¿Me puede dar asientos de palco?** *meh PWEH-deh dahr ah-SYEHN-tohs deh PAHL-koh*
Wow! What a game!	**¡Caray! ¡Que juego!** *kah-RAH-ee keh HWEH-goh*
Go Go Go!	**¡Dale, dale, dale!** *DAH-leh, DAH-leh, DAH-leh*
Oh No!	**¡O no!** *oh NOH*
Give it to them!	**¡Dale!** *DAH-leh*
Go for it!	**¡Ve por él!** *Veh pohr ehl*
Score!	**¡Anota!** *ah-NOH-tah*
What's the score?	**¿Cuál es la puntuación?** *kwahl ehs lah poon-twah-SYOHN*
Who's winning?	**¿Quién está ganando?** *kyehn ehs-TAH gah-NAHN-doh*

HIKING

Where can I find a guide to hiking trails?	**¿Dónde puedo encontrar un guía para los senderos de excursionismo?** *DOHN-deh PWEH-doh ehn-kohn-TRAHR oon GEE-ah PAH-rah lohs sehn-DEH-rohs deh ehs-koor-syoh-NEES-moh*

Do we need to hire a guide?	**¿Necesitamos contratar a un guía?** *neh-seh-see-TAH-mohs kohn-trah-TAHR ah oon GEE-ah*
Where can I rent equipment?	**¿Dónde puedo alquilar equipo?** *DOHN-deh PWEH-doh ahl-kee-LAHR eh-KEE-poh*
Do they have rock climbing there?	**¿Tienen escalada de rocas ahí?** *TYEH-nehn ehs-kah-LAH-dah deh RROH-kahs ah-EE*
We need more ropes and carabiners.	**Necesitamos más cuerda y carabineros.** *neh-seh-see-TAH-mohs mahs KWEHR-dah ee kah-rah-bee-NEH-rohs*
Where can we go mountain climbing?	**¿Dónde podemos ir de alpinismo?** *DOHN-deh poh-DEH-mohs eer deh ahl-pee-NEES-moh*
Are the routes ____	**¿Todas las rutas están ____** *TOH-dahs lahs ROO-tahs ehs-TAHN*
well marked?	**bien marcadas?** *byehn mahr-KAH-dahs*
in good condition?	**en buenas condiciones?** *ehn BWEH-nahs kohn-dees-YOH-nehs*

What is the altitude there?
¿Cuál es la altitud allí?
kwahl ehs lah ahl-tee-TOOD ah-YEE

How long will it take?
¿Cuánto tomará?
KWAHN-toh toh-mah-RAH

Is it very difficult?
¿Es muy difícil?
ehs MOO-ee dee-FEE-seel

I'd like a challenging climb but I don't want to take oxygen.
Me gustaría un ascenso desafiante, pero no quiero tener que llevar oxígeno.
meh goos-tah-REE-ah oon ah-SEHN-soh deh-sah-fee-AHN-teh peh-roh noh KYEH-roh teh-NEHR keh yeh-VAHR ohk-SEE-heh-noh

I want to hire someone to carry my excess gear.
Quisiera contratar a alguien para cargar mi exceso de equipo.
kee-SYEH-rah kohn-trah-TAHR ah AHLG-yehn PAH-rah kahr-GAHR mee ehk-SEH-soh deh eh-KEE-poh

We don't have time for a long route.
No tenemos tiempo para una ruta larga.
noh teh-NEH-mohs TYEHM-poh PAH-rah OO-nah RROO-tah LAHR-gah

I don't think it's safe to proceed.
No creo que sea seguro continuar.
noh KREH-oh keh SEH-ah seh-GOO-roh kohn-tee-NWAHR

Do we have a backup plan?
¿Tenemos un plan de respaldo?
teh-NEH-mohs oon plahn deh rrehs-PAHL-dah

If we're not back by tomorrow, send a search party.
Si no hemos regresado para mañana, envía un grupo de rescate.
see noh EH-mohs rreh-greh-SAH-doh PAH-rah mah-NYAH-nah ehn-VEE-ah oon GROO-poh deh rrehs-KAH-teh

Are the campsites marked?	**¿Los campamentos están marcados?** *lohs kahm-pah-MEHN-tohs ehs-TAHN mahr-KAH-dohs*
Can we camp off the trail?	**¿Podemos acampar a lejos del sendero?** *poh-DEH-mohs ah-kahm-PAHR ah LEH-hohs dehl sehn-DEH-roh*
Is it okay to build fires here?	**¿Está bien construir fogatas aquí?** *ehs-TAH byehn kohn-stroo-EER foh-GAH-tahs ah-KEE*
Do we need permits?	**¿Necesitamos permisos?** *neh-seh-see-TAH-mohs pehr-MEE-sohs*

For more camping terms, see p79.

BOATING OR FISHING

When do we sail?	**¿Cuándo partimos / salimos?** *KWAHN-doh pahr-TEE-mohs / sah-LEE-mohs*
Where are the life preservers?	**¿Dónde están los salvavidas?** *DOHN-deh ehs-TAHN lohs sahl-vah-VEE-dahs*
Can I purchase bait?	**¿Puedo comprar carnada?** *PWEH-doh kohm-PRAHR kahr-NAH-dah*
Can I rent a pole?	**¿Puedo alquilar una caña de pescar?** *PWEH-doh ahl-kee-LAHR OO-nah KAH-nyah deh pehs-KAHR*

How long is the voyage?	**¿Cuán largo es el viaje?**
	kwahn LAHR-goh ehs ehl
	VYAH-heh
Are we going up river or down?	**¿Vamos río arriba o río abajo?**
	VAH-mohs REE-oh ah-RREE-bah oh
	REE-oh ah-BAH-hoh
How far are we going?	**¿Por cuanta distancia vamos?**
	pohr KWAHN-tah dee-STAHN-
	seeah VAH-mohs
How fast are we going?	**¿Qué tan rápido vamos?**
	keh tahn RRAH-pee-doh VAH-
	mohs
How deep is the water here?	**¿Cuán profunda es el agua aquí?**
	kwahn proh-FOON-dah ehs ehl
	AH-wah ah-KEE
I got one!	**¡Pesqué uno!**
	pehs-KEH OO-noh
I can't swim.	**No sé nadar.**
	noh seh nah-DAHR
Can we go ashore?	**¿Podemos ir a la orilla?**
	poh-DEH-mohs eer ah lah oh-
	REE-yah

For more boating terms, see p62.

DIVING

I'd like to go snorkeling.	**Quisiera bucear con tubo respiratorio.**
	kee-SYEH-rah boo-seh-AHR kohn
	TOO-boh rehs-pee-rah-TOH-ryoh
I'd like to go scuba diving.	**Quisiera ir de buceo con tanques de oxígeno.**
	kee-SYEH-rah eer deh boo-SEH-oh
	kohn TAHN-kehs deh ohk-SEE-
	heh-noh

I have a NAUI / PADI certification.	**Tengo certificación NAUI / PADI.** *TEHNG-goh sehr-tee-fee-kah-SYOHN EH-neh ah oo ee / peh ah deh ee*
I need to rent gear.	**Necesito alquilar equipo.** *neh-seh-SEE-toh ahl-kee-LAHR eh-KEE-poh*
We'd like to see some shipwrecks if we can.	**Quisiéramos ver algunos naufragios si podemos.** *kee-SYEH-rah-mohs vehr ahl-GOO-nohs now-FRAH-hyohs see poh-DEH-mohs*
Are there any good reef dives?	**¿Hay buenos lugares para buceo de arrecifes?** *aye BWEH-nohs loo-GAH-rehs PAH-rah boo-SEH-oh deh ah-rreh-SEE-fehs*
I'd like to see a lot of sea-life.	**Quisiera ver mucha vida marina.** *kee-SYEH-rah vehr MOO-chah VEE-dah mah-REE-nah*
Are the currents strong?	**¿Las corrientes son fuertes?** *lahs koh-RRYEHN-tehs sohn FWEHR-tehs*
How clear is the water?	**¿Qué tan clara es el agua?** *keh tahn KLAH-rah ehs ehl AH-wah*
I want / don't want to go with a group	**Quiero / No quiero ir con un grupo.** *KYEH-roh / NOH kyeh-roh eer kohn oon GROO-poh*
Can we charter our own boat?	**¿Podemos fletar nuestro propio bote?** *poh-DEH-mohs fleh-TAHR NWEHS-troh PROH-pyoh BOH-teh*

SURFING

I'd like to go surfing.	**Quisiera ir de surfing.** *kee-SYEH-rah eer deh soor-FEENG*
Are there any good beaches?	**¿Hay buenas playas?** *aye BWEH-nahs PLAH-yahs*
Can I rent a board?	**¿Puedo alquilar una tabla?** *PWEH-doh ahl-kee-LAHR OO-nah TAH-blah*
How are the currents?	**¿Cómo son las corrientes?** *KOH-moh sohn lahs koh-RRYEHN-tehs*
How high are the waves?	**¿Cuán altas son las olas?** *kwahn AHL-tahs sohn lahs OH-lahs*
Is it usually crowded?	**¿Generalmente está llena de personas?** *heh-neh-rahl-MEHN-teh ehs-TAH YEH-nah deh pehr-SOH-nahs*
Are there facilities on that beach?	**¿Hay facilidades en esa playa?** *aye fah-see-lee-DAH-dehs ehn EH-sah PLAH-yah*
Is there wind surfing there also?	**¿Hay windsurfing allí también?** *aye weend-soor-FEENG ah-YEE tahm-BYEHN*

GOLFING

I'd like to reserve a tee-time, please.	**Quisiera reservar tiempo para jugar golf, por favor.** *kee-SYEH-rah rreh-sehr-VAHR TYEHM-poh PAH-rah hoo-GAHR gohlf, pohr fah-VOHR*
Do we need to be members to play?	**¿Tenemos que ser miembros para jugar?** *teh-NEH-mohs keh sehr MYEHM-brohs PAH-rah hoo-GAHR*
How many holes is your course?	**¿De cuántos hoyos es su campo?** *deh KWAHN-tohs OH-yohs ehs soo KAHM-poh*
What is par for the course?	**¿Qué es par para el campo?** *keh ehs PAHR PAH-rah ehl KAHM-poh*
I need to rent clubs.	**Necesito alquilar los palos.** *neh-seh-SEE-toh ahl-kee-LAHR lohs PAH-lohs*
I need to purchase a sleeve of balls.	**Necesito alquilar una funda de bolas.** *neh-seh-SEE-toh ahl-kee-LAHR OO-nah FOON-dah deh BOH-lahs*
I need a glove.	**Necesito un guante.** *neh-seh-SEE-toh oon GWAHN-teh*
I need a new hat.	**Necesito un sombrero nuevo.** *neh-seh-SEE-toh oon sohm-BREH-roh NWEH-voh*

Do you require soft spikes?	**¿Ustedes requieren zapatos con púas blandas?** *oos-TEH-dehs rreh-KYEH-rehn sah-PAH-tohs kohn POO-ahs BLAHN-dahs*
Do you have carts?	**¿Tienen carritos?** *TYEH-nehn kah-RREE-tohs*
I'd like to hire a caddy.	**Quisiera contratar a alguien que cargue mis palos.** *kee-SYEH-rah kohn-trah-TAHR ah AHLG-yehn keh KAHR-geh mees PAH-lohs*
Do you have a driving range?	**¿Tienen un campo de práctica?** *TYEH-nehn oon KAHM-poh deh PRAHK-tee-kah*
How much are the greens fees?	**¿Cuánto es la cuota por jugar?** *KWAHN-toh ehs lah KWOH-tah PAH-rah hoo-GAHR*
Can I book a lesson with the pro?	**¿Puedo reservar una lección con el profesional?** *PWEH-doh rreh-sehr-VAHR OO-nah lehk-SYOHN kohn ehl proh-feh-syoh-NAHL*
I need to have a club repaired.	**Necesito reparar un palo de golf.** *neh-seh-SEE-toh rreh-pah-RAHR oon PAH-loh deh gohlf*
Is the course dry?	**¿El campo está seco?** *ehl KAHM-poh ehs-TAH SEH-koh*
Are there any wildlife hazards?	**¿Hay peligros de vida silvestre?** *aye peh-LEEG-rohs deh VEE-dah seel-VEHS-treh*
How many meters is the course?	**¿De cuántos metros es el campo?** *deh KWAHN-tohs MEH-trohs ehs ehl KAHM-poh*
Is it very hilly?	**¿Está lleno de colinas pequeñas?** *ehs-TAH YEH-noh deh koh-LEE-nahs peh-KEH-nyahs*

CHAPTER TEN

For coverage of movies and cultural events, see p144, Chapter Seven, "Culture."

NIGHTCLUBBING

Where can I find ____	**¿Dónde puedo encontrar ____** *DOHN-deh PWEH-doh ehn-kohn-TRAHR*
a good nightclub?	**un buen club nocturno?** *oon bwehn kloob nohk-TOOR-noh*
a club with a live band?	**un club con banda en vivo?** *oon kloob kohn BAHN-dah ehn VEE-voh*
a reggae club?	**un club de reggae?** *oon kloob deh RREH-geh*
a hip hop club?	**un club de música hip-hop?** *oon kloob deh MOO-see-kah EEP-ohp / HEEP-hohp*
a techno club?	**un club de música techno?** *oon kloob deh MOO-see-kah TEHK-noh*
a jazz club?	**un club de jazz?** *oon kloob deh jahs*
a country-western club?	**un club de música country?** *oon kloob deh MOO-see-kah KOHN-tree*
a gay / lesbian club?	**un club de gays?** *oon kloob deh gehs*
a club where I can dance?	**un club dónde pueda bailar?** *oon kloob DOHN-deh PWEH-dah bah-ee-LAHR*

a club with Spanish / Mexican music?	**un club con música latina / mexicana?**
	oon kloob kohn MOO-see-kah lah-TEE-nah / meh-hee-KAH-nah
the most popular club in town?	**el club más popular en el pueblo?**
	ehl kloob mahs poh-poo-LAHR ehn ehl PWEH-bloh
a singles bar?	**una cantina para solteros?**
	OO-nah kahn-TEE-nah PAH-rah sohl-TEH-rohs
a piano bar?	**una cantina con piano?**
	OO-nah kahn-TEE-nah kohn PYAH-noh
the most upscale club?	**el club de más clase?**
	ehl kloob deh mahs KLAH-seh
What's the hottest bar these days?	**¿Cuál es la cantina más popular de estos días?**
	kwahl ehs lah kahn-TEE-nah mahs poh-poo-LAHR deh EHS-tohs DEE-ahs
What's the cover charge?	**¿Cuánto es el cargo de entrada?**
	KWAHN-toh ehs ehl KAHR-goh deh ehn-TRAH-dah
Do they have a dress code?	**¿Tienen un código de vestimenta?**
	TYEH-nehn oon KOH-dee-goh deh vehs-tee-MEHN-tah

NIGHTLIFE

Cover Your Culo

Be careful with the verb culear. *Culear* is "to shake one's bottom" or "dance," but in Colombia it means "to have sex." Because *el culo* is a vulgar term for derriere, *culear* may mean "to have anal sex" in many Latin American countries.

Is it expensive?	**¿Es caro?** *ehs KAH-roh*
What's the best time to go?	**¿A qué hora es lo mejor para ir?** *ah keh OH-rah ehs loh meh-HOHR* *PAH-rah eer*
What kind of music do they play there?	**¿Qué tipo de música tocan ahí?** *keh TEE-poh deh MOO-see-kah* *TOH-kahn ah-EE*
Is it smoking?	**¿Permiten fumar?** *pehr-MEE-tehn foo-MAHR*
Is it nonsmoking?	**¿Se prohíbe fumar?** *seh proh-EE-beh foo-MAHR*
I'm looking for _____	**Estoy buscando _____** *ehs-TOY boos-KAHN-doh*
a good cigar shop.	**una buena tienda de cigarros.** *OO-nah BWEH-nah TYEHN-dah* *deh see-GAH-rrohs*
a pack of cigarettes.	**un paquete de cigarrillos.** *oon pah-KEH-teh deh see-gah-* *REE-yohs*

Do You Mind If I Smoke?

¿Tiene un cigarrillo? *TYEH-neh oon see-gah-* *RREE-yoh*	Do you have a cigarette?
¿Tiene lumbre? *TYEH-neh LOOM-breh*	Do you have a light?
¿Le puedo ofrecer lumbre / encender su cigarrillo? *leh PWEH-doh oh-freh-SEHR* *LOOM-breh / ehn-sehn-DEHR* *so see-gah-RREE-yoh*	May I offer you a light?
Prohibido fumar. *proh-ee-BEE-doh foo-MAHR*	Smoking not permitted.

I'd like ____	**Quisiera ____**
	kee-SYEH-rah
a drink please.	**una bebida por favor.**
	OO-nah beh-BEE-dah pohr fah-VOHR
a bottle of beer please.	**una botella de cerveza.**
	OO-nah boh-TEH-yah deh sehr-VEH-sah
A beer on tap please.	**una cerveza de barril por favor.**
	OO-nah sehr-VEH-sah deh bah-RREEL pohr fah-VOHR
a shot of ____ please.	**un trago de ____ por favor.**
	oon TRAH-goh deh ____ pohr fah-VOHR

For a full list of drinks, see p88.

Make it a double please!	**¡Hazlo doble por favor!**
	AHS-loh DOH-bleh pohr fah-VOHR
With ice, please.	**Con hielo, por favor.**
	kohn YEH-loh pohr fah-VOHR
And one for the lady / the gentleman!	**¡Y uno para la dama / el caballero!**
	ee OO-noh PAH-rah lah DAH-mah / ehl kah-bah-YEH-roh
How much for a bottle / glass of beer?	**¿Cuánto por una botella / un copa de cerveza?**
	KWAHN-toh pohr OO-nah boh-TEH-yah / oon KOH-pah deh sehr-VEH-sah
I'd like to buy a drink for that girl / guy over there.	**Quisiera comprarle una bebida a aquella chica / aquel chico allá.**
	kee-SYEH-rah kohm-PRAHR-leh OO-nah beh-BEE-dah ah ah-KEH-yah CHEE-kah / ah-KEHL CHEE-koh ah-YAH
A pack of cigarettes, please.	**Un paquete de cigarrillos, por favor.**
	oon pah-KEH-teh deh see-gah-RREE-yohs pohr fah-VOHR

Do you have a lighter or matches?	**¿Tiene un encendedor o fósforos?** *TYEH-neh oon ehn-sehn-dah-DOHR oh FOHS-foh-rohs*
Do you smoke?	**¿Usted fuma?** *oos-TEHD FOO-mah*
Would you like a cigarette?	**¿Le gustaría un cigarrillo?** *leh goos-tah-REE-yah oon see-gah-RREE-yoh*
May I run a tab?	**¿Puedo crear una cuenta?** *PWEH-doh kreh-AHR OO-nah KWEHN-tah*
What's the cover?	**¿Cuánto es el cargo de entrada?** *KWAHN-toh ehs ehl KAHR-goh deh ehn-TRAH-dah*

ACROSS A CROWDED ROOM

Excuse me; may I buy you a drink?	**¿Con permiso, ¿puedo comprarle una bebida?** *kohn pehr-MEE-soh PWEH-doh kohm-PRAHR-leh OO-nah beh-BEE-dah*
You look amazing.	**Se ve maravilloso -a.** *seh veh mah-rah-vee-YOH-soh -sah*

You look like the most interesting person in the room.	**Usted se ve como la persona más interesante aquí.**
	oos-TEHD seh veh koh-moh lah pehr-SOH-nah mahs een-teh-reh-SAHN-teh ah-KEE
Would you like to dance?	**¿Le gustaría bailar?**
	leh goos-tah-REE-ah bah-ee-LAHR
Do you like to dance fast or slow?	**¿Le gusta bailar rápido o lento?**
	leh GOOS-tah bah-ee-LAHR RRAH-pee-doh oh LEHN-toh
Give me your hand.	**Déme su mano.**
	DEH-meh soo MAH-noh
What would you like to drink?	**¿Qué le gustaría tomar?**
	keh leh goos-tah-REE-ah toh-MAHR
You're a great dancer.	**Usted es un gran bailador / una gran bailadora.**
	oos-TEHD ehs oon grahn bah-ee-lah-DOHR / OO-nah grahn bah-ee-lah-DOH-rah
I don't know that dance!	**¡Yo no se ese baile!**
	yoh noh seh EH-seh BAYE-leh
Do you like this song?	**¿Le gusta esta canción?**
	leh GOOS-tah EHS-tah kahn-SYOHN
You have nice eyes!	**¡Usted tiene / Tú tienes ojos lindos!**
	oo-STEHD TYEH-neh / too TYEH-nehs OH-hohs LEEN-dohs

For a full list of features, see p118.

| May I have your phone number? | **¿Me puede dar su número de teléfono?** |
| | *meh PWEH-deh dahr soo NOO-meh-roh deh teh-LEH-foh-noh* |

GETTING CLOSER

You're very attractive.

Tú eres muy atractivo -a.
too EH-rehs MOO-ee ah-trahk-TEE-voh -vah

I like being with you.

Me gusta estar contigo.
meh GOOS-tah ehs-TAHR kohn-TEE-goh

I like you.

Me gustas.
meh GOOS-tahs

I want to hold you.

Quiero abrazarte.
KYEH-roh ah-brah-SAHR-teh

Kiss me.

Bésame.
BEH-sah-meh

May I give you ____

¿Te puedo dar ____
teh PWEH-doh dahr

  a hug?

  un abrazo?
  oon ah-BRAH-soh

  a kiss?

  un beso?
  oon BEH-soh

Would you like ____

¿Te gustaría ____
teh goos-tah-REE-ah

  a back rub?

  un masaje en la espalda?
  oon mah-SAH-heh ehn lah ehs-PAHL-dah

  a massage?

  un masaje?
  oon mah-SAH-heh

GETTING INTIMATE

Would you like to come inside?	**¿Te gustaría entrar?** *teh goos-tah-REE-ah ehn-TRAHR*
May I come inside?	**¿Puedo entrar?** *PWEH-doh ehn-TRAHR*
Let me help you out of that.	**Déjame ayudarte a quitarte eso.** *DEH-hah-meh ah-yoo-DAHR-teh ah kee-TAHR-teh EH-soh*
Would you help me out of this?	**¿Me puedes ayudar a quitarme esto?** *meh PWEH-dehs ah-yoo-DAHR ah kee-TAHR-meh EHS-toh*
You smell so good.	**Hueles tan bueno.** *WEH-lehs tahn BWEH-noh*
You're beautiful / handsome.	**Eres bella / guapo.** *EH-rehs BEH-yah / GWAH-poh*
May I?	**¿Puedo?** *PWEH-doh*
OK?	**¿Está bien?** *ehs-TAH byehn*
Like this?	**¿Así?** *ah-SEE*
How?	**¿Cómo?** *KOH-moh*

HOLD ON A SECOND

Please don't do that.	**Por favor no hagas eso.** *pohr fah-VOHR noh AH-gahs EH-soh*
Stop, please.	**Para por favor.** *PAH-rah pohr fah-VOHR*
Do you want me to stop?	**¿Quieres que pare?** *KYEH-rehs keh PAH-reh*
Let's just be friends.	**Seamos sólo amigos.** *seh-AH-mohs SOH-loh ah-MEE-gohs*

Don't Mix the Message

Te deseo. *teh deh-SEH-oh*	I desire you. This is pretty much a physical expression.
Te quiero. *teh KYEH-roh*	While this literally means "I want you," in Spanish, it implies "I love you" in the romantic and erotic sense.
Te amo. *teh AH-moh*	This is used very seriously. If you're not the person's parent or grandparent, you'd better not be saying this without a ring in your pocket.

Do you have a condom?	**¿Tienes un condón?** *TYEH-nehs oon kohn-DOHN*
Are you on birth control?	**¿Estás usando anticonceptivos?** *ehs-TAHS oo-SAHN-doh ahn-tee-kohn-sehp-TEE-vohs*
I have a condom.	**Tengo un condón.** *TEHNG-goh oon kohn-DOHN*
Do you have anything you should tell me first?	**¿Tienes que decirme algo primero?** *TYEH-nehs keh deh-SEER-meh AHL-goh pree-MEH-roh*

BACK TO IT

That's it.	**Eso es.** *EH-soh ehs*
That's not it.	**Eso no es.** *EH-soh noh ehs*
Here.	**Ahí.** *ah-EE*
There.	**Allá.** *ah-YAH*

For a full list of features, see p118.
For a full list of body parts, see p190.

More.	**Más.** *mahs*
Harder	**Más duro.** *mahs DOO-roh*
Faster	**Más rápido.** *mahs RRAH-pee-doh*
Deeper	**Más profundo.** *mahs proh-FOON-doh*
Slower.	**Más lento.** *mahs LEHN-toh*
Easier.	**Más suave.** *mahs SWAH-veh*

COOLDOWN

You're great.	**Eres tremendo -a.** *EH-rehs treh-MEHN-doh -dah*
That was great.	**Eso estuvo fabuloso.** *EH-soh ehs-TOO-voh fah-boo-LOH-soh*
Would you like ____	**¿Te gustaría ____** *teh goos-tah-REE-ah*
a drink?	**un trago?** *oon TRAH-goh*
a snack?	**un bocadillo?** *oon boh-kah-DEE-yoh*
a shower?	**una ducha?** *OO-nah DOO-cha*
May I stay here?	**¿Puedo quedarme aquí?** *PWEH-doh keh-DAHR-meh ah-KEE*
Would you like to stay here?	**¿Te gustaría quedarte aquí?** *teh goos-tah-REE-ah keh-DAHR-teh ah-KEE*
I'm sorry. I have to go now.	**Lo siento. Me tengo que ir ahora.** *loh SYEHN-toh meh TEHN-goh keh eer ah-OH-rah*
Where are you going?	**¿Adónde vas?** *ah-DOHN-deh vahs*

I have to work early.	**Tengo que trabajar temprano.**
	TEHN-goh keh trah-bah-HAHR
	tehm-PRAH-noh
I'm flying home in the morning.	**Regreso a casa en la mañana.**
	rreh-GREH-soh ah KAH-sah ehn lah
	mah-NYAH-nah
I have an early flight.	**Tengo un vuelo temprano.**
	TEHNG-goh oon VWEH-loh tehm-
	PRAH-noh
I think this was a mistake.	**Creo que esto fue un error.**
	KREH-oh keh EHS-toh fweh oon
	eh-RROHR
Will you make me breakfast too?	**¿Puedes hacerme desayuno también?**
	PWEH-dehs ah-SEHR-meh deh-sah-
	YOH-noh tahm-BYEHN
Stay. I'll make you breakfast.	**Quédate. Te haré desayuno.**
	KEH-dah-teh teh ah-REH deh-sah-
	YOO-noh

IN THE CASINO

How much is this table?	**¿Cuánto cuesta esta mesa?**
	KWAHN-toh KWEHS-tah EHS-tah
	MEH-sah
Deal me in.	**Repártame las cartas.**
	reh-PAHR-tah-meh lahs KAHR-tahs
Put it on red!	**¡Ponlo en rojo!**
	POHN-loh ehn ROH-hoh
Put it on black!	**¡Ponlo en negro!**
	POHN-loh ehn NEH-groh
Let it ride!	**¡Déjalo ir!**
	DEH-hah-loh eer
21!	**¡21!**
	veh-een-TYOO-noh
Snake-eyes!	**¡Ojos de serpiente!**
	OH-hohs deh sehr-PYEHN-teh

Seven.	**Siete.** *SYEH-teh*

For a full list of numbers, see p7.

Damn, eleven.	**Maldición, once.** *mahl-dees-YOHN OHN-seh*
I'll pass.	**Paso.** *PAH-soh*
Hit me!	**¡Dame!** *DAH-meh*
Split.	**Rompa.** *RROHM-pah*

Are the drinks complimentary?	**¿Las bebidas son complementarias?** *lahs beh-BEE-dahs sohn kohm-pleh-mehn-TAH-ryahs*
May I bill it to my room?	**¿Puedo facturarlo a mi habitación?** *PWEH-doh fahk-too-RAHR-loh ah mee ah-bee-tah-SYOHN*
I'd like to cash out.	**Quisiera llevarme el dinero.** *kee-SYEH-rah yeh-VAHR-meh ehl dee-NEH-roh*
I'll hold.	**Me quedo.** *meh KEH-doh*
I'll see your bet.	**Veo tu apuesta.** *VEH-oh too ah-PWEHS-tah*
I call.	**Igualo tu apuesta.** *ee-GWAH-loh too ah-PWEHS-tah*
Full house!	**¡Full house!** *fool OWS*
Royal flush.	**Escalera real.** *ehs-kah-LEH-rah reh-AHL*
Straight.	**Escalera.** *ehs-kah-LEH-rah*

CHAPTER ELEVEN

HEALTH & SAFETY

This chapter covers the terms you'll need to maintain your health and safety—including the most useful phrases for the pharmacy, the doctor's office, and the police station.

AT THE PHARMACY

Please fill this prescription.	**Por favor, despache esta receta.**
	pohr fah-VOHR dehs-PAH-cheh EHS-tah rreh-SEH-tah
Do you have something for ____	**¿Tiene algo para ____**
	TYEH-neh AHL-goh PAH-rah
a cold?	**un resfriado?**
	oon rrehs-FRYAH-doh
a cough?	**la tos?**
	lah TOHS
I need something ____	**Necesito algo para ____**
	neh-seh-SEE-toh AHL-goh PAH-rah
to help me sleep.	**ayudarme a dormir.**
	ah-yoo-DAHR-meh ah dohr-MEER
to help me relax.	**ayudarme a relajarme.**
	ah-yoo-DAHR-meh ah rreh-lah-HAHR-meh
I want to buy ____	**Quiero comprar ____**
	KYEH-roh kohm-PRAHR
condoms.	**condones.**
	kohn-DOH-nehs
an antihistamine.	**un antihistamínico.**
	oon ahn-tee-ees-tah-MEE-nee-koh
antibiotic cream.	**una crema antibiótica.**
	OO-nah KREH-mah ahn-tee-BYOH-tee-koh

aspirin.	**aspirina.** *ahs-pee-REE-nah*
non-aspirin pain reliever.	**un analgésico sin aspirina.** *oon ah-nahl-HEH-see-koh seen* *ahs-pee-REE-nah*
medicine with codeine.	**medicina con codeína.** *meh-dee-SEE-nah kohn koh-deh-* *EE-nah*
insect repellant.	**repelente contra insectos.** *rreh-peh-LEHN-teh KOHN-trah* *een-SEHK-tohs*
I need something for _____	**Necesito algo para _____.** *neh-seh-SEE-toh AHL-goh PAH-rah*
corns.	**los callos.** *lohs KAH-yohs*
congestion.	**la congestión.** *lah kohn-hehs-TYOHN*
warts.	**las verrugas.** *lahs veh-RROO-gahs*
constipation.	**el estreñimiento.** *ehl ehs-treh-nyee-MYEHN-toh*
diarrhea.	**la diarrea.** *lah dyah-RREH-ah*
indigestion.	**la indigestión.** *lah een-dee-hehs-TYOHN*
nausea.	**la náusea.** *lah NOW-seh-ah*
motion sickness.	**el enfermedad de movimiento.** *ehl ehn-fehr-mee-DAHD deh moh-* *vee-MYEHN-toh*
seasickness.	**el mareos.** *ehl mah-REH-ohs*
acne.	**el acné.** *ehl ahk-NEH*

HEALTH & SAFETY

AT THE DOCTOR'S OFFICE

I would like to see ____	**Quisiera ver a ____.**
	kee-SYEH-rah vehr ah
a doctor.	**un doctor.**
	oon dohk-TOHR
a chiropractor.	**un quiropráctico.**
	oon kee-roh-PRAHK-tee-koh
a gynecologist.	**un ginecólogo.**
	oon hee-neh-KOH-loh-goh
an eye / ears / nose / throat specialist.	**un especialista en ojos / oídos / nariz / garganta.**
	oon ehs-peh-syah-LEES-tah ehn OH-hohs / oh-EE-dohs / nah-REES / gahr-GAHN-tah
a dentist.	**un dentista.**
	oon dehn-TEES-tah
an optometrist.	**un optómetra.**
	oon ohp-TOH-meh-trah
Do I need an appointment?	**¿Necesito una cita?**
	neh-seh-SEE-toh OO-nah SEE-tah
I have an emergency.	**Tengo una emergencia.**
	TEHNG-goh OO-nah eh-mehr-HEHN-syah
I need an emergency prescription refill.	**Necesito un reabastecimiento de emergencia de mi receta.**
	neh-seh-SEE-toh oon rreh-ah-bahs-teh-see-MYEHN-toh deh eh-mehr-HEHN-syah deh mee rreh-SEH-tah
Please call a doctor.	**Por favor llame a un doctor.**
	pohr fah-VOHR YAH-meh ah oon dohk-TOHR
I need an ambulance.	**Necesito una ambulancia.**
	neh-seh-SEE-toh OO-nah ahm-boo-LAHN-syah

SYMPTOMS

For a full list of body parts, see p190.

My ____ hurts.	**Me duele mi ____.**
	meh DWEH-leh mee
My ____ is stiff.	**Mi ____ está tenso.**
	mee ____ ehs-TAH TEHN-soh
I think I'm having a heart attack.	**Creo que estoy teniendo un ataque cardiaco.**
	KREH-oh keh ehs-TOY teh-NYEHN-doh oon ah-TAH-keh kahr-DYAH-koh
I can't move.	**No me puedo mover.**
	noh meh PWEH-doh moh-VEHR
I fell.	**Me caí.**
	meh kah-EE
I fainted.	**Me desmayé.**
	meh dehs-mah-YEH
I have a cut on my ____.	**Tengo un corte en mi ____.**
	TEHNG-goh oon KOHR-teh ehn mee
I have a headache.	**Tengo dolor de cabeza.**
	TEHNG-goh doh-LOHR deh kah-BEH-sah
My vision is blurry	**Mi visión está borrosa.**
	mee vee-SYOHN ehs-TAH boh-RROH-sah
I feel dizzy.	**Me siento mareado.**
	meh-SYEHN-toh mah-reh-AH-doh
I think I'm pregnant.	**Creo que estoy embarazada.**
	KREH-oh keh ehs-TOY ehm-bah-rah-SAH-dah
I don't think I'm pregnant.	**No creo estar embarazada.**
	noh KREH-oh ehs-TAHR ehm-bah-rah-SAH-dah
I'm having trouble walking.	**Tengo dificultad al caminar.**
	TEHNG-goh dee-fee-kool-TAHD ahl kah-mee-NAHR

HEALTH & SAFETY

el cuello
los senos
el ombligo
las caderas
las muñecas
el trasero
la vagina
los muslos
las piernas

los tobillos

los hombros
las manos
los dedos
los brazos
el pecho
el torso
el estómago
la cintura
el pene
las pantorrillas

los pies
los dedos del pie

I can't get up.	**No me puedo levantar.** *noh meh PWEH-doh leh-vahn-TAHR*
I was mugged.	**Me asaltaron.** *meh ah-sahl-TAH-rohn*
I was raped.	**Me violaron.** *meh vee-oh-LAH-rohn*
A dog attacked me.	**Me atacó un perro.** *meh ah-tah-KOH oon PEH-rroh*
A snake bit me.	**Me mordió una serpiente.** *meh mohr-dee-OH OO-nah sehr-PYEHN-teh*
I can't move my _____ without pain.	**No puedo mover mi _____ sin sentir dolor.** *noh PWEH-doh moh-VEHR mee _____ seen sehn-TEER doh-LOHR*
I think I sprained my ankle.	**Creo que me torcí el tobillo.** *KREH-oh keh meh tohr-SEE ehl toh-BEE-yoh*

MEDICATIONS

I need morning-after pills.	**Necesito píldoras para la mañana siguiente.** *neh-seh-SEE-toh PEEL-doh-rahs PAH-rah lah mah-NYAH-nah see-GYEHN-teh*
I need birth control pills.	**Necesito píldoras anticonceptivas.** *neh-seh-SEE-toh PEEL-doh-rahs ahn-tee-kohn-sehp-TEE-vahs*
I lost my eyeglasses and need new ones.	**Perdí mis gafas y necesito unos nuevos.** *pehr-DEE mees GAH-fahs ee neh-seh-SEE-toh OO-nohs NWEH-vohs*
I need new contact lenses.	**Necesito lentes de contacto nuevos.** *neh-seh-SEE-toh LEHN-tehs deh kohn-TAHK-toh NWEH-vohs*
I need erectile dysfunction pills.	**Necesito píldoras para la disfunción eréctil.** *neh-seh-SEE-toh PEEL-doh-rahs PAH-rah lah dees-foon-SYOHN eh-REHK-teel*
It's cold in here!	**¡Hace frío aquí!** *AH-seh FREE-oh ah-KEE*
I am allergic to ____	**Soy alérgico a ____** *soy ah-LEHR-hee-koh ah*
penicillin.	**la penicilina.** *lah peh-nee-see-LEE-nah*
antibiotics.	**los antibióticos.** *lohs ahn-tee-BYOH-tee-kohs*
sulfa drugs.	**los sulfonamides.** *lohs sool-foh-nah-MEE-dehs*
steroids.	**los esteroides.** *lohs ehs-teh-ROH-EE-dehs*
I have asthma.	**Tengo asma.** *TEHNG-goh AHS-mah*

HEALTH & SAFETY

DENTAL PROBLEMS

I have a toothache.	**Tengo dolor de dientes.** *TEHNG-goh doh-LOHR deh* *DYEHN-tehs*
I chipped a tooth.	**Se me partió un diente.** *seh meh pahr-tee-OH oon* *DYEHN-teh*
My bridge came loose.	**Mi puente se soltó.** *mee PWEHN-teh seh sohl-TOH*
I lost a crown.	**Perdí una corona.** *pehr-DEE OO-nah koh-ROH-nah*
I lost a denture plate.	**Perdí mi dentadura postiza.** *pehr-DEE mee dehn-tah-DOO-rah* *pohs-TEE-sah*

AT THE POLICE STATION

I'm sorry, did I do something wrong?	**Lo siento, ¿hice algo mal?** *loh SYEHN-toh EE-seh AHL-goh* *mahl*
I am ____	**Soy ____** *soy*
an American.	**americano.** *ah-meh-ree-KAH-noh*
British.	**británico.** *bree-TAH-nee-koh*
a Canadian.	**canadiense.** *kah-nah-DYEHN-seh*
Irish.	**irlandés.** *eer-lahn-DEHS*
an Australian.	**australiano.** *ows-trah-LYAH-noh*
a New Zealander.	**de Nueva Zelanda.** *deh NWEH-vah seh-LAHN-dah*
The car is a rental.	**El auto es alquilado.** *ehl OW-toh ehs ahl-kee-LAH-doh*

Listen Up: Police Lingo

Su licencia, registro y seguro por favor.	Your license, registration and insurance, please.
soo lee-SEHN-syah rreh-HEES-troh ee seh-GOO-roh pohr fah-VOHR	
La multa es diez dólares y me la puede pagar directo.	The fine is $10. You can pay me directly.
lah MOOL-tah ehs dyehs DOH-lah-rehs ee meh lah PWEH-deh pah-GAHR dee-REHK-toh	
Su pasaporte, por favor.	Your passport please?
soo pah-sah-POHR-teh pohr fah-VOHR	
¿A dónde va?	Where are you going?
ah DOHN-deh vah	
¿Por qué tiene tanta prisa?	Why are you in such a hurry?
pohr keh TYEH-neh TAHN-tah PREE-sah	

Do I pay the fine to you?	**¿Le pago la multa a usted?**
	leh PAH-goh lah MOOL-tah ah oos-TEHD
Do I have to go to court?	**¿Tengo que ir a corte?**
	TEHNG-goh keh eer ah KOHR-teh
When?	**¿Cuándo?**
	KWAHN-doh
I'm sorry, my Spanish isn't very good.	**Lo siento, mi español no es muy bueno.**
	loh SYEHN-toh mee ehs-pah-NYOHL noh ehs MOO-ee BWEH-noh

I need an interpreter.	**Necesito un intérprete.**
	neh-seh-SEE-toh oon een-TEHR-preh-teh
I'm sorry, I don't understand the ticket.	**Lo siento, no entiendo la multa.**
	loh SYEHN-toh noh ehn-TYEHN-doh lah MOOL-tah
May I call my embassy?	**¿Puedo llamar a mi embajada?**
	PWEH-doh yah-MAHR ah mee ehm-bah-HA-dah
I was robbed.	**Me robaron.**
	meh rroh-BAH-rohn
I was mugged.	**Me asaltaron.**
	meh ah-sahl-TAH-rohn
I was raped	**Me violaron.**
	meh vee-oh-LAH-rohn
Do I need to make a report?	**¿Tengo que hacer un informe?**
	TEHNG-goh keh ah-SEHR oon een-FOHR-meh
Somebody broke into my room.	**Alguien entró en mi habitación.**
	AHLG-yehn ehn-TROH ehn mee ah-bee-tahs-YOHN
Someone stole my purse / wallet.	**Alguien robó mi bolso / cartera.**
	AHLG-yehn rroh-BOH mee BOHL-soh / kahr-TEH-rah

ENGLISH—SPANISH

DICTIONARY KEY

n	noun	m	masculine
v	verb	f	feminine
adj	adjective	s	singular
prep	preposition	pl	plural
adv	adverb		

All verbs are listed in infinitive (to + verb) form, cross-referenced to the appropriate conjugations page. Adjectives are listed first in masculine singular form, followed by the feminine ending.

For food terms, see the Menu Reader (p91) and Grocery section (p100) in Chapter 4, Dining.

A

able, to be able to (can) v poder **p31**

above adj sobre **p78**

accept, to accept v aceptar **p22**
  Do you accept credit cards? ¿Acepta tarjetas de crédito? **p38**

accident n el accidente m **p57**
  I've had an accident. He tenido un accidente.

account n la cuenta f **p134**
  I'd like to transfer to / from my checking / savings account. Quisiera transferir a / de mi cuenta de cheques / ahorros.

acne n el acné m **p187**

across prep a través de, al otro lado de **p6**
  across the street al otro lado de la calle

actual adj actual **p16**

adapter plug n el enchufe adaptador m

address n la dirección f **p124**
  What's the address? ¿Cuál es la dirección?

admission fee n el precio de entrada m **p148**

in advance por adelantado

African-American adj afroamericano -a **p119**

afternoon n la tarde f **p13**
  in the afternoon en la tarde

age n la edad f **p116**
  What's your age? ¿Cuántos años tiene?

agency n la agencia f **p50**
  car rental agency la agencia de alquiler de autos

agnostic adj agnóstico -a

air conditioning n el aire acondicionado m **p68**
  Would you lower / raise the air conditioning? ¿Puede bajar / subir el aire acondicionado?

airport n el aeropuerto m

I need a ride to the airport.
Necesito llegar al aeropuerto.

How far is it from the airport? *¿Cuán lejos está del aeropuerto?*

airsickness bag n *la bolsa para mareos* f p48

aisle (in store) n *el pasillo* m

Which aisle is it in? *¿En qué pasillo está?*

alarm clock n *el reloj despertador* m p75

alcohol n *el alcohol* m p88

Do you serve alcohol? *¿Sirven alcohol?*

I'd like nonalcoholic beer. *Quisiera una cerveza sin alcohol.*

all n *el todo* m p11

all adj *todo -a* p11

all of the time *todo el tiempo*

That's all, thank you. *Eso es todo, gracias.*

allergic adj *alérgico -a* p76

I'm allergic to ___. *Soy alérgico -a a ___.* See p87 and 191 for common allergens.

altitude n *la altitud* f p167

aluminum n *el aluminio* m

ambulance n *la ambulancia* f

American adj *americano -a*

amount n *la cantidad* f p63

angry adj *enojado -a*

animal n *el animal* m

another adj *otro -a* p48, 72

answer n *la contestación* f

answer, to answer (phone call, question) v *contestar* p22

Answer me, please. *Contéstame por favor.*

antibiotic n *el antibiótico* m

I need an antibiotic. *Necesito un antibiótico.*

antihistamine n *el antihistamínico* m p186

anxious adj *ansioso -a* p121

any adj *cualquier, cualquiera*

anything n *cualquier cosa*

anywhere adv *dondequiera, cualquier lugar*

April n *abril* p15

appointment n *la cita* f p148

Do I need an appointment? *¿Necesito una cita?*

are v See *be, to be.* p27, 28

Argentinian adj *argentino -a*

arm n *el brazo* m p16

arrive, to arrive v *llegar* p22

arrival(s) n *las llegadas* f

art n *el arte* m

exhibit of art *exhibición de arte* See p148 for art types.

art adj *de arte*

art museum *museo de arte*

artist n *el artista* m, *la artista* f

Asian adj *asiático -a* p80

ask for (request) v *pedir* p32

ask a question v *preguntar* p22

aspirin n *la aspirina* f p187

assist v *asistir* p23

assistance n la asistencia f

asthma n el asma f p191

> **I have asthma.** Tengo asma.

atheist adj ateo -a p127

ATM n el cajero automático m

> **I'm looking for an ATM.** Estoy buscando un cajero automático.

attend v asistir p23

audio adj audio, auditivo p65

August n agosto p15

aunt n la tía f p115

Australia n Australia

Australian adj australiano -a

autumn n el otoño m p15

available adj disponible p147

B

baby n el / la bebé m / f p117

baby adj de bebés, para bebés p100

> **Do you sell baby food?** ¿Venden comida para bebés?

babysitter n la niñera f

> **Do you have babysitters who speak English?** ¿Tiene niñeras que hablen inglés?

back n la espalda f p190

> **My back hurts.** Me duele la espalda.

back rub n el masaje de espalda m p180

backed up (toilet) adj tapado -a

> **The toilet is backed up.** El inodoro está tapado.

bag n la bolsa f, el bolso m

airsickness bag bolsa para mareos p48

> **My bag was stolen.** Mi bolsa fue robada.
>
> **I lost my bag.** Perdí mi bolsa.

bag v empacar p22

baggage n el equipaje m p39

baggage adj de equipaje p39

baggage claim reclamo de equipaje

bait n la carnada f, el cebo m

balance (on bank account) n el balance m p134

balance v balancear p22

balcony n el balcón m p66

ball (sport) n la bola f

ballroom dancing n el baile de salón m p145

band (musical ensemble) n la banda f p174

band-aid n vendaje m, venda f

bank n el banco m p133

> **Can you help me find a bank?** ¿Puede ayudarme a encontrar un banco?

bar n la cantina f, la taberna f

barber n el barbero m p158

bass (instrument) n el contrabajo m

bath n el baño m

bathroom (restroom) n el baño m p68

> **Where is the nearest public bathroom?** ¿Dónde está el baño público más cercano?

bathtub n la bañera f, la tina de baño f p68

bathe, to bathe oneself v bañarse p22, 35

battery (for flashlight) n la pila f

battery (for car) n la batería f, el acumulador m, la acumuladora f

bee n la abeja f

I was stung by a bee. Me picó una abeja.

be, to be (temporary state, condition, mood) v estar p27

be, to be (permanent quality) v ser p28

beach n la playa p130

beach v varar, encallar p22

beard n barba f

beautiful adj bello -a p117

bed n la cama f p67

beer n la cerveza f p88

beer on tap cerveza de barril

begin v comenzar, empezar p22

behave v comportar p22

behind adv detrás p5

below adv debajo p78

belt n el cinturón m p46

conveyor belt correa transportadora

berth n el camarote m

best mejor

bet, to bet v apostar p22

better mejor

big adj grande p12

bilingual adj bilingüe

bill (currency) n el billete m

bill v facturar p22

biography n la biografía f

biracial adj biracial p119

bird n el pájaro m

birth control n los anticonceptivos m p182, 191

birth control adj anticonceptivo -a p182, 191

I'm out of birth control pills. Se me acabaron las pastillas anticonceptivas.

I need more birth control pills. Necesito más pastillas anticonceptivas.

bit (small amount) n un poco m

black adj negro -a p118

blanket n la cobija f, la frazada f p47

bleach n el blanqueador m

blind adj ciego -a

block v bloquear p22

blond(e) adj rubio -a p117

blouse n la blusa f p152

blue adj azul p119

blurry adj borroso -a p189

board n bordo

on board a bordo

board v abordar p22

boarding pass n la boleta de abordaje f p45

boat n el barco m

Bolivian adj boliviano -a

bomb n la bomba f p16

book n el libro m p166

bookstore n la librería f p166

boss n el jefe m, la jefa f

bottle n la botella f p177
  May I heat this (baby) bottle someplace? ¿Puedo calentar esta botella en algún lugar?
box (seat) n el palco m p165
box office n la boletería f
boy n el niño m
boyfriend n el novio m p115
braid n la trenza f p160
braille, American n el braille americano m
brake n el freno m p55
  emergency brake el freno de emergencia
brake v frenar p22
brandy n el brandy m p89
bread n el pan m p100
break v romper p22
breakfast n el desayuno m
  What time is breakfast? ¿A qué hora es el desayuno?
bridge (across a river, dental) n el puente m p192
briefcase n el maletín m p49
bright adj brillante
broadband n la banda ancha f
bronze adj bronce
brother n el hermano m p115
brown adj café, castaño -a, moreno -a, pardo -a p119
brunette n el moreno m, la morena f p117
Buddhist n el budista m, la budista f p127
budget n el presupuesto m
buffet n el bufé m

bug n el insecto m, el bicho m
bull n el toro m
bullfight n la corrida de toros f
bullfighter n el torero m, el matador m
burn v quemar p22
  Can I burn a CD here? ¿Puedo quemar un CD aquí? p139
bus n el autobús m p57
  Where is the bus stop? ¿Dónde es la parada de autobuses?
  Which bus goes to ____? ¿Cuál autobús va hacia ____? p60
business n el negocio m p44
business adj de negocios p73
  business center centro de negocios
busy adj concurrido -a (restaurant), ocupado -a (phone)
butter n la mantequilla f p86
buy, to buy v comprar p22

C

café n el café m p37
  Internet café cibercafé
call, to call v llamar (shout) telefonear (phone) p22
camp, to camp v acampar p22
camper n el campista m
camping adj para acampar
  Do we need a camping permit? ¿Necesitamos un permiso para acampar?

campsite *n* el campamento *m*

can *n* la lata *f*

can (able to) *v* poder **p31**

Canada *n* Canadá

Canadian *adj* canadiense

cancel, to cancel *v* cancelar **p22**

> **My flight was canceled.** *Mi vuelo fue cancelado.*

canvas *n* el lienzo *m* (for painting), la lona *f* **p49** (material)

cappuccino *n* el cappuccino *m*

car *n* el auto *m*

> **car rental agency** *agencia de alquiler de autos*
>
> **I need a rental car.** *Necesito un auto alquilado.*

card *n* la tarjeta *f* **p122**

> **Do you accept credit cards?** *¿Aceptan tarjetas de crédito?*
>
> **May I have your business card?** *¿Me puede dar su tarjeta de presentación?*

car seat (child's safety seat) *n* el asiento para niños *m*

> **Do you rent car seats for children?** *¿Ustedes alquilan asientos para niños para el auto?*

carsickness *n* el mareo de auto *m*

cash *n* el efectivo *m* **p133**

> **cash only** *efectivo solamente* **p134**

cash, to cash *v* hacer efectivo **p30**

> **to cash out (gambling)** *hacer efectivo* **p185**

cashmere *n* el cachemir *m*

casino *n* el casino *m* **p66**

cat *n* el gato *m*, la gata *f*

Catholic *adj* católico -a **p127**

cavity (tooth cavity) *n* la carie *f*

> **I think I have a cavity.** *Creo que tengo una carie.*

CD *n* el CD *m*, el disco compacto *m* **p139**

CD player *n* el lector de discos compactos *m* **p51**

celebrate, to celebrate *v* celebrar **p22**

cell phone *n* el teléfono celular *m* **p134**

centimeter *n* el centímetro *m*

chamber music *n* la música de cámara *f*

change (money) *n* el cambio *m*

> **I'd like change, please.** *Quisiera obtener cambio, por favor.*
>
> **This isn't the correct change.** *Esto no es el cambio correcto.*

change (to change money, clothes) *v* cambiar **p22**

changing room *n* el cuarto de cambio *m*

charge, to charge (money) *v* cobrar **p22**

charge, to charge (a battery) *v* recargar **p22**

charmed *adj* encantado -a

charred (meat) adj achicharrado -a p84

charter, to charter v fletar
p22

cheap adj barato -a p52

check n el cheque m p90

**Do you accept travelers'
checks?** ¿Aceptan cheques
de viajero?

check, to check v comprobar,
verificar p22

checked (pattern) adj a
cuadros

check-in n registro p36

What time is check-in? ¿A
qué hora es el registro?

check-out n la salida f

check-out time la hora de
salida

What time is check-out? ¿A
que hora es la salida?

check out, to check out v despedirse p32, 35

cheese n el queso m p100

chicken n el pollo m p96

child n el niño m, la niña f

children n los niños m p45

Are children allowed? ¿Se
permiten niños?

**Do you have children's pro-
grams?** ¿Tienen programas
para niños?

**Do you have a children's
menu?** ¿Tienen un menú
para niños?

Chinese adj chino -a p120

chiropractor n el quiropráctico m p188

church n la iglesia f p127

cigar n el cigarro m p151

cigarette n el cigarrillo m

a pack of cigarettes un
paquete de cigarrillos

cinema n el cine m, el cinema m

city n la ciudad f p68

claim n el reclamo m

I'd like to file a claim.
Quisiera presentar un
reclamo.

clarinet n el clarinete m

class n la clase f p41

business class clase de
negocios

economy class clase
económica

first class primera clase

classical (music) adj clásico -a

clean adj limpiado -a

clean, to clean v limpiar p22

**Please clean the room
today.** Por favor limpia la
habitación hoy.

clear v aclarar p22

clear adj claro -a p170

climbing n la escalada f p166

climb, to climb v escalar,
subir p22, 23

to climb a mountain escalar
una montaña

to climb stairs subir las
escaleras

close, to close v cerrar p22

close (near) cerca, cercano p5

closed adj cerrado -a p56

cloudy adj nublado -a p125

clover n el trébol m

go clubbing, to go clubbing v ir a los clubes nocturnos p25

coat n el abrigo m p153

cockfight n la pelea de gallos f

coffee n el café m p91

iced coffee café helado

cognac n el coñac m p89

coin n la moneda f

cold n el resfriado m p111

I have a cold. Tengo un resfriado.

cold adj frío -a p125

I'm cold. Tengo frío.

It's cold out. Hace frío.

coliseum n el coliseo m

collect adj a cobro revertido

I'd like to place a collect call. Quisiera hacer una llamada a cobro revertido.

collect, to collect v recolectar p22

college n la universidad f

Colombian adj colombiano -a

color n el color m

color v colorear p22

computer n la computadora f

concert n el concierto m p130

condition n la condición f

in good / bad condition en buena / mala condición

condom n el condón m p182

Do you have a condom? ¿Tienes un condón?

not without a condom no sin un condón

condor n el cóndor m

confirm, to confirm v confirmar p22

I'd like to confirm my reservation. Quisiera confirmar mi reservación.

confused adj confundido -a

congested adj congestionado -a

connection speed n la velocidad de conexión f p140

constipated adj estreñido -a

I'm constipated. Estoy estreñido -a.

contact lens n el lente de contacto m

I lost my contact lens. Perdí mi lente de contacto.

continue, to continue v continuar p22

convertible n el convertible m

cook, to cook v cocinar p22

I'd like a room where I can cook. Quisiera una habitación donde pueda cocinar.

cookie n la galleta f p6

copper adj cobre

corner n la esquina f

on the corner en la esquina

correct v corregir p23

correct adj correcto -a p58

Am I on the correct train? ¿Estoy en el tren correcto?

cost, to cost v costar p22

How much does it cost? ¿Cuánto cuesta?

Costa Rican adj costarricense

costume *n* el disfraz *m*

cotton *n* el algodón *m* p152

cough *n* la tos *f* p186

cough *v* toser p23

counter (in bar) *n* el mostrador *m* p36

country-and-western *n* la música country *f* p128

court (legal) *n* la corte *f* p193

court (sport) *n* la cancha *f*

courteous *adj* cortés p78

cousin *n* el primo *m*, la prima *f*

cover charge (in bar) *n* el cargo de entrada *m* p175

cow *n* la vaca *f*

crack (in glass object) *n* la grieta *f*

craftsperson *n* el artesano *m*, la artesana *f* p122

cream *n* la crema *f* p94

credit card *n* la tarjeta de crédito *f* p133

> **Do you accept credit cards?** ¿Aceptan tarjetas de crédito?

crib *n* la cuna *f* p69

crown (dental) *n* la corona *f*

curb *n* el borde de la acera *m*

curl *n* el rizo *m*

curly *adj* rizado -a p118

currency exchange *n* el cambio de moneda *m* p37, 133

> **Where is the nearest currency exchange?** ¿Dónde está el cambio de moneda más cercano?

current (water) *n* la corriente *f*

customs *n* aduana *f* p39

cut (wound) *n* el corte *m*, la cortadura *f* p189

> **I have a bad cut.** Tengo una cortadura seria.

cut, to cut *v* cortar p22

cybercafé *n* el cibercafé *m*

> **Where can I find a cybercafé?** ¿Dónde puedo encontrar un cibercafé?

D

damaged *adj* dañado -a p49

Damn! *expletive* ¡Maldición!

dance *v* bailar p22

danger *n* el peligro *m* p56

dark *n* la oscuridad *f*

dark *adj* oscuro -a

daughter *n* la hija *f* p117

day *n* el día *m* p161

> **the day before yesterday** el día antes de ayer / anteayer p14
>
> **these last few days** estos últimos días

dawn *n* la madrugada *m* p13

> **at dawn** al amanecer

deaf *adj* sordo -a

deal (bargain) *n* la ganga *f*

> **What a great deal!** ¡Que ganga increíble!

deal (cards) *v* repartir p23

> **Deal me in.** Repárteme.

December *n* diciembre p15

declined *adj* rechazado -a

> **Was my credit card declined?** ¿Mi tarjeta de crédito fue rechazada?

declare v declarar **p22**

I have nothing to declare. *No tengo nada que declarar.*

deep adj profundo -a **p169**

delay n el retraso m **p44**

How long is the delay? *¿Cuán largo es el retraso?*

delighted adj deleitado -a

democracy n la democracia f

dent v abollar **p22**

He / She dented the car. *Él / Ella abolló el auto.*

dentist n el dentista m **p188**

denture n la dentadura f

denture plate *dentadura*

departure n la salida f

designer n el diseñador m, la diseñadora f **p122**

dessert n el postre m **p88**

dessert menu *el menú de postres*

destination n el destino m

diabetic adj diabético -a **p84**

dial (a phone) v marcar **p22**

dial direct *marcar directo*

diaper n el pañal m

Where can I change a diaper? *¿Dónde puedo cambiar un pañal?*

diarrhea n la diarrea f **p187**

dictionary n el diccionario m

different (other) adj diferente **p154**

difficult adj difícil **p167**

dinner n la cena f **p130**

directory assistance (phone) n la asistencia telefónica f

disability n la incapacidad f

disappear v desaparecer **p23**

disco n el disco m **p128**

disconnected adj desconectado -a **p138**

Operator, I was disconnected. *Operadora, fui desconectado -a.*

discount n el descuento m

Do I qualify for a discount? *¿Cualifico para un descuento?*

dish n el plato m **p85**

dive v bucear **p22**

scuba dive *buceo con tanques de oxígeno* **p169**

divorced adj divorciado -a

dizzy adj mareado -a **p189**

do, to do v hacer **p30**

doctor n el doctor m, la doctora f **p122, 188**

doctor's office n la oficina del doctor m

dog n el perro m **p43**

service dog *perro de servicio* **p70**

dollar n el dólar m

door n la puerta f **p78**

double adj doble **p8**

double bed *cama doble* **p67**

double vision *visión doble*

down adj abajo **p5**

download v descargar **p22**

downtown n el centro de la ciudad m **p149**

dozen n la docena f **p11**

drain n el drenaje m

drama n el drama m

drawing (work of art) n el dibujo m

dress (garment) n el vestido m

dress (general attire) n la vestimenta f p175

What's the dress code? ¿Cuál es el código de vestimenta?

dress v vestirse p23, 35

Should I dress up for that affair. Debería vestirme para ese evento.

dressing (salad) n el aderezo m

dried adj secado -a p109

drink n la bebida f p177

I'd like a drink. Quisiera una bebida.

drink, to drink v beber p23

drip v gotear p22

drive v guiar, manejar p22

driver n el chofer m p57

driving range n el campo para golpear pelotas m

drum n el tambor m

dry adj seco -a

This towel isn't dry. Esta toalla no está seca.

dry, to dry v secar p22

I need to dry my clothes. Necesito secar mi ropa.

dry cleaner n la tintorería f

dry cleaning n la limpieza en seco f

duck n el pato m

duty-free adj libre de impuestos p38

duty-free shop n la tienda libre de impuestos f p38

DVD n el DVD m p51

Do the rooms have DVD players? ¿Las habitaciones tienen lectores de DVD?

Where can I rent DVDs or videos? ¿Dónde puedo alquilar DVD o videos?

E

early adj temprano -a p13

It's early. Es temprano.

eat v comer p23

to eat out comer afuera

economy n la economía f

Ecuadorian adj ecuatoriano -a

editor n el editor m, la editora f p122

educator n el educador m, la educadora f p122

eight n el ocho m p7

eighteen n el dieciocho m p7

eighth n el octavo m p9

eighty n el ochenta m p7

election n la elección f p125

electrical hookup n la conexión eléctrica f p79

elevator n el elevador m p69

eleven n el once m p7

e-mail n el e-mail m124

May I have your e-mail address? ¿Me puede dar su dirección de e-mail?

e-mail message mensaje de e-mail

e-mail, to send e-mail v enviar un e-mail p22

embarrassed adj avergonzado -a p16

embassy n la embajada f

emergency n la emergencia f

emergency brake n el freno de emergencia m

emergency exit n la salida de emergencia f p41

employee n el empleado m, la empleada f p123

employer n el patrono m

engine n el motor m p55

engineer n el ingeniero m, la ingeniera f p122

England n Inglaterra

English n, adj el inglés m, la inglesa f p72

Do you speak English? ¿Habla inglés? p2

enjoy, to enjoy v disfrutar p22

enter, to enter v entrar p22

Do not enter. No entre.

enthusiastic adj entusiasmado -a p121

entrance n la entrada f p39

envelope n el sobre m p143

environment n el ambiente m

escalator n la escalera mecánica f

espresso n el café expreso m

exchange rate n la tasa de cambio f p133

What is the exchange rate for US / Canadian dollars? ¿Cuál es la tasa de cambio para los dólares americanos / canadienses?

excuse (pardon) v excusar, perdonar p22

Excuse me. Perdone.

exhausted adj exhausto -a

exhibit n la exhibición f

exit n la salida f p39

not an exit no es salida

exit v salir p23

expensive adj caro -a p176

explain v explicar p22

express adj expreso -a p41, 60

express check-in registro expreso

extra (additional) adj adicional p74

extra-large adj extra grande

eye n el ojo m p188

eyebrow n la ceja f

eyeglasses n los espejuelos m

eyelash n la pestaña f

F

fabric n la tela f

face n la cara f p119

faint v desmayar p22

fall (season) n el otoño m

fall v caer p23

family n la familia f p115

fan n el abanico m

far lejos p5

How far is it to _____? ¿Cuán lejos es hasta _____?

fare n la tarifa f

fast adj rápido -a p57, 140

fat adj gordo -a p12, 19

father n el padre m p115

faucet n el grifo m

fault n la culpa f p57

I'm at fault. Es mi culpa.

It was his fault. *Fue su culpa.*

fax *n* el fax *m* p123

February *n* febrero p14

fee *n* el honorario *m*

female *adj* hembra

fiancé(e) *n* el prometido *m*, la prometida *f* p115

fifteen *adj* el quince *m* p7

fifth *adj* el quinto -a *m* p9

fifty *adj* el cincuenta *m* p7

find *v* encontrar, hallar p22

fine (for traffic violation) *n* la multa *f* p193

fine *bien* p1

I'm fine. *Estoy bien.*

fire! *n* el fuego *m*

first *adj* primero -a p9

fishing pole *n* la caña de pescar *f*

fitness center *n* el centro de gimnasia *m* p66

fit (clothes) *v* entallarse p22, 35

Does this look like it fits? *¿Esto parece que me entalla?*

fitting room *n* el probador *m*

five *adj* cinco p7

flight *n* el vuelo *m* p39

Where do domestic flights arrive / depart? *¿Adónde llegan / De dónde salen los vuelos domésticos?*

Where do international flights arrive / depart? *¿Adónde llegan / De dónde salen los vuelos internacionales?*

What time does this flight leave? *¿A qué hora sale este vuelo?*

flight attendant *asistente de vuelo*

floor *n* el piso *m* p69

ground floor *planta baja*

second floor *primer piso*

*Note that in Spanish, the second floor is called the first, the third is the second, etc.

flower *n* la flor *f*

flush (gambling) *n* la escalera *f*

flush, to flush *v* bajar el inodoro p22

This toilet won't flush. *El inodoro no baja.*

flute *n* la flauta *f*

food *n* la comida *f* p87

foot (body part, measurement) *n* el pie *m*

forehead *n* la frente *f*

formula *n* la fórmula *f*

Do you sell infants' formula? *¿Venden fórmula para infantes?*

forty *adj* cuarenta p7

forward *adj* delante p6

four *adj* cuatro p7

fourteen *adj* catorce p7

fourth *adj* cuarto -a p9

one-fourth *un cuarto*

fragile *adj* frágil p141

freckle *n* la peca *f*

French *adj* francés p120

fresh *adj fresco -a* p102
Friday *n el viernes m* p14
friend *n el amigo m la amiga f* p115
front *adj delantero* p42
 front desk *la recepción* p73
 front door *la puerta principal l puerta del frente*
fruit *n la fruta f* p101
fruit juice *n el jugo de fruta m*
full, to be full (after a meal) *adj lleno -a* p90
Full house! *n ¡Full house!*
fuse *n el fusible m*

G
gallon *n el galón m* p11
garlic *n el ajo m* p108
gas *n el combustible m, la gasolina f* p55
 gas gauge *indicador de combustible*
 out of gas *sin combustible*
gate (at airport) *n la puerta de salida f* p36
German *adj alemán, alemana*
gift *n el regalo m*
gin *n la ginebra f* p89
girl *n la chica f, la muchacha f*
girlfriend *n la novia f* p115
give, to give *v dar* p22
glass *n la copa f* p84

 Do you have it by the glass? *¿Lo tienen por la copa?*

 I'd like a glass please. *Quisiera una copa por favor.*

glasses (eye) *n las gafas f*
 I need new glasses. *Necesito gafas nuevas.*

glove *n el guante m* p172
go, to go *v ir* p25
goal (sport) *n el gol m*
goalie *n el portero m* p164
gold *adj oro*
golf *n el golf m* p49
golf, to go golfing *v jugar golf* p22
good *adj bueno -a* p111
goodbye *n el adiós m* p112
grade (school) *n el grado m*
gram *n el gramo m*
grandfather *n el abuelo m*
grandmother *n la abuela f*
grandparent *n el abuelo m, la abuela f*
grape *n la uva f*
gray *adj gris*
great *adj grandioso -a*
Greek *adj griego -a* p81
Greek Orthodox *adj ortodoxo griego* p127
green *adj verde* p119
groceries *n los comestibles m*
group *n el grupo m* p44
grow, to grow (get larger) *v crecer* p23
 Where did you grow up? *¿Dónde creciste?*

guard n el guardia m p37

security guard guardia de
seguridad

Guatemalan adj guatemalteco -a p120

guest n el invitado m, la invitada f

guide (of tours) n el / la guía m
f p148

guide (publication) n la guía f

guide, to guide v guiar p22

guided tour n la excursión
guiada f

guitar n la guitarra f p129

gym n el gimnasio m p161

gynecologist n el ginecólogo m

H

hair n el pelo m, el cabello m

haircut n el recorte de pelo m

I need a haircut. Necesito
un recorte de pelo.

How much is a haircut?
¿Cuánto cuesta un recorte
de pelo?

hairdresser n el peluquero m,
la peluquera f

hair dryer n la secadora de
pelo f p75

half n la mitad f

one-half medio p8

hallway n el pasillo m

hand n la mano f p179

handicapped-accessible adj
accesible para personas
con impedimentos

handle, to handle v manejar
p22

handsome adj guapo -a, bien
parecido -a p117

hangout (hot spot) n el lugar
de reunión m

hang out (to relax) v pasar el
rato p22

**hang up (to end a phone
call)** v colgar p22

hanger n la percha f

happy adj alegre p121

hard adj difícil (difficult),
duro -a (firm) p49

hat n el sombrero m, el gorro m

have v tener p29

hazel adj color café p119

headache n el dolor de
cabeza m p111

headlight n el foco delantero m

headphones n los audífonos m

hear v escuchar p22

hearing-impaired adj con
impedimentos auditivos

heart n el corazón m p189

heart attack n el ataque cardiaco m, el ataque al
corazón m p189

hectare n la hectárea f p10

hello n hola p1

Help! n ¡Ayuda!

help, to help v ayudar p22

hen n la gallina f

her adj de ella p3

herb n la hierba f

here n aquí p5

high adj alto -a p171

highlights (hair) n los destellos m p160

highway *n la autopista f*

hike, to hike *v excursionar* p22

him *pron él* p3

Hindu *adj hindú* p120

hip-hop *n hip-hop* p174

his *adj de él*

historical *adj histórico -a*

history *n la historia f* p131

hobby *n el pasatiempo m*

hold, to hold *v sujetar* p22

to hold hands *sujetar las manos*

Would you hold this for me? *¿Sujetas esto por mí?*

hold, to hold (to pause) *v esperar* p22

Hold on a minute! *¡Espera un minuto!*

I'll hold. *Espero.*

hold, to hold (gambling) *v quedar* p22

holiday *n el día de fiesta m*

home *n el hogar m, la residencia f*

homemaker *n la ama de casa f*

Honduran *adj hondureño -a*

horn *n la bocina f*

horse *n el caballo m*

hostel *n la hospedería f* p66

hot *adj caliente* p89

hot chocolate *n el chocolate caliente m* p89

hotel *n el hotel m* p66

Do you have a list of local hotels? *¿Tiene una lista de hoteles locales?*

hour *n la hora f* p139

hours (at museum) *n el horario m*

how *adv cómo, cuánto (how much), cuántos (how many)* p3, 12

humid *adj húmedo -a* p125

hundred *n cien m, cientos m*

hurry *v apresurar* p35

I'm in a hurry. *Tengo prisa.* Hurry, please! *¡Apresúrate por favor!*

hurt, to hurt *v herir* p23

Ouch! That hurts! *¡Ay! ¡Eso duele!*

husband *n el esposo m* p114

I

I *pron yo* p3

ice *n el hielo m* p87

identification *n la identificación f* p46

inch *n la pulgada f* p10

indigestion *n la indigestión f*

inexpensive *adj económico -a, barato -a* p38

infant *n el infante m*

Are infants allowed? *¿Se permiten infantes?*

information *n la información f*

information booth *n el puesto de información m*

injury *n la lesión f* p16

insect repellent *n el repelente para insectos m* p187

inside *adentro* p84

insult *v insultar* p22

insurance n el seguro m p193

intercourse (sexual) n el coito m

interest rate n la tasa de interés f p133

intermission n el interludio m

Internet n el Internet m p38

High-speed Internet Internet de alta velocidad

Do you have Internet access? ¿Tienen acceso al Internet?

Where can I find an Internet café? ¿Dónde puedo encontrar un ciber-café?

interpreter n el / la intérprete m f p194

I need an interpreter. Necesito un intérprete.

introduce, to introduce v introducir p23

I'd like to introduce you to _____. Quisiera introducirle a _____.

Ireland n Irlanda

Irish adj irlandés, irlandesa

is v See be (to be). p27, 28

Italian adj italiano -a p120

J

jacket n la chaqueta f p46

January n enero p14

Japanese adj japonés / japonesa p120

jazz n el jazz m p128

Jewish adj judío -a p127

jog, to run v trotar p22

juice n el jugo m p100

June n junio p15

July n julio p15

K

keep, to keep v guardar p22

kid n el niño m

Are kids allowed? ¿Se permiten niños?

Do you have kids' programs? ¿Tienen programas para niños?

Do you have a kids' menu? ¿Tienen un menú para niños?

kilo n el kilo m p10

kilometer n el kilómetro m

kind n el tipo m, la clase F (type)

What kind is it? ¿Qué clase es?

kiss n el beso m p180

kitchen n la cocina f p73

know, to know (something) v saber p33

know, to know (someone) v conocer p33

kosher adj kósher p85

L

lactose-intolerant adj intolerante a la lactosa p86

land, to land v aterrizar p22

landscape n el paisaje m

language n el lenguaje m

laptop n la computadora portátil f p158

large *adj grande* p16
last, to last *v durar* **p22**
last *adv último -a* p9
late *adj tarde* p13
  Please don't be late. *Por favor no estés tarde.*
later *adv luego, más tarde*
  See you later. *Te veo luego.*
laundry *n la lavandería f* p74
lavender *adj lavanda*
law *n la ley f*
lawyer *n el abogado f* p122
least *n al menos f*
least *adj mínimo*
leather *n el cuero m* p50
leave, to leave (depart) *v salir* **p23**
left *adj izquierdo -a* p5
  on the left *a la izquierda*
leg *n la pierna f*
lemonade *n la limonada f*
less *adj menos* p156
lesson *n la lección f* p173
license *n la licencia f* p193
  driver's license *licencia de conducir*
life preserver *n el salvavidas m*
light *n (lamp) la luz f* p55
light (for cigarette) *n la lumbre f* p176
  May I offer you a light? *¿Puedo ofrecerle lumbre?*
lighter (cigarette) *n el encendedor m* p178
like, desire *v gustar (to please)* p34

I would like ____. *Me gustaría ____.*
like, to like *v gustar (to please)* p34
  I like this place. *Me gusta este lugar.*
limo *n la limosina f* p57
liquor *n el licor m* p45
liter *n el litro m* p10
little *adj pequeño -a (size), poco -a (amount)*
live, to live *v vivir* **p23**
  Where do you live? *¿Dónde vives?*
living *n la vida f* p122
  What do you do for a living? *¿Qué haces para ganarte la vida?*
local *adj local* p60
lock *n el candado m* p162
lock, to lock *v cerrar con llave* **p22**
  I can't lock the door. *No puedo cerrar la puerta con llave.*
  I'm locked out. *Me quedé fuera sin llave.*
locker *n el casillero m* p161
  storage locker *casillero de almacén*
  locker room *vestuario* p163
long *adv mucho tiempo, bastante* p12
  For how long? *¿Por cuánto tiempo?*
long *adj largo -a* p70
look, to look *v (to observe) mirar* **p22**

I'm just looking. *Sólo estoy mirando.*

Look here! *¡Mira aquí!*

look, to look *v (to appear) ver* p33

How does this look? *¿Cómo se ve esto?*

look for, to look for *(to search) v buscar* p22

I'm looking for a porter. *Estoy buscando un portero.*

loose *adj suelto -a* p153

lose, to lose *v perder* p23

I lost my passport. *Perdí mi pasaporte.*

I lost my wallet. *Perdí mi cartera.*

I'm lost. *Estoy perdido -a.*

lost. See lose *perdido -a* p45

loud *adj ruidoso -a* p78

loudly *adv ruidosamente*

lounge *n el salón público m*

lounge, to lounge *v relajarse* p35

love *n el amor m*

love, to love *v amar* p22

to love (family) *amar*

to love (a friend) *amar, querer*

to love (a lover) *amar*

to make love *hacer el amor*

low *adj bajo -a* p85

lunch *n el almuerzo m* p82

luggage *n el equipaje m* p37

Where do I report lost luggage? *¿Dónde reporto el equipaje perdido?*

Where is the lost luggage claim? *¿Dónde está el reclamo de equipaje?*

M

machine *n la máquina f* p74

made of *adj hecho de*

magazine *n la revista f*

maid (hotel) *n la camarera f*

maiden *adj soltera*

That's my maiden name. *Ese es mi apellido de soltera.*

mail *n el correo m*

air mail *correo aéreo*

registered mail *correo certificado*

mail *v enviar* p22

make, to make *v hacer* p30

makeup *n el maquillaje m*

make up, to make up (apologize) *v hacer las paces* p30

make up, to make up (apply cosmetics) *v maquillar* p22

male *n el varón m* p45

male *adj masculino*

mall *n el centro comercial m*

man *n el hombre m*

manager *n el / la gerente m f*

manual (instruction booklet) *n el manual m* p53

many *adj muchos -as* p11

map *n el mapa m* p51

March (month) *n marzo* p15

market *n el mercado m* p154

flea market *mercado de pulgas / pulguero* p151

open-air market *mercado al aire libre*

married *adj casado -a* p116

marry, to marry *v casarse* p22, 35

massage, to massage *v dar masaje* p22 p180

match (sport) *n el partido m*

match *n el fósforo m*

book of matches *libro de fósforos*

match, to match *v igualar, hacer juego* p22, 30

Does this ___ match my outfit? *¿Este ___ hace juego con mi vestido?*

May (month) *n mayo* p15

may *v aux poder* p31

May I ___? *¿Puedo?*

meal *n la comida f* p42

meat *n la carne f* p87

meatball *n la albóndiga f*

medication *n la medicina f*

medium (size) *adj mediano -a*

medium rare (meat) *adj a medio cocer* p84

medium well (meat) *adj medio bien cocido* p85

member *n el miembro m*

menu *n el menú m* p82

May I see a menu? *¿Puedo ver un menú?*

children's menu *menú para niños*

diabetic menu *menú diabético*

kosher menu *menú kósher*

metal detector *n el detector de metales m*

meter *n el metro m* p10

Mexican *adj mexicano -a*

middle *adj de en medio* p28

midnight *n la medianoche f*

mile *n la milla f* p10

military *n el ejército m, la milicia f*

milk *n la leche f* p90

milk shake *batido de leche*

milliliter *n el mililitro m*

millimeter *n el milímetro m*

minute *n el minuto m* p4

in a minute *en un minuto*

miss, to miss (a flight) *v perder* p23

missing *adj perdido -a, ausente*

mistake *n el error m* p78

moderately priced *adj de precio moderado* p66

mole (facial feature) *n el lunar m*

Monday *n el lunes m* p14

money *n el dinero m* p132

money transfer *transferencia de dinero*

month *n el mes m* p4

morning *n la mañana f* p13

in the morning *en la mañana*

mosque *n la mezquita f*

mother *n la madre f* p115

mother, to mother *v cuidar* p22

motorcycle *n la motocicleta f*

mountain n la montaña f
mountain climbing escalado
de montaña p166
mouse n el ratón m
mouth n la boca f
move, to move v mover p23
movie n la película f p145
much n mucho m, la gran
cantidad f p11
mug, to mug (someone) v
asaltar p22
mugged adj asaltado -a
museum n el museo m p130
music n la música f p128
live music música en vivo
musician n el músico m, la
musica f p123
muslim adj musulmán p127
mustache n el bigote m
mystery (novel) n la novela
de misterio f

N
name n el nombre m p114
My name is ___. Me llamo
___. p1
What's your name? ¿Cómo
se llama? / ¿Cuál es su
nombre?
napkin n la servilleta f
narrow adj angosto -a p12
nationality n la nacionalidad f
nausea n la náusea f p187
near adj cercano -a p5
nearby adj cercano -a p81
neat (tidy) adj limpio -a
need, to need v necesitar p22

neighbor n el vecino m, la
vecina f p115
nephew n el sobrino m p115
network n la red f
new adj nuevo -a p162
newspaper n el periódico m
newsstand n el puesto de
periódicos m p38
New Zealand n Nueva
Zelanda
New Zealander adj neoze-
landés, neozelandesa
next prep próximo, al lado
next to al lado de
the next station la próxima
estación
Nicaraguan adj nicaragüense,
nicaragüeña p120
nice adj agradable
niece n la sobrina f p115
night n la noche f p13
at night en la noche
per night por noche p70
nightclub n el club nocturno m
nine adj nueve p7
nineteen adj diecinueve p7
ninety adj noventa p7
ninth adj noveno -a p9
no adv no p1
noisy adj ruidoso -a p77
none n el ninguno p11
nonsmoking adj de no fumar
nonsmoking area área de
no fumar
nonsmoking room
habitación de no fumar
noon n el mediodía m p13

nose *n* la nariz *f* p188

novel *n* la novela *f*

November *n* noviembre p15

now *adv* ahora p4

number *n* el número *m* p124

Which room number? ¿Cuál es el número de la habitación?

May I have your phone number? ¿Me puede dar su número de teléfono?

nurse *n* la enfermera *f* p123

nurse *v* amamantar p22

Do you have a place where I can nurse? ¿Tienen un lugar dónde pueda amamantar?

nursery *n* la guardería infantil *f*

Do you have a nursery? ¿Tienen una guardería infantil?

nut *n* la nuez *f*

O

o'clock *adv* en punto p4

two o'clock dos en punto

October *n* octubre p15

offer, to offer *v* ofrecer p33

officer *n* el oficial *m*, la oficial *f* p45

oil *n* el aceite *m* p55, 86

okay *adv* OK, de acuerdo

old *adj* viejo -a p26

olive *n* la aceituna *f*

one *adj* uno -a p7

one way (traffic sign) *adj* en una sola dirección

open (business) *adj* abierto -a p154

Are you open? ¿Están abierto?

opera *n* la ópera *f* p128

operator (phone) *n* el operador *m*, la operadora *f*

optometrist *n* el optómetra *m*, la optometra *f*

orange (color) *adj* naranjo -a

orange juice *n* el jugo de naranja *m* p47

order, to order (demand) *v* pedir p32

order, to order (request) *v* ordenar p22

organic *adj* orgánico -a

Ouch! *interj* ¡ay!

outside *n* afuera p84

overcooked *adj* sobrecocido -a

overheat, to overheat *v* sobrecalentarse p22, 35

The car overheated. El auto se sobrecalentó.

overflowing *adv* desbordante

oxygen tank *n* el tanque de oxígeno *m*

P

package *n* el paquete *m* p110

pacifier *n* el chupete *m*

page, to page (someone) *v* mandar a llamar p22

paint, to paint *v* pintar p22

painting *n* la pintura *f*

pale *adj* pálido -a p118

Panamanian *adj* panameño -a

paper n el papel p100

parade n la parada f

Paraguayan adj paraguayo -a

parent n el padre m

park n el parque m p130

park, to park v estacionar p22

no parking no estacione

parking fee tarifa de estacionamiento

parking garage estacionamiento

partner n el compañero m, la compañera f

party n el partido m p126

party n la fiesta f

political party partido político

pass, to pass v pasar p22

I'll pass. Yo paso.

passenger n el pasajero m, la pasajera f

passport n el pasaporte m

I've lost my passport. Perdí mi pasaporte.

pay, to pay v pagar p22

peanut n el cacahuate m

pedestrian adj peatonal

pediatrician n el pediatra m, la pediatra f

Can you recommend a pediatrician? ¿Puede recomendar un pediatra?

permit n el permiso m

Do we need a permit? ¿Necesitamos un permiso?

permit, to permit v permitir p23

Peruvian adj peruano -a

phone n el teléfono m p179

May I have your phone number? ¿Me puede dar su número de teléfono?

Where can I find a public phone? ¿Dónde puedo encontrar un teléfono público?

phone operator operadora

Do you sell prepaid phones? ¿Venden teléfonos prepagados?

phone adj telefónico -a

Do you have a phone directory? ¿Tiene un directorio telefónico?

phone call n la llamada telefónica f

I need to make a collect phone call. Necesito hacer una llamada telefónica con cargos revertidos.

an international phone call una llamada internacional

photocopy, to photocopy v fotocopiar p22

piano n el piano m p129

pillow n la almohada f p47

down pillow almohada de plumas

pink adj rosado -a

pint n la pinta f p11

pizza n la pizza f p80

place, to place v colocar p22

plastic n el plástico m p50

play n la obra de teatro f

play, to play (a game) v jugar p22

play, to play (an instrument) v tocar **p22**

playground n el patio de recreo m

Do you have a playground? ¿Tienen un patio de recreo?

please (polite entreaty) adv por favor

please, to be pleasing to v agradar **p22**

pleasure n el placer m **p1**

It's a pleasure. Es un placer.

plug n el enchufe m **p158**

plug, to plug v enchufar **p22**

point, to point v señalar, apuntar **p22**

Would you point me in the direction of___? ¿Me pude señalar la dirección de___?

police n la policía f **p37**

police station n la estación de policías f **p37**

pool n la piscina f **p66**

pool (the game) n el billar m

pop music n la música pop f

popular adj popular **p175**

port (beverage) n el oporto m

port (for ship) n el puerto

porter n el portero m, la portera f **p36**

portion n la porción f

portrait n el retrato m

postcard n la postal f

post office n el correo m

Where is the post office? ¿Dónde está el correo?

poultry n las aves de corral f pl

pound n la libra f **p110**

prefer, to prefer v preferir **p23**

pregnant adj embarazada

prepared adj preparado -a

prescription n la receta f **p45**

price n el precio m

print, to print v imprimir **p23**

private berth / cabin n el camarote privado m **p62**

problem n el problema m **p2**

process, to process v procesar **p22**

product n el producto m

professional adj profesional

program n el programa m

May I have a program? ¿Me puede dar un programa?

Protestant n protestante m

publisher n el editor m

Puerto Rican adj puertorriqueño -a m / f

pull, to pull v halar **p22**

pump n la bomba f **p16**

purple adj morado -a

purse n la cartera f, el bolso m

push, to push v empujar **p22**

put, to put v poner **p29** (like tener)

Q

quarter adj un cuarto **p8**

one-quarter un cuarto

quiet adj tranquilo -a **p82**

R

rabbit n el conejo m **p91**

radio n el radio m **p51**

satellite radio *radio por satélite*

rain, to rain *v llover* **p31** (like *poder*)

Is it supposed to rain? *¿Se supone que llueva?*

rainy *adj lluvioso -a* **p125**

It's rainy. *Está lluvioso.*

ramp, wheelchair *n la rampa para sillas de ruedas f* **p65**

rare (meat) *adj crudo -a* **p84**

rate (for car rental, hotel) *n la tarifa f* **p52**

What's the rate per day? *¿Cuál es la tarifa por día?*

What's the rate per week? *¿Cuál es la tarifa por semana?*

rate plan (cell phone) *n el plan de tarifa m*

rather *adv preferiblemente*

read, to read *v leer* **p23**

really *adv verdaderamente*

receipt *n el recibo m* **p133**

receive, to receive *v recibir* **p23**

recommend, to recommend *v recomendar* **p22**

red *adj rojo -a* **p184**

redhead *n el pelirrojo m, la pelirroja f* **p117**

reef *n el arrecife m* **p170**

refill (of beverage) *n el relleno m*

refill (of prescription) *n el reabastecimiento m* **p188**

reggae *adj reggae* **p128**

relative (family) *n el pariente m*

remove, to remove *v remover* **p23**

rent, to rent *v alquilar* **p22**

I'd like to rent a car. *Quisiera alquilar un auto.*

repeat, to repeat *v repetir* **p32** (like *pedir*)

Would you please repeat that? *¿Puede repetir eso por favor?* **p2**

reservation *n la reservación m*

I'd like to make a reservation for ____. *Quisiera hacer una reservación para ____.* **p70** See p7 for numbers.

restaurant *n el restaurante? m*

Where can I find a good restaurant? *¿Dónde puedo encontrar un buen restaurante.* **p80**

restroom *n el baño m* **p36**

Do you have a public restroom? *¿Tienen un baño público?*

return, to return (to a place) *v regresar* **p22**

return, to return (something to a store) *v devolver* **(p31,** like *poder*)

ride, to ride *v correr* **p23**

right *adj derecho -a* **p55**

It is on the right. *Está a mano derecha.*

Turn right at the corner. *Vira a la derecha en la esquina.*

rights *n pl los derechos m*

civil rights *derechos civiles*

river *n el río m* p169

road *n la carretera f* p56

road closed sign *n el letrero de carretera cerrada m* p56

rob, to rob *v robar* p22

  I've been robbed. *Me han robado.*

rock and roll *n rock and roll*

rock climbing *n la escalada de rocas f*

rocks (ice) *n las rocas f* p88

  I'd like it on the rocks. *Lo quisiera en las rocas.*

romance (novel) *n la novela de romance f*

romantic *adj romántico -a*

room (hotel) *n la habitación f*

  room for one / two *habitación para uno / dos*

  room service *servicio de habitaciones*

rope *n la cuerda f* p16

rose *n la rosa f*

royal flush *n la escalera real f*

rum *n el ron m* p89

run, to run *v correr* p23

S

sad *adj triste* p121

safe (for storing valuables) *n la caja fuerte* p75

  Do the rooms have safes? *¿Las habitaciones tienen cajas fuertes?*

safe (secure) *adj seguro -a*

  Is this area safe? *¿Esta área es segura?*

sail *n la vela f*

sail, to sail *v zarpar* p22

  When do we sail? *¿Cuándo zarpamos?* p28

salad *n la ensalada f* p110

salesperson *n el vendedor m, la vendedora f* p122

salt *n la sal f* p108

  Is that low-salt? *¿Eso es bajo en sal?*

Salvadorian *adj salvadoreño -a* p121

satellite *n el satélite m* p51

  satellite radio *radio satélite*

  satellite tracking *rastreo por satélite*

Saturday *n el sábado m* p14

sauce *n la salsa f*

say, to say *v decir* (p32, like pedir)

scan, to scan *v (document) escanear* p22

schedule *n el itinerario m*

school *n la escuela f*

scooter *n la motoneta f* p51

score *n la puntuación f* p165

Scottish *adj escocés*

scratched *adj rayado -a* p53

  scratched surface *superficie rayada*

scuba dive, to scuba dive *v bucear con tanques de oxígeno* p22

sculpture *n la escultura f*

seafood *n los mariscos m* p81

search *n la búsqueda f*

  hand search *búsqueda a mano*

ENGLISH–SPANISH

search, to search v buscar
p22

seasick adj mareado -a p62

I am seasick. Estoy
mareado -a.

seasickness pill n la píldora
para el mareo f

seat n el asiento m p41, 146

child seat asiento de niño

second adj segundo -a p9

security n la seguridad f p37

security checkpoint punto
de control de seguridad

security guard guardia de
seguridad

sedan n el sedán m p50

see, to see v ver p23 (like ser)

May I see it? ¿Puedo verlo?

self-serve adj auto servicio

sell, to sell v vender p23

seltzer n el seltzer m p88

send, to send v enviar p22

separated (marital status)
adj separado -a p116

September n el septiembre
m p15

serve, to serve v servir p32

service n el servicio m p43

out of service fuera de servicio p136

services (religious) n el servicio m p127

service charge n el cargo por
servicio m p72

seven adj siete p7

seventy adj setenta p7

seventeen adj diecisiete p7

seventh adj séptimo -a p9

sew, to sew v coser p23

sex (gender) n el sexo m

sex, to have (intercourse) v
tener relaciones p29

shallow adj poco profundo -a

sheet (bed linen) n la sábana f

shellfish n el crustáceo m p87

ship n el barco m p63

ship, to ship v enviar p22

**How much to ship this to
____?** ¿Cuánto cuesta
enviar esto ____?

shipwreck n el naufragio m

shirt n la camisa f

shoe n el zapato m p150

shop n la tienda f p150

shop v comprar, ir de compras p23

**I'm shopping for mens'
clothes.** Estoy comprando
ropa de hombres.

**I'm shopping for womens'
clothes.** Estoy comprando
ropa de mujer.

**I'm shopping for childrens'
clothes.** Estoy comprando
ropa para niños.

short adj corto -a p10

shorts n los pantalones cortos m p83

shot (liquor) n el trago m

shout v gritar p22

show (performance) n el
espectáculo m, la función f

What time is the show? ¿A
qué hora es el espec-
táculo?

show, to show v *mostrar* p31
(like *poder*)

Would you show me?
¿Puede mostrarme?

shower n *la ducha* f p68

Does it have a shower?
¿Tiene una ducha?

shower, to shower v
ducharse p22, 35

shrimp n *el camarón* m p102

shuttle bus n *el autobús de
transbordo* m

sick adj *enfermo -a* p48

I feel sick. *Me siento
enfermo -a.*

side n *el lado* m p86

**on the side (e.g., salad
dressing)** *por el lado*

sidewalk n *la acera* f

sightseeing n *el excursionismo* m

sightseeing bus n *el autobús
de excursión* m

sign, to sign v *firmar* p22

Where do I sign? *¿Dónde
firmo?*

silk n *la ceda* f p152

silver adj *plato -a*

sing, to sing v *cantar* p22

single (unmarried) adj
soltero -a p116

Are you single? *¿Estás
soltero -a?*

single (one) adj *sencillo -a,
individual*

single bed *cama individual*

sink n *el fregadero* m

sister n *la hermana* f p115

sit, to sit v *sentar*

six adj *seis* p7

sixteen adj *dieciséis* p7

sixty adj *sesenta* p7

size (clothing, shoes) n *la
talla* f p151

skin n *la piel* f

sleeping berth n *el camarote
para dormir* m

slow adj *lento -a* p179

slow, to slow v *reducir la
velocidad* p33

Slow down! *¡Reduzca la
velocidad!* p58

slow(ly) adv *lentamente*

Speak more slowly. *Hable
más lentamente.* p112

slum n *el suburbio* m p16

small adj *pequeño -a* p11

smell, to smell v *oler*

smoke, to smoke v *fumar* p22

smoking n *el fumar* m p37

smoking area *área de fumar*

No Smoking *No fumar* p39

snack n *el bocadillo* m p183

Snake eyes! n *¡Ojos de serpiente!, ¡Par de ases!* p184

snorkel n *el tubo de respiración* m

soap n *el jabón* m p16

sock n *la media* f

soda n *la soda* f, *el refresco
m, la gaseosa* f p47

diet soda *refresco de dieta*

soft adj *suave*

software n *el software* m

sold out adj *vendido -a*

some adj *algún, alguno -a*

someone n alguien p38

something n algo p48

son n el hijo m p117

song n la canción f p179

sorry adj apenado -a

 I'm sorry. Lo siento.

soup n la sopa f p16

spa n el balneario m p67

Spain n España

Spanish adj español p2

spare tire n la llanta de respuesta f

speak, to speak v hablar p22

 Do you speak English? ¿Habla inglés?

 Would you speak louder, please? ¿Podría hablar más alto, por favor?

 Would you speak slower, please? ¿Podría hablar más lento, por favor?

special (featured meal) n el especial m

specify, to specify v especificar p22

speed limit n el límite de velocidad m p56

 What's the speed limit? ¿Cuál es el límite de velocidad?

speedometer n el velocímetro m

spell, to spell v deletrear p22

 How do you spell that? ¿Cómo se deletrea eso?

spice n la especie f

spill, to spill v derramar p22

split (gambling) n la división f

sports n los deportes m p130

spring (season) n la primavera f p15

stadium n el estadio m p163

staff (employees) n el personal m p78

stamp (postage) n la estampilla f

stair n la escalera f

 Where are the stairs? ¿Dónde están las escaleras?

 Are there many stairs? ¿Hay muchas escaleras?

stand, to stand v pararse p22, 35

start, to start (commence) v comenzar

start, to start (a car) v encender p31 (like querer)

state n el estado m

station n la estación f p58

 Where is the nearest_____? ¿Dónde está ____ más cercana?

 gas station la gasolinera

 bus station la estación de autobuses

 subway station la estación del metro

 train station la estación del tren

stay, to stay v quedarse p22, 35

 We'll be staying for ____ nights. Me quedaré por ____ noches. Numbers, p7.

steakhouse n el restaurante de parrilla m p80

steal, to steal v robar **p22**

stolen adj robado -a **p49**

stop n la parada f **p59**

> **Is this my stop?** ¿Ésta es mi parada?
>
> **I missed my stop.** Perdí mi parada.

stop, to stop v detener **p29**

> **Please stop.** Por favor deténgase.
>
> **STOP (traffic sign)** PARE
>
> **Stop, thief!** ¡Alto, ladrón!

store n la tienda f **p150**

straight adj recto -a, derecho -a, lacio -a **(hair) p118**

> **straight ahead** hacia delante **p5**
>
> **straight (drink)** sencillo
>
> **Go straight. (giving directions)** Siga derecho. **p55**

straight (gambling) n la escalera f **p185**

street n la calle f **p6**

> **across the street** al cruzar la calle
>
> **down the street** calle abajo
>
> **Which street?** ¿En cuál calle?
>
> **How many more streets?** ¿Cuántas calles más?

stressed adj estresado -a

striped adj a rayas

stroller n el cochecito para niños / bebés m

> **Do you rent baby strollers?** ¿Alquilan cochecitos para bebés?

substitution n la sustitución f

suburb n el barrio m **p16**

subway n el metro m **p63**

> **subway line** línea del metro
>
> **subway station** estación del metro
>
> **Which subway do I take for ____?** ¿Cuál metro tomo para ____?

subtitle n el subtítulo m

suitcase n la maleta f **p49**

suite n la suite f **p69**

summer n el verano m **p15**

sun n el sol m

sunburn n la quemadura de sol f

> **I have a bad sunburn.** Tengo una quemadura de sol mala.

Sunday n domingo m **p14**

sunglasses n las gafas de sol f

sunny adj soleado -a **p125**

> **It's sunny out.** Está soleado afuera.

sunroof n el techo corredizo m

sunscreen n el bloqueador de sol m

> **Do you have sunscreen SPF ____?** ¿Tienen bloqueador de sol SPF ____? See numbers **p7**.

supermarket n el supermercado m

surf v surfear **p22**

surfboard n la tabla de surfear f

suspiciously adv sospechosamente **p48**

swallow, to swallow v *tragar* p22

sweater n *el suéter* m p46

swim, to swim v *nadar* p22

Can one swim here?
¿Puedo nadar aquí?

swimsuit n *el traje de baño* m

swim trunks n *el pantalón de traje de baño* m

symphony n *la sinfonía* f

T

table n *la mesa* f p21

table for two *mesa para dos*

tailor n *el sastre* m p74

Can you recommend a good tailor? *¿Puede recomendar un buen sastre?*

take, to take v *tomar, llevar* p22

Take me to the station. *Lléveme a la estación.*

How much to take me to _____? *¿Cuánto cuesta llevarme a _____?*

takeout menu n *el menú para llevar* m

talk, to talk v *hablar* p22

tall adj *alto -a* p119

tanned adj *bronceado -a*

taste (flavor) n *el sabor* m

taste n (discernment) *el gusto* m

taste, to taste v *probar* p22

tax n *el impuesto* m p156

value-added tax (VAT) *impuesto al valor agregado (IVA)*

taxi n *el taxi* m p57

Taxi! *¡Taxi!*

Would you call me a taxi? *¿Me puede llamar un taxi?*

tea n *el té* m p90

team n *el equipo* m p164

Techno n *el techno* m p128

television n *la televisión* f

temple n *el templo* m p126

ten adj *diez* p7

tennis n *el tenis* m p67

tennis court *cancha de tenis*

tent n *la tienda de campaña* f

tenth adj *décimo -a* p9

terminal n (airport) *el terminal* m p39

Thank you. *Gracias.* p1

that (near) adj *ese / eso / esa*

that (far away) adj *aquel / aquello / aquella*

theater n *el teatro* m p145

them (m/f) *ellos / ellas* p3

there (demonstrative) adv *ahí* (nearby), *allí* (far)

Is / Are there ? *¿Hay ?*

over there *allí*

these adj *éstos -as* p6

thick adj *grueso -a, espeso -a*

thin adj *delgado -a, flaco -a, fino -a* p119

third adj *tercero -a* p9

thirteen adj *trece* p7

thirty adj *treinta* p7

this adj *este, esto, esta* p6

those adj *aquellos -as, esos -as*

thousand *mil* p7

three *tres* p7

Thursday n el jueves m p14

ticket n el boleto m p36

　ticket counter mostrador de venta de boletos

　one-way ticket boleto de ida p38

　round-trip ticket boleto de ida y vuelta p38

tight adj apretado -a p153

time n el tiempo m p167

　Is it on time? ¿Está a tiempo?

　At what time? ¿A qué hora?

　What time is it? ¿Qué hora es?

timetable n (train) el itinerario m p59

tip (gratuity) la propina f p90

tire n la llanta f p53

　I have a flat tire. Tengo una llanta vacía.

tired adj cansado -a p121

today n hoy

toilet n el inodoro m p76

　The toilet is overflowing. El inodoro se está desbordando.

　The toilet is backed up. El inodoro está tapado.

toilet paper n el papel higiénico m

　You're out of toilet paper. Se le acabó el papel higiénico.

toiletries n los artículos de tocador m p100

toll n el peaje m p56

tomorrow n mañana p4

ton n la tonelada f

too (excessively) adv demasiado -a

too (also) adv también p184

tooth n el diente m p192

　I lost my tooth. Perdí mi diente.

toothache n el dolor de dientes m

　I have a toothache. Tengo dolor de dientes.

total n el total m

　What is the total? ¿Cuál es el total?

tour n la excursión f

　Are guided tours available? ¿Hay excursiones guiadas disponibles?

　Are audio tours available? ¿Hay excursiones por audio disponibles?

towel n la toalla f

　May we have more towels? ¿Me puede dar más toallas?

toy n el juguete m

　toy store n la juguetería f

　Do you have any toys for the children? ¿Tiene juguetes para niños?

traffic n el tráfico m, el tránsito m p153

　How's traffic? ¿Cómo está el tráfico?

　traffic rules reglas de tránsito

trail n el sendero m p168
  Are there trails? ¿Hay senderos?

train n el tren m p59
  express train tren expreso
  local train tren local
  Does the train go to _____? ¿El tren va a _____?
  May I have a train schedule? ¿Me puede dar un itinerario de trenes?
  Where is the train station? ¿Dónde está la estación del tren?

train, to train v entrenar p22

transfer, to transfer v transferir p29
  I need to transfer funds. Necesito transferir fondos.

transmission n la transmisión f
  automatic transmission transmisión automática
  standard transmission transmisión manual

travel, to travel v viajar p22

travelers' check n el cheque de viajero m
  Do you cash travelers' checks? ¿Ustedes cambian cheques de viajero?

trim, to trim (hair) v recortar p22

trip n el viaje m p111

triple adj triple p8

trumpet n la trompeta f

trunk n el baúl m (luggage) p49, el portaequipajes m (in car)

try, to try (attempt) v intentar p22, tratar p22

try, to try on (clothing) v medir p32

try, to try (food) v probar

Tuesday n el martes m p14

turkey n el pavo m p96

turn, to turn v virar, girar p22
  to turn left / right vire a la izquierda / derecha
  to turn off / on encender / apagar p22

twelve adj doce p7

twenty adj veinte p7

twine n la cuerda f p141

two adj dos p7

U

umbrella n la sombrilla f

uncle n el tío m p115

undercooked adj crudo -a

understand, to understand v entender p29
  I don't understand. No entiendo.
  Do you understand? ¿Entiende?

underwear n la ropa interior f

university n la universidad f

up adv arriba p5

update, to update v actualizar p22

upgrade n la mejora de categoría f p52

upload, to upload v cargar p22

upscale adj de más clase p72

Uruguayan adj uruguayo -a p121

us pron nosotros -as p3

USB port n el puerto USB m

use, to use v usar p22

V

vacation n la vacación m p44

on vacation de vacaciones

to go on vacation ir de vacaciones

vacancy n el vacante m

van n la furgoneta f, la van f

VCR n la videograbadora f

Do the rooms have VCRs? ¿Las habitaciones tienen videograbadoras?

vegetable n el vegetal m

vegetarian n el vegetariano m, la vegetariana f p42

vending machine n la máquina de venta f

Venezuelan adj venezolano -a p121

version n la versión f

very muy p78

video n el video m

Where can I rent videos or DVDs? ¿Dónde puedo alquilar videos o DVD?

view n la vista f p68

beach view vista a la playa

city view vista a la ciudad

vineyard n el viñedo m

vinyl n el vinilo m p50

violin n el violín m

visa n la visa f

Do I need a visa? ¿Necesito una visa?

vision n la visión f p189

visit, to visit v visitar p22

visually-impaired adj con impedimentos visuales f

vodka n el vodka m p89

voucher n el vale m p44

W

wait, to wait v esperar p22

Please wait. Por favor espere.

How long is the wait? ¿Cuán larga es la espera?

waiter n el camarero f

waiting area n la área de espera f p36

wake-up call n la llamada de despertar f p75

wallet n la cartera f, la billetera f p46

I lost my wallet. Perdí mi cartera.

Someone stole my wallet. Alguien me robó mi billetera.

walk, to walk v caminar p22

walker (ambulatory device) n el andador m p43

walkway n la pasarela f

moving walkway pasarela mecánica

want, to want v querer p31

war n la guerra f p126

warm adj caliente p89, 125

watch, to watch v observar p22

water n el agua m p46

Is the water potable? ¿El agua es potable?

Is there running water? ¿Hay agua de llave? p79

wave, to wave v agitar las manos p22

waxing n la depilación con cera f

weapon n el arma m p16

wear, to wear v usar p22

weather forecast n el pronóstico del tiempo m

Wednesday n el miércoles m

week n la semana f p4, 14

this week esta semana

last week la semana pasada

next week la próxima semana

weigh v pesar p22

I weigh ____. Yo peso ____.

It weighs ____. Pesa ____.
See p7 for numbers.

weights n las pesas f p161

welcome adv bienvenido

You're welcome. Está bienvenido.

well adv bien

well done (meat) bien cocido p85

well done (task) bien hecho

I don't feel well. No me siento bien.

western adj occidental, de vaqueros

whale n la ballena f

what adv qué p3

What sort of ____? ¿Qué clase de ____?

What time is ____? ¿A qué hora es ___? p12
See p112 for questions.

wheelchair n la silla de ruedas f p43

wheelchair access acceso para sillas de ruedas p70

wheelchair ramp rampa para sillas de ruedas

power wheelchair silla de ruedas eléctricas

wheeled (luggage) adj con ruedas

when adv cuándo p3
See p112 for questions.

where adv dónde p3

Where is it? ¿Dónde está?
See p112 for questions.

which adv cuál p3

Which one? ¿Cuál?
See p112 for questions.

white adj blanco -a

who adv quién p3

whose adj de quién

wide adj ancho -a p12

widow, widower n la viuda f, el viudo m p116

wife n la esposa f p114

wi-fi n la red inalámbrica f

window n la ventana f, la ventanilla f p41, 142

drop-off window ventanilla de entregas

pickup window ventanilla de recogido

windshield n el parabrisas m

windshield wiper n el limpiaparabrisas m

windy adj ventoso -a p125

wine n el vino m p47, 84

winter n el invierno m p15

wiper n el limpiaparabrisas m

with prep con p87

withdraw v retirar p22

I need to withdraw money.
Necesito retirar dinero.

without prep sin p87

woman n la mujer f

work, to work v trabajar,
funcionar p22

This doesn't work. Esto no
funciona.

workout n el ejercicio m

worse peor

worst lo peor

write, to write v escribir p23

**Would you write that down
for me?** ¿Podría escribir
eso para mí?

writer n el escritor m p122

X

x-ray machine n la máquina
de rayos X f

Y

yellow adj amarillo -a

Yes. adv Sí.

yesterday n ayer m p4

the day before yesterday
anteayer p14

yield sign n la señal de ceda
el paso f

you pron usted, tú, ustedes,
vosotros -as p3

you (singular, informal) tú

you (singular, formal) usted

you (plural informal)
vosotros -as **(rare)**

you (plural formal) ustedes

your, yours adj suyo -a, tuyo -a

young adj joven p116

Z

zoo n el zoológico m p130

A

abajo *down adv* p5

el abanico *m fan (hand-held) n*

la abeja *f bee n*

abierto -a *open (business) adj*

el / la abogado *m lawyer n* p122

la abolladura *f dent n*

abordar *to board v* p22

el abrigo *m coat n* p153

el abril *m April n* p15

la abuela *f grandmother n*

el abuelo *m grandfather n*

acampar *to camp v* p22

el accidente *m accident n*

el aceite *m oil n* p55, 86

la aceituna *f olive n*

aceptar *to accept v* p22

Se aceptan tarjetas de crédito. *Credit cards accepted.*

la acera *f sidewalk n*

achicharrado -a *charred (meat) adj* p84

aclarar *to clear v* p22

el acné *m acne n* p187

actual *actual adj* p16

actualizar *to update v* p22

de acuerdo *Okay. adj adv*

el acumulador *m,* la acumuladora *f battery (for car) n*

adelante *forward adj* p6

el adelanto *m advance n*

adentro *inside adj* p84

el aderezo *m dressing (salad) n*

adicional *extra adj* p74

el adiós *m goodbye n* p112

la aduana *f customs n* p39

el aeropuerto *m airport n*

afroamericano -a *African American adj* p119

afro, africano *afro adj*

afuera *outside n* p84

¡Agarren al ladrón! *Stop, thief!*

la agencia *f agency n* p50

la agencia de alquiler de autos *f car rental agency*

la agencia de crédito *f credit bureau n* p133

el agnóstico *m,* la agnóstica *f agnostic m, adj* p127

el agosto *m August n* p15

agotado -a *exhausted (person) adj, sold out (thing) adj*

agradable *nice adj*

agradar *to please v, to be pleasing to v* p22

el agua *m water n* p46

el agua caliente *hot water*
el agua frío *cold water*

el águila *m eagle n*

ahí *there (nearby) adv (demonstrative)* p182

ahora *now adv* p4

el aire acondicionado *m air conditioning n* p68

el ajo *m garlic n* p108

la albóndiga *f meatball n*

el alcohol *m alcohol n* p88

alegre *happy adj* p121

el alemán *m,* la alemana *f German n adj* p80

la alergia *f allergy n*

alérgico -a *allergic adj* p5, 76
  **Soy alérgico / alérgica
  a ____.** *I'm allergic to ____.*
algo *m something n* p48
el algodón *m cotton n* p152
alguien *someone n* p38
algún, alguno -a *some adj*
allá *over there adv*
allí *there (far) adv (demonstrative)* p5
la almohada *f pillow n* p47
  la almohada de plumas
  down pillow
el almuerzo *m lunch n* p82
alquilar *to rent v*
el alpinismo *m mountain
  climbing n*
alto -a *high adj, tall adj* p171
  alto *high adj* p171
  más alto *higher*
  lo más alto *highest*
la altitud *f altitude n* p167
el aluminio *m aluminum n*
amable *kind (nice) n*
la ama de casa *f homemaker n*
amamantar *to breastfeed v*
  p22
el amanecer *m dawn n* p13
  al amanecer *at dawn*
amar *to love v* p22
amarillo -a *yellow adj*
el ambiente *m environment n*
la ambulancia *f ambulance n*
americano -a *American adj*
el amigo *m* / **la amiga** *f
  friend n* p115
el amor *m love n*
ancho -a *wide adj* p12

el andador *m walker (ambulatory device) n* p43
el animal *m animal n*
ansioso -a *anxious adj* p121
el antibiótico *m antibiotic n*
  Necesito un antibiótico.
  I need an antibiotic.
los anticonceptivos *m pl
  birth control n* p182, 191
  **Estoy usando anticoncep-
  tivos.** *I'm on birth control.*
anticonceptivo -a *birth control adj*
  **Se me acabaron las pastillas
  anticonceptivas.** *I'm out of
  birth control pills.*
el antihistamínico *m antihistamine n* p186
el año *m year n*
  ¿Cuántos años tiene?
  What's your age?
apagar *to turn off (lights) v*
  p22
el apellido *m last name*
  **Me quedé con mi apellido
  de soltera.** *I kept my
  maiden name.*
apenado -a *sorry adj*
  Lo siento. *I'm sorry.*
apostar *to bet v* p22
apresurarse *to hurry v* p22, 35
  ¡Apresúrate por favor!
  Hurry, please!
apretado -a *tight adj* p153
la apuesta *f bet n* p185
  Igualo tu apuesta. *I'll see
  your bet.* p185

apuntar to point v **p22**

aquel / aquello that (far away) adj **p6**

aquellos / aquellas those adj pl

aquí here adv **p5**

argentino -a Argentinian adj **p120**

el arma m weapon n **p16**

el arrecife m reef n **p170**

arriba up adv **p5**

el arte m art n

la exhibición de arte exhibit of art

de arte art adj

el museo de arte art museum

el artesano m, **la artesana** f craftsperson / artisan n

los artículos de tocador m toiletries n **p100**

el / la artista m f artist n

asaltar to mug (assault) v **p22**

asaltado to get mugged

asiático -a Asian adj **p80**

el asiento m seat n **p41**

el asiento a nivel de orquesta orchestra seat

la asistencia f assistance n

la asistencia telefónica f directory assistance

asistir to attend v / to assist v **p23**

el asma f asthma n **p191**

Yo tengo asma. I have asthma.

la aspirina f aspirin n **p187**

el asunto m matter, affair

No te metas en mis asuntos. Mind your own business.

el ataque cardiaco m, **el ataque al corazón** m heart attack

ateo -a atheist adj

aterrizar to land v **p22**

el ático de lujo m penthouse n

los audífonos m headphones n

el audio m audio n **p148**

audio -a, auditivo -a audio adj **p65**

ausente missing adj

el Australia m Australia n

australiano -a Australian adj

el auto m, **el automóvil** m, **el carro** m car n

la agencia de alquiler de autos car rental agency

el autobús m bus n **p57**

la parada de autobuses bus stop

el autobús de transbordo shuttle bus

el autobús de excursión sightseeing bus

la autopista f highway n

de auto servicio self-serve adj

el avance m advance n

avergonzado -a embarrassed adj **p16**

las aves de corral f pl poultry n

¡Ay! Ouch! interj

ayer *m yesterday adv* p4

el día antes de ayer / anteayer *the day before yesterday adv* p14

la ayuda *f help n* p56

¡Ayuda! *Help! n*

ayudar *to help v* **p22**

azul *blue adj* p119

B

el baile de salón *m ballroom dancing n* p145

bajar el inodoro *to flush v* **p22**

bajo -a *low adj* p85

bajo *low adj* p85

más bajo *lower*

lo más bajo *lowest*

el balance *m balance (on bank account) n* p134

balancear *to balance v* **p22**

el balcón *m balcony n* p66

el balneario *m spa n*

bancario -a *bank adj*

la cuenta bancaria *bank account*

la tarjeta bancaria *bank card*

el banco *m bank n* p133

la banda *f band n*

la banda ancha *f broadband n*

bañarse *to bathe v* **p22, 35**

la bañera *f,* **la tina de baño** *f bathtub n* p68

el baño *m bathroom, restroom n, bath n* p36

¿Tienen un baño público? *Do you have a public restroom?*

el baño de caballeros *men's restroom*

el baño de damas *women's restroom*

barato *cheap adj* p52

barato *cheap* p52

más barato *cheaper* p52

lo más barato *cheapest*

el barbero *m barber n* p158

el barco *m boat n, ship n* p63

el barrio *m suburb n* p16

la batería *f battery (for car) n*

el baúl *m trunk (luggage) n*

el / la bebé *m f baby n* p117

de bebés, para bebés *for babies adj*

coches para bebés *baby strollers?*

comida para bebés *baby food*

beber *to drink v* **p23**

la bebida *f drink n* p177

la bebida complementaria *complimentary drink*

Quisiera una bebida. *I'd like a drink.*

bello -a *beautiful adj* p117

el beso *m kiss n* p180

bien *okay adv*

¿Está bien? *Are you okay?*

bien *well adv*

bien *fine adj* p1

Estoy bien. *I'm fine.*

bien parecido *m handsome adj*

bienvenido -a *welcome adj*

Está bienvenido. *You're welcome.*

bilingüe *bilingual adj*

el billar *m* *pool (the game) n*

el billete *m* *bill (currency) n*

la billetera *f* *wallet n*

biracial *biracial adj*

blanco -a *white, off-white adj*

el blanqueador *m* *bleach n*

el bloque *m* *block n*

el bloqueador de sol *m* *sunscreen n*

bloquear *to block v* **p22**

la blusa *f* *blouse n* **p152**

la boca *f* *mouth n*

el bocadillo *m* *snack n* **p183**

la bocina *f* *horn n*

la bola *f* *ball (sport) n*

la boleta de abordaje *f* *boarding pass n* **p45**

la boletería *f* *box office n*

el boleto *m* *ticket n* **p36**

el mostrador de venta de boletos *ticket counter* **p36**

el boleto de ida *one-way ticket* **p38**

el boleto de ida y vuelta *round-trip ticket* **p38**

boliviano -a *Bolivian adj* **p120**

la bolsa *f* / **el bolso** *m* *bag n*

el bolso *m* *purse n* **p49**

la bomba *f* *bomb n* **p16**

la bomba *f* *pump n*

el borde de la acera *m* *curb n*

el bordo *m* *board n*

a bordo *on board*

borroso -a *blurry adj* **p189**

la botella *f* *bottle n* **p177**

el braille americano *m* *braille (American) n*

el brandy *m* *brandy n* **p89**

el brazo *m* *arm n* **p16**

brillante *bright adj*

bronceado -a *tanned adj*

bronze (color de) *bronze (color) adj*

bucear *to dive v* **p22**

bucear con tanques de oxígeno *to scuba dive v*

Buceo con tanques de oxígeno. *I scuba dive.*

bucear con tubo de respiración *to snorkel v*

el budista *m,* **la budista** *f* *Buddhist n* **p127**

bueno -a *good adj* **p111**

buenos días *good morning*

buenas noches *good evening* **p111**

buenas noches *good night*

buenas tardes *good afternoon* **p111**

el bufé *m* *buffet n*

de tipo bufé *buffet-style adj*

el burro *m* *donkey n*

buscar *to look for (to search) v* **p22**

la búsqueda *f* *search n*

búsqueda a mano *hand search*

C

el caballo *m* *horse n*

el cabello *m* *hair n*

la cabra *f* *goat n* **p101**

el cacahuate m *peanut* n

el cachemir m *cashmere* n

caer *to fall* v **p23**

café (color de) *brown* adj
p119

el café m *café* n, *coffee* n

el café helado *iced coffee*
el café expreso m *espresso* n
el cibercafé *Internet café*

la caja fuerte *safe (for storing valuables)* n p75

el cajero automático m *ATM* n

caliente *hot* adj, *warm* adj

el calipso m *calypso (music)* n

callado -a *quiet* adj

la calle f *street* n p6

calle abajo *down the street*
al cruzar la calle *across the
street*

la cama f *bed* n

la camarera f *maid (hotel)* n

el camarero m *waiter* n

el camarón m *shrimp* n p102

el camarote m *berth* n

cambiar *to change (money)* v
/ *to change (clothes)* v **p22**

el cambio m *change (money)* n

el cambio de moneda m *currency exchange* n p37, 133

la caminadora f *treadmill* n

caminar *to walk* v **p22**

la caminata f *walk* n

la camisa f *shirt* n

el campamento m *campsite* n

el campista m *camper* n

el campo para golpear
pelotas m *driving range* n

Canadá m *Canada* n

canadiense *Canadian* adj
p192

cancelar *to cancel* v **p22**

la cancha f *court (sport)* n

la canción f *song* n p179

el candado m *lock* n p162

cansado -a *tired* adj p121

cantar *to sing* v **p22**

la cantidad f *amount* n p63

la cantina f *bar* n p37

la cantina de piano *piano bar*
la cantina para solteros *sin-
gles bar* p175

la caña de pescar f *fishing
pole* n

el cappuccino m *cappuccino* n

la cara f *face* n p119

cargar *to upload* v **p22**

el cargo de entrada m *cover
charge (in bar)* n p175

el cargo por servicio m *service charge* n p72

la carie f *cavity (tooth cavity)* n

la carnada f *bait* n p168

la carne f *meat* n p87

caro -a *expensive* adj p176

la carretera f *road* n p56

el carro para dormir m *sleeping car* n

la cartera f *purse* n, *wallet* n

Perdí mi cartera. *I lost my
wallet.*
Alguien me robó mi cartera.
Someone stole my wallet.

casado -a *married* adj p116

casarse *to marry* v **p22, 35**

el casillero *m* locker *n* p161
casillero del gimnasio gym locker
casillero de almacén storage locker
el casino *m* casino *n* p66
el católico *m*, la católica *f* Catholic *n adj* p127
catorce fourteen *n adj* p7
el CD *m*, el disco compacto *m* CD *n* p139
el cebo *m* bait *n*
la ceda *f* silk *n* p152
la ceja *f* eyebrow *n*
celebrar to celebrate *v* p22
la cena *f* dinner *n*
el centímetro *m* centimeter *n*
el centro comercial *m* mall *n*
el centro de la ciudad *m* downtown *n* p149
el centro de gimnasia *m* fitness center *n* p66
cerca close, near *adj* p5
cerca close p5
más cerca closer p5
lo más cerca closest p5
cercano -a near, nearby *adj*
cercano near *adj*
más cercano nearer (comparative)
lo más cercano nearest (superlative)
el cerdo *m* pig *n*
cerrado -a closed *adj* p56
la cerradura *f* lock *n*
cerrar to close *v* p22
cerrar con llave to lock *v* p22

la cerveza *f* beer *n* p88
cerveza de barril beer on tap, draft beer p177
la chaqueta *f* jacket *n* p46
el cheque *m* check *n* p90
el cheque de viajero *m* travelers' check *n*
la chica *f* girl *n* p177
chino -a Chinese *adj* p120
el chocolate caliente *m* hot chocolate *n* p89
el chofer *m* driver *n* p57
el chupete *m* pacifier *n*
el cibercafé *m* cybercafé *n*
ciego -a blind *adj*
cien *m*, cientos *m* hundred *n adj* p7
el cigarrillo *m* cigarette *n*
el paquete de cigarrillos pack of cigarettes
el cigarro *m* cigar *n*
cinco five *n adj* p7
el cincuenta *m* fifty *n adj* p7
el cine *m*, el cinema *m* cinema *n*
el cinturón *m* belt *n* p46
el cisne *m* swan *n*
la cita *f* appointment *n* p148
la ciudad *f* city *n* p68
el clarinete *m* clarinet *n*
claro -a clear *adj* p170
la clase *f* kind (type) *n*
¿Qué clase es? What kind is it?
la clase *f* class *n* p41
la clase de negocios business class p41

la clase económica *economy class* p41

la primera clase *first class* p41

clásico -a *classical (music)* adj

el club nocturno *m nightclub n*

la cobija *f blanket n* p47

cobrar *to charge (money)* v p22

cobre (color de) *copper adj*

a cobro revertido *collect adj*

el cochecito para niños / bebés *m stroller n*

la cocina *f kitchen n* p73

la cocina pequeña *f kitchenette n* p69

cocinar *to cook* v p22

el coito *m intercourse (sexual) n*

el colegio *m college n, high school n*

colérico -a, enojado -a *angry adj* p121

colgar *hang up (to end a phone call)* v p22

el coliseo *m coliseum n*

colocar *to place* v p22

colombiano -a *Colombian adj*

el color *m color n* p154

colorear *to color* v p22

el combustible *m gas n* p55

el indicador de combustible *gas gauge*

sin combustible *out of gas*

comenzar *to begin v, to start (commence)* v p22

comer *to eat* v p23

comer afuera *to eat out*

los comestibles *m groceries n*

la comida *f food n* p87

la comida *f meal n* p42

la comida diabética *diabetic meal* p42

la comida kósher *kosher meal* p42

la comida vegetariana *vegetarian meal* p42

cómo *how adv* p3

el compañero *m,* **la compañera** *f partner n*

compensar *to make up (compensate)* v p22

comportar *to behave* v p22

comprar *to shop* v p22

comprobar, verificar *to check* v p22

la computadora *f computer n*

la computadora portátil *f laptop n* p158

con *with prep* p87

el concierto *m concert n* p130

concurrido *busy (restaurant) adj*

la condición *f condition n*

en buena / mala condición *in good / bad condition*

el condón *m condom n* p182

¿Tienes un condón? *Do you have a condom?* p182

no sin un condón *not without a condom*

el conejo *m rabbit n* p91

la conexión eléctrica *f electrical hookup n* p79

la **confirmación** f confirmation n

confirmar to confirm v **p22**

confundido -a confused adj

la **congestión** f congestion (sinus) n **p187**

congestionado -a congested adj **p16**

la **congestión de tránsito** f congestion (traffic) n

conocer to know (someone) v **p33**

la **consola de juegos** f game console n **p157**

el **contacto de emergencia** m emergency contact n

la **contestación** f answer n

Necesito una contestación. I need an answer.

contestar to answer (phone call) v, to answer (respond to a question) v **p22**

Contésteme por favor. Answer me, please.

continuar to continue v **p22**

el **contrabajo** m bass (instrument) n

la **contraseña** f password n

el **convertible** m convertible n

el **coñac** m cognac n **p89**

la **copa** f glass (drinking) n

¿Lo tienen por la copa? Do you have it by the glass?

Quisiera una copa por favor. I'd like a glass please.

el **corazón** m heart n **p189**

la **corona** f crown (dental) n

la **correa** f belt n

la **correa transportadora** conveyor belt **p46**

correcto -a correct adj **p58**

corregir to correct v **p23**

el **correo** m mail n / post office n **p141**

el **correo aéreo** air mail

el **correo certificado** certified mail

el **correo expreso** express mail

el **correo de primera clase** first class mail

el **correo certificado** registered mail

¿Dónde está el correo? Where is the post office?

correr to ride v / to run v **p23**

la **corrida de toros** f bullfight n

la **corriente** f current (water) n

la **cortadura** f cut (wound) n

cortar to cut v **p22**

la **corte** f court (legal) n **p193**

la **corte de tránsito** traffic court

cortés courteous adj **p78**

corto -a short adj **p10**

coser to sew v **p23**

costarricense Costa Rican n adj **p120**

costear to cost v **p22**

cuánto how (much) adv **p3**

¿Cuánto? How much? **p3**

¿Por cuánto tiempo? For how long?

cuántos how (many) adv

country (la música) f country-and-western adj

crecer to grow (get larger) v p23

¿Dónde creciste? Where did you grow up?

la crema f cream n p94

cremoso -a off-white adj

crudo -a rare (meat) adj, undercooked adj p84

el crustáceo m shellfish n p87

a cuadros checked (pattern) adj

cuál which adv p3

cualquier -a any adj

cualquier cosa anything n

cuándo when adv p3

cuarenta forty n adj

cuarto fourth n adj p9

un cuarto one quarter, one fourth

el cuarto de cambio m changing room n

el cuarto de degustación m tasting room n

el cuarto de galón m quart n

cuatro four n adj p7

el cubismo m Cubism n

cuenta f account n p134

la cuerda f rope n, twine n

el cuero m leather n p50

cuidar to mother v p22

la culpa f fault n p57

Es mi culpa. I'm at fault. p57
Fue su culpa. It was his fault.

la cuna f crib n p69

D

dañado -a damaged adj p49

dar to give v p25 (like ir)

dar masaje to massage v p22

debajo below adj p78

décimo -a tenth adj p9

decir to say v p32

declarar to declare v p22

delantero -a front adj p42

deleitado -a delighted adj

deletrear to spell v p22

¿Cómo se deletrea eso? How do you spell that?

delgado -a thin (slender) adj

demasiado -a too (excessively) adv

la democracia f democracy n

la dentadura f dentures, denture plate n p192

el dentista m dentist n p188

la depilación con cera f waxing n

los deportes m pl sports n

derecho -a right adj, straight adv p55

Está a mano derecha. It is on the right. p55
Vira a la derecha en la esquina. Turn right at the corner.
Siga derecho. Go straight. (giving directions)

los derechos m pl rights n pl

los derechos civiles civil rights

derramar to spill v p22

desacelerar to slow v p22

desaparecer to disappear v p33 (like conocer)

el desayuno m breakfast n

la descarga f download n

descargar to download v p22

desconectar to disconnect v p22

el descuento m discount n

el descuento de niños children's discount

el descuento de personas mayores de edad senior discount

el descuento de estudiantes student discount

el desfile m parade n

desmayar to faint v p22

despedirse to check out (of hotel) v p23, 25

los destellos m pl highlights (hair) n p160

el destino m destination n

el detector de metales m metal detector n

detener to stop v p29

Deténgase por favor. Please stop.

detrás behind adj

devolver to return (something) v p31 (like poder)

el día m day n p161

el día antes de ayer / anteayer the day before yesterday p14

estos últimos días these last few days

diabético -a diabetic adj p84

el día de fiesta m holiday n

la diarrea f diarrhea n p187

dibujar m drawing (activity) v p22

el dibujo m drawing (work of art) n p129

el diccionario m dictionary n

el diciembre m December n

diecinueve nineteen n adj p7

dieciocho eighteen n adj p7

dieciséis sixteen n adj p7

diecisiete seventeen n adj p7

el diente m tooth n p192

diez ten n adj p7

diferente different (other) adj p154

difícil difficult adj p167

el dinero m money n p132

la transferencia de dinero money transfer p132

la dirección f direction

en una sola dirección one way (traffic sign)

la dirección f address n p124

¿Cuál es la dirección? What's the address?

el disco m disco n p128

el diseñador m, **la diseñadora** f designer n p122

el disfraz m costume n

disfrutar to enjoy v p22

disponible available adj p147

la división f split (gambling) n

divorciado -a divorced adj

doble double adj p8

doce twelve n adj p7

la docena f dozen n p11

el doctor m / **la doctora** f doctor n p122, 188

el dólar *m dollar n*

doler *to hurt (to feel painful) v* p23

> **¡Ay! ¡Eso duele!** *Ouch! That hurts!*
>
> **el dolor de cabeza** *m headache n* p111
>
> **el dolor de dientes** *m toothache n*
>
> **Tengo dolor de dientes.** *I have a toothache.*

el domingo *m Sunday n* p14

dónde *where adv* p3

> **¿Dónde está?** *Where is it?*

dondequiera, cualquier lugar *anywhere adv*

dorado -a *golden adj*

dos *two n adj* p7

el drama *m drama n*

el drenaje *m drain n*

la ducha *f shower n* p68

ducharse *to shower v* p22, 35

durar *to last v* p22

duro *hard (firm) adj* p49

el DVD *m DVD n* p51

E

la economía *f economy n*

económico -a, barato -a *inexpensive adj* p38

ecuatoriano -a *Ecuadorian adj*

la edad *f age n* p116

> **¿Qué edad tienes?** *What's your age?*

el editor *m,* **la editora** *f editor, publisher n* p122

el educador *m,* **la educadora** *f educator n* p122

el efectivo *m cash n* p133

> **efectivo solamente** *cash only* p134

el ejercicio *m workout n*

el ejército *m military n*

él *him pron* p3

de él *his adj*

la elección *f election n* p125

el elefante *m elephant n*

el elevador *m elevator n* p69

ella *f she pron* p3

de ella *hers adj* p3

ellos / ellas *them pron pl* p3

el e-mail *m e-mail n* p124

> **¿Me puede dar su dirección de e-mail?** *May I have your e-mail address?* p124
>
> **el mensaje de e-mail** *e-mail message* p124

la embajada *f embassy n*

embarazada *pregnant adj*

embarcar *to ship v* p22

la emergencia *f emergency n*

empacar *to bag v* p22

el empleado *m,* **la empleada** *f employee n* p123

empujar *to push v* p22

encallar *to beach v* p22

encantado -a *charmed adj*

el encendedor *m lighter (cigarette) n* p178

encender *to start (a car) v, to turn on v* p31 (like *querer*)

enchufar *to plug v* p22

el enchufe *m plug n* p158

el enchufe adaptador *m* *adapter plug* *n*

encontrar, hallar *to find* *v* **p22**

el enero *m* *January* *n* **p14**

la enfermera *f* *nurse* *n* **p123**

enfermo -a *sick* *adj* **p48**

la ensalada *f* *salad* *n* **p110**

entallar *to fit (clothes)* *v* **p22**

entender *to understand* *v* **p23**

No entiendo. *I don't understand.*

¿Entiende? *Do you understand?*

la entrada *f* *entrance* *n* **p39**

entrar *to enter* *v* **p22**

No entre. *Do not enter.*

Prohibida la entrada. *Entry forbidden.*

entrenar *to train* *v* **p22**

entusiasmado -a *enthusiastic* *adj* **p121**

enviar *to send* *v* **p22**

enviar un e-mail *to send e-mail* *v* **p22**

el equipaje *m* *baggage, luggage* *n* **p39**

el equipaje perdido *lost baggage*

de equipaje *baggage* *adj* **p39**

reclamo de equipaje *baggage claim* **p39**

el equipo *m* *team* *n* / *equipment* *n* **p37**

el error *m* *mistake* *n* **p78**

la escalada *f* *climbing* *n* **p166**

la escalada de rocas *rock climbing* **p166**

para escalar *climbing* *adj*

el equipo para escalar *climbing gear*

escalar, subir *to climb* *v* **p22, 23**

escalar una montaña *to climb a mountain*

subir las escaleras *to climb stairs*

la escalera *f* *stair* *n* / *flush, straight (gambling)* *n* **p185**

la escalera real *royal flush*

la escalera mecánica *f* *escalator* *n*

escanear *to scan (document)* *v* **p22**

escocés *Scottish* *adj*

escribir *to write* *v* **p23**

¿Podría escribir eso para mí? *Would you write that down for me?*

el escritor *m* *writer* *n* **p122**

escuchar *to listen* *v* **p22**

la escuela *f* *school* *n*

la escuela intermedia *junior high / middle school*

la escuela de leyes *law school*

la escuela de medicina *medical school*

la escuela primaria *primary school*

la escuela superior / secundaria *high school*

la escultura *f* *sculpture* *n*

ese / eso / esa *that (near)* *adj*

esos / esas *those (near)* *adj pl*

la espalda *f* *back* *n* **p190**

español *Spanish n adj* p2

el especial *m special (featured meal) n*

la especie *f spice n*

especificar *to specify v* **p22**

el espectáculo *m show (performance) n*

los espejuelos *m eyeglasses n*

la espera *f wait n* p82

esperar *to hold (to pause) v, to wait v* **p22**

espeso -a *thick adj*

la esposa *f wife n* p114

el esposo *m husband n* p114

la esquina *f corner n*

   en la esquina *on the corner*

la estación *f station n* p58

   ¿Dónde está la gasolinera más cercanía? *Where is the nearest gas station?*

la estación de policías *f police station n* p37

estacionamiento *parking adj*

estacionar *to park v* **p22**

   no estacione *no parking*

el estadio *m stadium n* p163

el estado *m state n*

estadounidense *American adj*

la estampilla *f stamp (postage) n*

estar *to be (temporary state, condition, mood) v* **p27**

este / esta *this adj* p6

esto *this n* p6

éstos / éstas *these n adj pl* p6

estrecho -a *narrow adj* p12

estreñido -a *constipated adj*

estresado -a *stressed adj*

la excursión *f tour n*

excursionar *to hike v* **p22**

la excursión guiada *f guided tour n*

el excursionismo *m sightseeing n*

excusar, perdonar *to excuse (pardon) v* **p22**

   Perdone. *Excuse me.*

exhausto -a *exhausted adj*

la exhibición *f exhibit n*

explicar *to explain v* **p22**

expreso *express adj* p41, 60

   el registro expreso *express check-in* p41

extra grande *extra-large adj*

F

facturar *to bill v* **p22**

la familia *f family n* p115

el fax *m fax n* p123

el febrero *m February n* p14

el festival *m festival n*

fino -a *thin (fine) adj*

firmar *to sign v* **p22**

   Firme aquí. *Sign here.*

flaco -a *thin (skinny) adj*

la flauta *f flute n*

fletar *to charter (transportation) v* **p22**

fleteado *charter adj*

   vuelo fleteado *charter flight*

la flor *f flower n*

el foco delantero m *head-light* n

el formato m *format* n p157

la fórmula f *formula* n

el fósforo m *match (fire)* n

fotocopiar *to photocopy* v **p22**

frágil *fragile* adj p141

francés m, **francesa** f *French* adj p120

la frazada f *blanket* n p47

el fregadero m *sink* n

frenar *to brake* v **p22**

el freno m *brake* n p55

la frente f *forehead* n

del frente *front* adj

fresco *fresh* adj p102

frío -a *cold* adj p125

la fruta f *fruit* n p101

el fuego m *fire* n

las fuerzas armadas f pl *armed forces* n pl

¡Full house! *Full house!* n

fumar *to smoke* v **p22**

el fumar m *smoking* n

la área de fumar *smoking area* p37

no fumar *no smoking* p39

la función f *show (performance)* n

funcionar *to work* v **p22**

la furgoneta f *van* n p50

el fusible m *fuse* n

G

las gafas f pl *glasses (spectacles)* n p162

las gafas de sol f pl *sunglasses* n p152

la galleta f *cookie* n p6

el galón m *gallon* n p11

la ganga f *deal (bargain)* n

la gasolina f *gas* n

el gato m, **la gata** f *cat* n

el / la gerente m f *manager* n

el gimnasio m *gym* n p161

la ginebra f *gin* n p89

el / la ginecólogo -a *gynecologist* n

girar *to turn* v **p22**

el gol m *goal (sport)* n

el golf m *golf* n p49

el campo de golf *golf course*

gordo -a *fat* adj p12, 119

el gorro m *hat* n

gotear *to drip* v **p22**

gracias *thank you*

el grado m *grade (school)* n

el gramo m *gram* n

la gran cantidad f *a lot* n

grande *big* adj, *large* adj p12

grande *big, large* p12, 16

más grande *bigger, larger* p77, 154

lo más grande *biggest, largest*

¡Grandioso! *Great!* interj

griego -a *Greek* adj p81

la grieta f *crack (in glass object)* n

el grifo m *faucet* n

gris *gray* adj

gritar *to shout* v **p22**

grueso -a *thick* adj

el grupo m group n p44

el guante m glove n p172

guapo handsome adj p117

guardar to keep v **p22**

la guardería infantil f nursery n

el guardia m guard n p37

el guardia de seguridad security guard p37

guatemalteco -a Guatemalan adj p120

la guerra f war n p126

la guía f guide (publication) n

el / la guía m f guide (of tours) n

guiar to guide v **p22**

guiar, manejar to drive v **p22**

la guitarra f guitar n p129

gustar See **p22** (explanation of gustar) to please v **p34**

el gusto m taste (discernment) n

H

la habitación f room (hotel) n

hablar to speak v, to talk v **p22**

Se habla Inglés aquí. English spoken here.

hacer to do v, to make v **p30**

hacer efectivo to cash v **p30**

hacer efectivo to cash out (gambling) **p30**, p185

hacer juego to match v **p30**

hacer las paces to make up (apologize) v **p30**

hacia toward prep

halar to pull v **p22**

¿Hay _____? Is / Are there _____?

hecho de made of adj

la hectárea f hectare n p10

la hermana f sister n

el hermano m brother n p115

el hielo m ice n p87

la máquina de hielo ice machine

la hierba f herb n

la hija f daughter n p117

el hijo m son n p117

el hindú m, **la hindú** f Hindu n

hip-hop hip-hop n p174

la historia f history n p131

histórico -a historical adj

el hogar m home n

la hoja del limpiaparabrisas f wiper blade n

hola hello n p1

el hombre m man n

hondureño -a Honduran adj

el honorario m fee n

la hora f hour n, time n p139

el horario m hours (at museum) n

la hospedería de cama y desayuno f bed-and-breakfast (B & B) n

la hospedería f hostel n p66

el hotel m hotel n p66

hoy today n p4

húmedo -a humid adj p125

I

la identificación f identification n p46

la iglesia f church n p127

igualar *to match* v **p22**

el impedimento m, **la persona con impedimento** f *handicap* n

con impedimentos auditivos *hearing-impaired* adj

el impresionismo m *Impressionism* n

imprimir *to print* v **p23**

el impuesto m *tax* n **p156**

impuesto al valor agregado (IVA) *value-added tax (VAT)*

la incapacidad f *disability* n

la indigestión f *indigestion* n

el infante m *infant* n

la información f *information* n

el ingeniero m, **la ingeniera** f *engineer* n **p122**

Inglaterra f *England* n

inglés, inglesa *English* adj **p72**

el inodoro m *toilet* n **p76**

el insecto m *bug* n **p87**

insultar *to insult* v **p22**

intentar *to try (attempt)* v **p22**

el interludio m *intermission* n

el Internet m *Internet* n **p38**

¿Dónde puedo encontrar un cibercafé? *Where can I find an Internet café?*

el / la intérprete m f *interpreter* n **p194**

intolerante a la lactosa *lactose-intolerant* adj **p86**

el invierno m *winter* n **p15**

el invitado m / **la invitada** f *guest* n

ir *to go* v (See Future **p25**)

ir a los clubes nocturnos *to go clubbing* v (See Future **p25**)

ir de compras *to shop* v (See Future **p25**)

Irlanda f *Ireland* n

irlandés, irlandesa *Irish* adj

italiano -a *Italian* adj **p120**

el itinerario m *schedule* n, *timetable (train)* n **p59**

izquierdo -a *left* adj **p5**

J

el jabón m *soap* n **p16**

japonés, japonesa *Japanese* adj **p120**

el jazz m *jazz* n **p128**

el jefe m, **la jefa** f *boss* n

joven *young* adj **p116**

judío -a *Jewish* adj **p127**

el jueves m *Thursday* n **p14**

jugar golf *to go golfing* v **p22**

jugar *to play (a game)* v **p22**

el jugo m *juice* n **p100**

el jugo de fruta m *fruit juice* n

el jugo de naranja m *orange juice* n

el juguete m *toy* n

la juguetería f *toy store* n

el julio m *July* n **p15**

el junio m *June* n **p15**

K

el kilo *m kilo n* p10

el kilómetro *m kilometer n* p10

kósher *kosher adj* p85

L

lacio -a *straight (hair) adj*

el lado *m side n* p86

   por el lado *on the side (e.g., salad dressing)* p86

al lado *next prep* p5

   del lado *next to*

largo *long adj* p10

   largo *long adj* p10

   más largo *longer*

   lo más largo *longest*

la lata *f can n*

el lavamanos *m sink n*

lavanda *lavender adj*

la lavandería *f laundry n* p74

la lección *f lesson n* p173

la leche *f milk n* p90

   el batido de leche *milk shake*

el lector de discos compactos *m CD player n*

leer *to read v* p23

lejos *far adj* p5

   más lejos *farther*

   lo más lejos *farthest*

el lenguaje *m language n*

lentamente *slowly adv*

el lente de contacto *m contact lens n*

lento -a *slow adj* p179

la lesión *f injury n* p16

el letrero de carretera cerrada *m road closed sign n*

la ley *f law n*

la libra *f pound n* p110

libre de impuestos *duty-free adj* p38

la librería *f bookstore n* p166

el libro *m book n* p166

la licencia *f license n* p193

   la licencia de conducir *driver's license*

   la placa de matrícula *automobile license plate*

el licor *m liqueur, liquor n*

el límite de velocidad *m speed limit n* p56

la limonada *f lemonade n*

la limosina *f limo n* p57

el limpiaparabrisas *m windshield wiper n*

limpiar *to clean v* p22

la limpieza en seco *f dry cleaning n*

limpio -a *clean neat (tidy) adj*

el litro *m liter n* p10

la llamada de despertar *f wake-up call n* p75

la llamada telefónica *f phone call n*

   la llamada con cargos revertidos *collect phone call*

   la llamada internacional *international phone call*

   la llamada de larga distancia *long-distance phone call*

llamar *to call (shout)* v **p22**

llamar, telefonear *to call (to phone)* v **p22**

la llanta f *tire* n p59

la llanta de repuesta *spare tire* n

las llegadas f pl *arrivals* n

llegar *to arrive* v **p22**

lleno -a *full* adj p90

llevar *to take* v **p22**

llover *to rain* v **p31** (like poder)

lluvioso -a *rainy* adj p125

local *local* adj p60

la lona f *canvas (fabric)* n p49

luego, más tarde *later* adv

Hasta luego. *See you later.*

el lugar de reunión m *hangout (hot spot)* n

de lujo *upscale* adj p175

la lumbre f *light (for cigarette)* n p176

¿Puedo ofrecerle lumbre? *May I offer you a light?*

el lunar m *mole (facial feature)* n

el lunes m *Monday* n p14

la luz f *light (lamp)* n p55

la luz indicadora *light (on car dashboard)*

la luz del freno *brake light*

la luz de examinar el motor *check engine light* p55

el foco delantero *headlight*

la luz del aceite *oil light* p55

M

la madre f *mother* n p115

¡Maldición! *Damn!* expletive

la maleta f *suitcase* n p49

el maletín m *briefcase* n p49

la mamá f *mom* n, *mommy* n

mandar a llamar *to page (someone)* v **p22**

manejar *to handle* v **p22**

Manejar con cuidado. *Handle with care* p141.

la mano f *hand* n p179

la mantequilla f *butter* n p86

el manual m *manual (instruction booklet)* n p53

el mañana m *tomorrow* n adv

la mañana f *morning* n p13

en la mañana *in the morning* p74

el mapa m *map* n p51

el mapa a bordo *onboard map* p51

el maquillaje m *makeup* n

maquillar *to make up (apply cosmetics)* v **p22**

la máquina f *machine* n p74

la máquina de rayos X *x-ray machine*

la máquina de venta *vending machine*

marcar *to dial (a phone number)* v **p22**

marcar directo *to dial direct*

mareado -a *dizzy* adj / *seasick* adj p62, 189

el mareo de auto m *carsickness* n

los mariscos *m* seafood *n* p81
el martes *m* Tuesday *n* p14
el marzo *m* March (month) *n*
el masaje de espalda *m* back rub *n* p180
masculino male *adj*
el matador *m* bullfighter *n*
el mayo *m* May (month) *n*
la media *f* sock *n*
media libra half-pound p110
mediano -a medium *adj* (size) p12
la medianoche *f* midnight *adv* p13
la medicina *f* medicine *n*, medication *n*
medio -a half *adj*, one-half *adj* una p8
en medio middle *adj* p28
medio bien cocido medium well (meat) *adj* p85
a medio cocer medium rare (meat) *adj*
el mediodía noon *n* p13
medir to measure *v* / to try on (clothing) *v* p32 (like pedir)
mejor best. See good
mejor better. See good
la mejora de categoría *f* upgrade *n* p52
la membresía *f* membership *n*
menos See poco p156
al menos *f* at least *n*
el menú *m* menu *n* p82
el menú para niños children's menu

el menú diabético diabetic menu
el menú de platos para llevar takeout menu
el mercado *m* market *n*
el mercado de pulgas / el pulguero flea market p151
el mercado al aire libre open-air market
el mes *m* month *n* p4
la mesa *f* table *n* p21
el metro *m* subway *n* / meter *n*
la línea del metro subway line
la estación del metro subway station
¿Cuál metro tomo para ____? Which subway do I take for ____?
mexicano -a Mexican *adj* p120
la mezquita *f* mosque *n* p126
el miembro *m* member *n*
el miércoles *m* Wednesday *n*
mil thousand *n* *adj* p7
el mililitro *m* milliliter *n*
el milímetro *m* millimeter *n*
la milla *f* mile *n* p10
el minibar *m* minibar *n*
el mínimo least. See little
el minuto *m* minute *n* p4
en un minuto in a minute
mirar to look (observe) *v* p22
¡Mira aquí! Look here!
la mitad *f* half *n*
la moneda *f* coin *n*

la montaña *f mountain n*

el escalado de montaña *mountain climbing*

morado -a *purple adj*

el moreno *m,* la morena *f brunette n* p117

el mostrador *m counter (in bar) n* p36

mostrar *to show v* p22

¿Puede mostrarme? *Would you show me?*

la motocicleta *f motorcycle n*

la motoneta *f scooter n* p165

el motor *m engine n* p55

mover *to move v* p2 *(like poder)*

la muchacha *f girl n*

mucho -a *much adj* p11

muchos -as *many adj* p11

la mujer *f woman n*

la multa *f fine (for traffic violation) n* p193

el museo *m museum n* p130

la música *f music n* p128

la música pop *pop music*

el musical *m musical (music genre) n*

músico -a *musical adj*

el músico *m musician n* p123

el musulmán *m,* la musulmana *f Muslim n adj* p127

muy *very* p78

N

la nacionalidad *f nationality n*

nadar *to swim v* p22

Nadar prohibido. *Swimming prohibited.*

la naranja *orange n, orange (color) adj*

la nariz *f nose n* p188

el naufragio *m shipwreck n*

la náusea *f nausea n* p187

necesitar *to need v* p22

el negocio *m business n* p44

de negocios *business adj* p73

el centro de negocios *business center* p73

negro -a *black adj* p118

neozelandés, neozelandesa *New Zealander adj*

nicaragüense, nicaragüeña *Nicaraguan adj* p120

ninguno -a *none n* p11

la niña *f little girl n* p115

la niñera *f babysitter n*

el niño *m boy n, kid n* p115

los niños *m pl children n pl*

no *no adj adv* p1

la noche *f night n* p13

a noche *at night* p13

en la noche *at night* p70

por noche *per night*

de no fumar *nonsmoking adj*

el área de no fumar *nonsmoking area*

el carro de no fumar *nonsmoking car*

la habitación de no fumar *nonsmoking room*

el nombre *m name n* p114

Me llamo ____. / Mi nombre es ____. *My name is ____.*

¿Cómo se llama? / ¿Cuál es su nombre? *What's your name?*

el primer nombre *first name*

nosotros -as *we, us* pron pl

la novela *f novel n*

la novela de misterio *mystery novel*

la novela de romance *romance novel*

noveno -a *ninth n adj* p9

noventa *ninety n adj* p7

la novia *f girlfriend n* p115

el noviembre *m November n*

el novio *m boyfriend n* p115

nublado -a *cloudy adj* p125

Nueva Zelanda *f New Zealand n*

nueve *nine n adj* p7

nuevo -a *new adj* p162

la nuez *f nut n*

el número *m number n* p124

O

la obra de teatro *f play n*

observar *to watch v* **p22**

occidental *western adj*

ochenta *m eighty n adj* p7

ocho *m eight n adj* p7

octavo -a *eighth n adj* p9

tres octavos *three eighths*

el octubre *m October n* p15

ocupado -a *busy adj* (phone line), *occupied adj* p138

el oficial *m officer n* p45

la oficina del doctor *m doctor's office n*

ofrecer *to offer v* **p23**

oír *to hear v*

el ojo *m eye n* p184

¡Ojos de serpiente! *Snake eyes! n*

oler *to smell v* **p23**

once *eleven n adj* p7

la onza *f ounce n* p10

la ópera *f opera n* p128

el operador *m,* **la operadora** *f operator (phone) n* p72

el oporto *m port (beverage) n*

el optómetra *m optometrist n*

ordenar *to order (request) v* **p22**

orgánico -a *organic adj*

el órgano *m organ n*

oro (color de) *gold (color) adj*

el oro *m gold n*

ortodoxo griego *Greek Orthodox adj* p127

la oscuridad *f darkness n*

oscuro -a *dark adj*

el otoño *m autumn (fall season) n* p15

otro -a *another adj* p48, 72

P

el padre *m father, parent n*

pagar *to pay v* **p22**

el paisaje *m landscape (painting) n*

el pájaro *m bird n*

el pájaro carpintero *m woodpecker n*

el palco *m box (seat) n* p165

pálido -a *pale adj* p118**

el pan *m bread n* p100

panameño -a *Panamanian adj* p120

el pantalón *m pair of pants n*

el pantalón de traje de baño *swim trunks n*

los pantalones cortos *shorts*

el pañal *m diaper n*

el pañal de paño *cloth diaper*

el pañal desechable *disposable diaper*

el papel *paper n* p100

el plato de papel *paper plate* p100

la servilleta de papel *paper napkin* p100

el papel higiénico *m toilet paper n*

el paquete *m package n* p110

el parabrisas *m windshield n*

la parada *f stop n* p59

la parada del autobús *bus stop*

paraguayo -a *Paraguayan adj* p121

pararse *to stand v* p22, 35

¡Par de ases! *Snake eyes! n*

PARE *STOP (traffic sign)*

el pariente *m*, la pariente *f relative n*

el parque *m park n* p130

el partido *m match (sport) n*

el partido político *m political party n* p126

el pasajero *m*, la pasajera *f passenger n* p48

el pasaporte *m passport n*

pasar *to pass (gambling) v* p22

la pasarela *f walkway n*

la pasarela mecánica *moving walkway*

pasar el rato *to hang out (relax) v* p22

el pasatiempo *m hobby n*

el pasillo *m aisle (in store) n / hallway n* p100

el patio de recreo *m playground n*

el pato *m duck n*

el patrono *m employer n*

el pavo *m turkey n* p96

el peaje *m toll n* p56

peatonal *pedestrian adj*

el distrito de compras peatonal *pedestrian shopping district*

la peca *f freckle n*

el / la pediatra *pediatrician n*

pedir *to order, request, demand v* p32

la pelea de gallos *f cockfight n*

la película *f movie n* p145

el peligro *m danger n* p56

el pelirrojo *m*, la pelirroja *f redhead n adj* p117

el pelo *m hair n* p118

el peluquero *m*, la peluquera *f hairdresser n*

el pensamiento *m thought n / pansy n*

peor *worse. See bad*

lo peor *worst. See bad*

pequeño -a *small adj, short adj, little adj* p11
pequeño *small, little* p11
más pequeño *smaller, littler*
lo mas pequeño *smallest, littlest*
la percha *f hanger n*
perder *to lose v / to miss (a flight) v* p23, 29 (like *tener*)
perdido -a *missing adj, lost adj* p45
el periódico *m newspaper n*
el permanente *m permanent (hair) n*
el permiso *m permit n*
permitir *to permit v* p23
el perro *m dog n* p43
el perro de servicio *service dog* p70
la persona *f person n*
la persona con impedimentos visuales *visually-impaired person*
el personal *m staff (employees) n* p78
el peruano *m,* **la peruana** *f Peruvian n adj* p121
pesar *to weigh v* p22
las pesas *f pl weights n* p161
la pestaña *f eyelash n*
el piano *m piano n* p129
el pie *m foot (body part) n, foot (unit of measurement) n* p10
la piel *f skin n*
la pierna *f leg n*

la pila *f battery (for flashlight) n*
la píldora *f pill n*
la píldora para el mareo *f seasickness pill*
la pinta *f pint n* p11
pintar *to paint v* p22
la pintura *f painting n*
la piscina *f pool (swimming) n*
el piso *m floor n* p69
el primer piso *ground floor, first floor* p69
la pizza *f pizza n* p80
el placer *m pleasure n* p1
Es un placer. *It's a pleasure.*
el plan de tarifa *m rate plan (cell phone) n*
¿Tiene un plan de tarifa? *Do you have a rate plan?*
el plástico *m plastic n* p50
plata *silver (color) adj*
la plata *f silver n*
plateado -a *silver adj*
el plato *m dish n* p85
la playa *f beach n* p130
poco -a *little adj* p11
un poco *m bit (small amount) n*
poco profundo -a *shallow adj*
poder *to be able to (can) v, may v aux* p31
¿Puedo _____? *May I _____?*
la policía *f police n* p37
el pollo *m chicken n* p96
poner *to put (gambling) v* p23
¡Ponlo en rojo / negro! *Put it on red / black!* p184

popular *popular adj* p175

por adelantado *in advance adv*

la porción *f portion (of food) n*

por favor *please (polite entreaty) adv* p1

el portaequipajes *m trunk (of car) n*

el portero *m,* **la portera** *f goalie n, porter n* p36, 164

la postal *f postcard n*

el postre *m dessert n* p88

el menú de postres *dessert menu* p88

el precio *m price n*

el precio de entrada *admission fee n* p148

de precio moderado *moderately priced* p66

preferiblemente *preferably adj*

preferir *to prefer v* p23

preguntar *to ask v* p22

preparado -a *prepared adj*

presentar *to introduce v* p22

Quisiera presentarle a ____. *I'd like to introduce you to ____.*

presupuestar *to budget v* p22

el presupuesto *m budget n*

la primavera *f spring (season) n* p15

primero -a *first adj* p9

el primo *m,* **la prima** *f cousin n*

el probador *m fitting room n*

probar *to taste v, to try (food) v* p22

el problema *m problem n* p2

procesar *to process (a transaction) v* p22

el producto *m product n*

profesional *professional adj*

profundo -a *deep adj* p169

el programa *m program n*

el prometido *m,* **la prometida** *f fiancé(e) n*

el pronóstico del tiempo *m weather forecast n*

la propina *f tip (gratuity)* p90

propina incluida *tip included* p90

protestante *Protestant n adj*

próximo -a *next prep* p4

la próxima estación *the next station*

el puente *m bridge (across a river) n / bridge (dental structure) n* p92

el puerco *m pig n*

la puerta *f door n* p78

la puerta de salida *gate (at airport)* p36

el puerto *port (for ship mooring) n* p62

el puerto USB *m USB port n*

puertorriqueño -a *Puerto Rican adj*

el puesto de información *m information booth n* p37

el puesto de periódicos *m newsstand n* p38

la pulgada *f inch n* p10

en punto *o'clock adv* p4

dos en punto *two o'clock*

la puntuación *f score n*

Q

qué *what adv* p3

   ¿Qué hubo? *What's up?*

quedar *to hold (gambling) v* p22

quedarse *to stay v* p22, 35

la quemadura de sol *f sunburn n*

quemar *to burn v* p22

querer *to want v* p31

el queso *m cheese n* p100

quién *who adv* p3

   ¿De quién es ___? *Whose is ___?*

quince *m fifteen n adj*

el quinto *m fifth n adj*

el quiropráctico *m chiropractor n* p188

R

la radio *m radio n* p51

   la radio por satélite *satellite radio* p51

la rampa para sillas de ruedas *f wheelchair ramp n*

rápido -a *fast adj* p57, 140

el rasguño *m scratch n*

el ratón *m mouse n*

rayado -a *scratched adj* p53

rayar *to scratch v* p22

a rayas *striped adj*

el rayazo *m scratch n*

el reabastecimiento *m refill (of prescription) n* p188

recargar *to charge (a battery) v* p22

la recepción *f front desk n*

la receta *f prescription n* p45

rechazado -a *declined adj*

   Su tarjeta de crédito fue rechazada. *Your credit card was declined.*

recibir *to receive v* p23

el recibo *m receipt n* p133

el reclamo *m claim n*

recolectar *to collect v* p22

recomendar *to recommend v* p22

recortar *to trim (hair) v* p22

el recorte de pelo *m haircut n*

recto -a *straight adj*

la red *f network n*

la red inalámbrica *f wi-fi n*

reducir la velocidad *to slow v* p33 (like *conocer*)

   ¡Reduzca la velocidad! *Slow down!* p58

el refresco *m soda n* p47

   el refresco de dieta *diet soda* p47

el regalo *m gift n*

el reggae *m reggae n* p128

el registro *check-in n* p36

   el registro al borde de la acera *curbside check-in*

   el registro electrónico *electronic check-in* p41

   el registro expreso *express check-in* p41

regresar *to return (to a place) v* p22

relajarse *to lounge v* p22, 35

el reloj *m clock n, watch n*

   el reloj despertador *alarm clock* p75

el relleno *refill (of beverage)* n

remover *to remove* v **p23, 31**
(like *poder*)

repartir *to deal (cards)* v **p23**
   Repárteme. *Deal me in.* p184

el repelente para insectos m
   insect repellent n p187

repetir *to repeat* v **p23, 32**
(like *pedir*)

   **¿Puede repetir eso por
   favor?** *Would you please
   repeat that?* p2

la reservación m *reservation* n

el resfriado m *cold (illness)* n

residencial *home* adj
   la dirección residencial
   home address
   **el número de teléfono resi-
   dencial** *home telephone
   number*

el restaurante m *restaurant* n
   el restaurante de parrilla
   steakhouse

retirar *to withdraw* v **p22**

el retiro m *withdrawal* n

el retraso m *delay* n p44

el retrato m *portrait* n

la revista f *magazine* n

el río m *river* n p169

rizado -a *curly* adj p118

el rizo m *curl* n

robado -a *stolen* adj p49

robar *to rob* v, *to steal* v **p22**

la roca f *rock* n p88
   en las rocas *on the rocks*

el rock and roll m *rock and
   roll* n p128

rojo -a *red* adj p184

romántico -a *romantic* adj

romper *to break* v **p23**

el ron m *rum* n p89

la ropa interior f *underwear* n

la rosa f *rose* n

rosado -a *pink* adj

el rubio m, **la rubia** f *blond(e)*
   n adj p117

con ruedas *wheeled (luggage)* adj

ruidoso -a *loud, noisy* adj 77

S

el sábado m *Saturday* n p14

la sábana f *sheet (bed linen)* n

saber *to know (something)* v
   p33

el sabor m *taste, flavor* n
   el sabor a chocolate *chocolate flavor*

la sal f *salt* n p108
   bajos en sal *low-salt*

la sala de espera f *waiting
   area* n p36

la salida f *check-out* n /
   departure n / *exit* n p39
   la hora de salida *check-out
   time*
   no es salida *not an exit*
   la salida de emergencia
   emergency exit p41

salir *to leave (depart)* v **p23**

el salón público m *lounge* n

la salsa f *sauce* n

salvadoreño -a *Salvadoran*
   adj p121

el salvavidas m *life preserver* n

el sastre *m* tailor *n* p74

el satélite *m* satellite *n* p51

la radio satélite satellite radio p51

rastreo por satélite satellite tracking p51

secado -a dried *adj* p109

la secadora de pelo *f* hair dryer *n* p75

secar to dry *v* p22

seco -a dry *adj*

el sedán *m* sedan *n* p50

segundo -a second *adj* p9

la seguridad *f* security *n* p37

el punto de control de seguridad security checkpoint

la guardia de seguridad security guard p37

el seguro *m* insurance *n* p193

el seguro para colisiones collision insurance

el seguro de responsabilidad civil liability insurance

seguro -a safe (secure) *adj*

seis six *n adj* p7

el seltzer *m* seltzer *n* p88

la semana *f* week *n* p4, 14

esta semana this week

la semana pasada last week

la próxima semana next week

una semana one week p14

dentro de una semana a week from now

sencillo -a single *n adj* / simple *adj*

sencillo straight up (drink)

el sendero *m* trail *n* p168

sentar to sit *v* p22

señalar to point *v* p22

la señal de ceda el paso *f* yield sign *n*

separado -a separated (marital status) *adj* p116

el septiembre *m* September *n*

séptimo -a seventh *n adj* p9

ser to be (permanent quality) *v* p28

el servicio *m* service *n* p43

fuera de servicio out of service p136

el servicio *m* service (religious) *n* p127

la servilleta *f* napkin *n*

servir to serve *v* p23, 32 (like pedir)

sesenta sixty *n adj* p7

setenta seventy *n adj* p7

el sexo *m* sex (gender) *n*

sí yes *adv* p1

siete seven *n adj* p7

la silla de ruedas *f* wheelchair *n* p43

el acceso para sillas de ruedas wheelchair access

rampa para sillas de ruedas wheelchair ramp

la silla de ruedas eléctrica power wheelchair

sin without *prep* p87

la sinfonía *f* symphony *n*

sobre above *adj* p78

el sobre *m* envelope *n* p143

sobrecalentar to overheat *v* p22

sobrecocido -a *overcooked adj*

la sobrina *f niece n* p115

el sobrino *m nephew n* p115

el socialismo *m socialism n*

la soda *f soda n* p47

el software *m software n*

el sol *m sun n*

soleado *sunny adj* p125

soltero -a *single (unmarried) adj* p116

¿Estás soltero / soltera? *Are you single?* p116

el sombrero *m hat n* p152

la sombrilla *f umbrella n*

la sopa *f soup n* p16

sordo -a *deaf adj*

sospechosamente *suspiciously adv* p48

suave *soft adj*

el subtítulo *m subtitle n*

el suburbio *m slum n* p16

suelto -a *loose adj* p153

el suéter *m sweater n* p46

la suite *f suite n* p69

sujetar *to hold v* p22

sujetar las manos *to hold hands*

el supermercado *m supermarket n*

surfear *to surf v* p22

la tabla de surf *surfboard n*

la sustitución *f substitution n*

suyo -a *your, yours adj sing (formal)*

T

la taberna *f bar n*

la talla *f size (clothing, shoes) n*

también *too (also) adv* p184

el tambor *m drum n*

el tanque de oxígeno *m oxygen tank n*

tarde *late adj* p13

Por favor no llegues tarde. *Please don't be late.*

la tarde *f afternoon n* p13

en la tarde *in the afternoon*

la tarifa *f fare n / rate n*

la tarjeta *f card n* p122

la tarjeta de crédito *credit card* p133

¿Aceptan tarjetas de crédito? *Do you accept credit cards?*

la tarjeta de presentación *business card*

la tasa de cambio *f exchange rate n* p133

la tasa de interés *f interest rate n* p133

el taxi *m taxi n* p57

¡Taxi! *Taxi!*

la parada de los taxis *taxi stand*

el té *m tea n* p90

el té con leche y azúcar *tea with milk and sugar*

el té con limón *tea with lemon*

el té de hierbas *herbal tea*

el teatro *m theater n* p145

el teatro de la ópera *m opera house n* p146

el techno *m techno n (music)*

el techo *m roof n*

el techo corredizo *sunroof*

la tela f fabric n
telefónico phone adj p179
el directorio telefónico phone directory
el teléfono m phone n
el teléfono celular cell phone p134
¿Me puede dar su número de teléfono? May I have your phone number? p179
el operador m / **la operadora** f **de teléfono** phone operator
teléfonos prepagados prepaid phones
la televisión f television n
la televisión por cable cable television p68
la televisión por satélite satellite television p68
el templo m temple n p126
temprano early adj p13
tener to have v p29
tener relaciones to have sex (intercourse)
el tenis m tennis n p67
tercero -a third n adj p9
el terminal m terminal (airport) n p39
la tía f aunt n p115
el tiempo m time n p167
la tienda f shop n, store n
la tienda de campaña f tent n
la tintorería f dry cleaner n
el tío m uncle n p115
el tipo m kind (sort, type) n
la toalla f towel n

tocar to touch v / to play (an instrument) v p22
todo -a all adj p11
todo el tiempo all the time
Eso es todo. That's all.
tomar to take v p22
¿Cuánto tiempo tomará esto? How long will this take?
la tonelada f ton n
el torero m bullfighter n
el toro m bull n
la tos f cough n
toser to cough v p23
el total m total n
¿Cuál es el total? What is the total?
trabajar to work v p22
Yo trabajo para ____. I work for ____.
el tráfico m traffic n p53
¿Cómo está el tráfico? How's traffic?
El tráfico es terrible. Traffic is terrible.
tragar to swallow v p22
el trago m shot (liquor) n
el traje de baño m swimsuit n
la transacción f transaction n
la transferencia f transfer n
la transferencia de dinero money transfer, wire transfer p132
transferir to transfer v p31 (like querer)
el tránsito m traffic n
las reglas de tránsito traffic rules

la **transmisión** f *transmission* n

la **transmisión automática** *automatic transmission* p52

la **transmisión manual** *standard transmission* p52

trece *thirteen* n adj p7

treinta *thirty* n adj p7

el **tren** m *train* n p59

el **tren expreso** *express train*

el **tren local** *local train*

la **trenza** f *braid* n p160

tres *three* n adj p7

triste *sad* adj p121

triple *triple* adj p8

la **trompeta** f *trumpet* n

trotar *jogging* n p22

trotar *to run* v p22

tú *you* pron sing (informal)

el **tubo de respiración** m *snorkel (breathing tube)* n

tuyo -a *your, yours* adj sing (informal)

U

último -a *last* adv p9

la **universidad** f *university* n

uno *one* n adj p7

la **uva** f *grape* n

el **uruguayo** m, la **uruguaya** f *Uruguayan* n p121

usar *to use* v / *to wear* v p22

usted *you* pron sing (formal)

ustedes *you* pron pl (formal)

V

la **vaca** f *cow* n

la **vacación** f *vacation* n p44

de vacaciones *on vacation*

ir de vacaciones *to go on vacation*

el **vacante** m *vacancy* n

no hay vacantes *no vacancy*

el **vale** m *voucher* n p44

el **vale para comida** *meal voucher* p44

el **vale para hospedaje** *room voucher* p44

la **van** f *van* n

de vaqueros *western* adj (movie)

varar *to beach* v p22

el **varón** m *male (person)* n

el **vecino** m, la **vecina** f *neighbor* n p115

el **vegetal** m *vegetable* n

el **vegetariano** m, la **vegetariana** f *vegetarian* n adj

veinte *twenty* n adj p7

la **vela** f *sail* n

la **velocidad de conexión** f *connection speed* n p140

el **velocímetro** m *speedometer* n

el **vendedor** m, la **vendedora** f *salesperson* n p122

el **vendedor callejero** m, la **vendedora callejera** f *street vendor*

vender *to sell* v p23

venezolano -a *Venezuelan* adj

la **ventana** f *window* n p41

la **ventanilla** f *window* n

la **ventanilla de entregas** *drop-off window* p142

la ventanilla de recogido
pickup window p142

ventoso -a *windy adj* p125

ver *to see v* p23

  ¿Puedo verlo? *May I see it?*

el verano *m summer n* p15

verdaderamente *really adj*

verde *green adj* p119

la verruga *f wart n*

verse *to look (appear) v* p23, 35

la versión *f version n* p140

el vestido *m dress (garment) n*

la vestimenta *f dress (general attire) n* p174

vestirse *to dress v* p32 (like pedir)* p35

el vestuario *m locker room n*

viajar *to travel v* p22

el viaje *m trip n* p111

la vida *f life n* p122

  ¿Qué haces para ganarte la vida? *What do you do for a living?* p122

el video *m video n*

la videograbadora *f VCR n*

viejo -a *old adj* p26

el viernes *m Friday n* p14

el vinilo *m vinyl n* p50

el vino *m wine n* p47

el viñedo *m vineyard n*

el violín *m violin n*

virar *to turn v* p22

  Vire a la izquierda / derecha. *Turn left / right.*

la visa *f visa n*

visitar *to visit v* p22

la vista *f view n / vision n* p68

  la vista a la playa *beach view* p68

  la vista a la ciudad *city view*

la viuda *f widow n* p116

el viudo *m widower n* p116

vivir *to live v* p23

  ¿Dónde vives? *Where do you live?*

el vodka *m vodka n*

vosotros -as *(Spain) you pron pl (informal)*

votar *to vote v* p22

el vuelo *m flight n* p39

  el / la asistente de vuelo *m f flight attendant*

W

windsurf *to windsurf v*

Y

yo *I pron* p3

Z

el zapato *m shoe n*

zarpar *to sail v* p22

  ¿Cuándo zarpamos? *When do we sail?*

el zoológico *m zoo n* p130